PENGUIN
RAW CON

'The best introduction to this mo
of British architecture – a lea
Simon Bradley, auth

'Calder provides the ideal eye-opening introduction for the curious general reader. It deserves a large audience ... This is a charmingly personal book, authoritatively knowledgeable and spikily argumentative.'
Literary Review

'A compelling and evocative read, one that is meticulously researched, and filled with insight and passion. Through Barnabas Calder's personal narrative we gain a deep understanding and appreciation of a tough subject.'
Kate Goodwin, Head of Architecture, Royal Academy of Arts

'A fascinating odyssey through Britain's Brutalist landscape. The journey is sometimes breathtaking, but always insightful and informed. By its end, we understand the complexity, skill, and vision, as well as the politics, that created the buildings he explores in such loving detail.'
Elizabeth Darling, author of *Re-forming Britain*

'Barnabas Calder is a self-outed lover of concrete, a man who doesn't visit buildings but makes "pilgrimages". He holds back on neither his praise for the objects of his passion, nor his wrath against those who threaten them. Buy this excellent book, read it and go out and hug your nearest lofty edifice in concrete and glass!'
Neil Baxter, The Royal Incorporation of Architects in Scotland

'This engrossing book by a fellow self-confessed concrete lover is both a witty travelogue and memoir and the clear-sighted history of Brutalist buildings. Barnabas Calder relishes the craftsmanship, the financial back stories, and the aims and ambitions of a diverse generation of architects, whose works deserve our sympathy.'
Catherine Croft, Director, Twentieth Century Society

'It's not a history book... It's chatty, anecdotal and thoroughly entertaining... My advice? Read the book, load up your mobile with some rock 'n' roll and Calder's online photos, and go hug some concrete.'
Times Higher Education

'Calder wants to make an argument about the greatness of Brutalism as an architectural style. He writes beautifully.'
Owen Hatherley, *London Review of Books*

'Eclectic and readable.'
Rowan Moore, *Observer*, Architecture Books of the Year

'Impressively well-written... Calder writes with the opinionated self-assurance of the young Ruskin. Compelling reading... thrilling... excellent.'
Adrian Forty, *RIBA Journal*

'Calder's book is the very antithesis of the recent glut of coffee-table-style, #brutalism, which focus primarily on appearance. By adopting a personal perspective, he humanises what is often demonised as an alienating material.'
Blueprint Magazine

'An excellent – and highly readable – guide... If you're interested in Brutalism as architecture and construction practice, if you're interested in its meaning and its context, buy this book.'
Municipal Dreams

ABOUT THE AUTHOR

Barnabas Calder is a historian of architecture specialising in British architecture since 1945. He is a Senior Lecturer at the University of Liverpool where he researches the relationship between architecture and energy throughout human history. His most recent book, *Architecture: From Prehistory to Climate Emergency*, was published in 2021.

Twitter and Instagram: @BarnabasCalder
#ArchitectureAndEnergy

Raw Concrete

The Beauty of Brutalism

BARNABAS CALDER

PENGUIN BOOKS

PENGUIN BOOKS

UK | USA | Canada | Ireland | Australia
India | New Zealand | South Africa

Penguin Books is part of the Penguin Random House group of companies
whose addresses can be found at global.penguinrandomhouse.com

First published by William Heinemann 2016
Published in Penguin Books 2022
005

Copyright © Barnabas Calder, 2016

The moral right of the author has been asserted

Photographs on pages 132–133, 137, 292, 295, 299 and 301 reproduced courtesy
of Lasdun Archive/RIBA collection (architecture.com/image-library).

The author and the publisher have made every effort to trace the holders
of copyright in illustrations and quotations. Any inadvertent omissions
or errors may be corrected in future editions.

Typeset in 10.58 pt/12.95pt Minion Pro Subhead
by Integra Software Services Pvt. Ltd, Pondicherry

Printed and bound in Great Britain by Clays Ltd, Elcograf S.p.A.

The authorised representative in the EEA is Penguin Random House Ireland,
Morrison Chambers, 32 Nassau Street, Dublin D02 YH68

A CIP catalogue record for this book is available from the British Library

ISBN: 978-1-529-15608-9

www.greenpenguin.co.uk

Penguin Random House is committed to a
sustainable future for our business, our readers
and our planet. This book is made from Forest
Stewardship Council® certified paper.

To my parents, and to Janet and
Tony Carter, who got me launched

Contents

AUTHOR'S NOTE ix

INTRODUCTION   Raw Concrete 1

One   The Seduction of Concrete: Hermit's Castle, Achmelvich 21
Two   Monuments to the People: Trellick Tower and Balfron Tower 51
Three   The Bankers' Commune: The Barbican 85
Four   'Preponderately Precinctual in Intention': New Court, Christ's College, Cambridge 121
Five   The Establishment's Radical: Professor Sir Leslie Martin, PhD 161
Six   'Too Commercial – No Convictions': Developers' Brutalism 203
Seven   Good Ordinary Brutalism: The University of Strathclyde Architecture Building and the Newbery Tower 237
Eight   A Concrete Violin: The National Theatre 273
Epilogue Destruction and Preservation 331

Endnotes 343
Acknowledgements 383
Index 385

Author's Note

The buildings featured in this book form a personal selection rather than an attempt at an objective UK top ten (though several of them would be hard to leave out of such a list). Their uneven geographical distribution reflects places where I happen to have spent time rather than especially rich concentrations of Brutalist architecture. There are very few towns on the planet where you will not find your own nearby examples of good Brutalism. Please feel free to add your own photos of other Brutalist buildings at: **barnabascalder.org/rcgroup**

At the start of each chapter there is a QR code box that you can scan to be taken to a webpage featuring further images of the building or buildings under discussion. Each page contains images of the buildings in full colour, and at much higher resolutions than are possible in this book. The URL of the site with the photos is given in text form too.

Introduction

Raw Concrete

(barnabascalder.org/rci/)

I am a lover of concrete. The great outburst of large concrete buildings in the 1960s and '70s, the style known as Brutalism, thrills me. I love the unapologetic strength of these buildings, and the dazzling confidence of their designers in making their substantial mark. I love the optimism they seem to embody, their architecture promising bullishly that new technologies can improve almost every corner of human life. Most of all, I love the way the buildings look: rough, raw concrete, streaked by rain and dirt, forming punchy, abstract shapes; soaring cliffs of tower block or entire cities within cities.

Brutalism is a controversial, muscular term for a controversial, muscular style. Brutalist buildings derive their aesthetic not from borrowed historical motifs, but from the proud flaunting of modern construction methods, especially concrete, and up-to-the-minute facilities like central heating and passenger lifts. The best buildings of the 1960s bring back the elation which so many in Britain felt at the rapid and substantial improvements of the period. More than the music of the Beatles, more than the photographs of David Bailey, the films of Antonioni, or the fashion of Carnaby Street, the architecture

Hermit's Castle, interior

of the 1960s gives me a taste of the joy felt by so many at the fast-developing, ever-freer world of that most exciting of decades.

I was not always such an admirer. Growing up in the 1980s and '90s, in a comfortable Edwardian suburb of London, concrete architecture represented everything which was frightening and other: urban motorways stinking, rowdy, and flanked by decaying buildings; reeking underpasses which seemed to have been expressly kinked to maximise the number of corners round which imaginary psychopaths could cluster; vast impersonal office buildings giving no indication of what was done within them; and above all council estates on whose raised walkways and deserts of patchy grass nameless but horrible crimes probably took place almost constantly.

My childhood views on Brutalism were shaped by the attitudes of an older generation who had seen the 1960s and '70s mass-demolition of Britain's Victorian and Georgian architecture and mourned it. Concrete Modernism was recent and had become associated with political corruption, rapacious developers, vainglorious utopianism and social failure.

Brutalism suffers from architecture's curious dual status. Architecture is present everywhere and used by everyone, yet at the same time it is the least understood of the major arts. Special architecture is visited and marvelled at on holiday – ancient temples, medieval cathedrals, or the colourful, cartoonish buildings of Antoni Gaudí. But the more recent structures that so many people use every day are perceived simultaneously as being banal in their ubiquity, and as being too intimidatingly technical to understand. With almost no architectural education in schools, off-the-peg opinions, sweeping generalisations and unquestioned prejudices thrive, and build strength from wide repetition. No style is as routinely victim to such adverse stereotypes as Brutalism. Even in January 2016, when high-profile campaigns were being fought by residents' groups in some London estates to keep their Brutalist social housing, the Prime Minister felt that post-war estates remained a safe target for a 1980s-style bashing: 'step outside in the worst estates, and you're confronted by concrete slabs dropped from on high, brutal high-rise towers and dark alleyways that are a gift to criminals and drug dealers.'[1] He then went on to blame the 2011 riots on their residents. With these attitudes proving hard to shift, it can take courage to see the good things in front of our noses.

Knowing a little about architecture can bring daily pleasure: what were the ideas and ideals which shaped it? What challenges were the designers up against? How do the built results embody the aspirations and priorities of clients and architects? The range and quality of buildings present in every British town and city is considerable, and our wealth of 1960s Brutalism is the equal of anywhere on earth. Understanding a building's materials, the techniques which went into making it, and the historical context of its creation can transform an inarticulate and faintly threatening heap of concrete into an ingenious and elegant piece of artistic design and skilled construction craft.

The uniform sobriety of concrete turns out, when you look at it more closely, to conceal a subtle gamut of textures and colours, beautiful in themselves and a permanent record of how the building was made. And in this tough, uneffusive material the best Brutalist architects were capable of producing landscapes more powerfully expressive than anything ever built before or since.

Today, 1960s architecture tends to be discussed in terms of taste and fashion – loved, then hated, now loved again by increasing numbers, in the way that music and clothing goes in and out of style. I have slowly come to believe that these buildings not only match the great architecture of any other period, but that they win out. The 1960s were objectively, almost measurably, the most exciting and artistically rich period in which to be an architect. There was never before such a fertile soil for those designing buildings, and there may never be again. Brutalism was the high point of architecture in the entire history of humanity. It takes only a fairly basic level of expertise to start to recognise it as one of the greatest ever flowerings of human creativity and ingenuity.

A Brief History of Brutalism

i: Architecture and Energy

The technological change which nourished this wonderful moment, and which lies in the background of every project of the period, was cheap energy. Putting up a building is one of humanity's most energy-hungry activities.[2] Until the Industrial Revolution, only the very powerful were able to summon the labour to build more than fairly modest functional buildings. Even the awe-inspiring achievements of the Pharaohs, the Roman Emperors or medieval Catholicism were circumscribed closely by the limitations on their access to energy: enough human strength can quarry and move any quantity of stone, but it cannot heat the furnaces to make the materials required for sophisticated engineering. The structures erected by the most powerful people and organisations the world had ever seen were restricted to the limited potential of heavy walls or columns of stone or mud brick, the largest interiors achievable only by domes or vaults which then dictated the form of the rest of the building through the immutable physics of the arch.

From around 1800 industrialising countries changed rapidly, and beyond recognition, using the cheap heat of coal and then oil, and later the flexible ubiquity of electricity. By the 1960s the exploitation of fossil fuels had given every British citizen access to more energy than was available to anyone in the pre-modern world. Architects were freed by unprecedented energy wealth from the age-old structural limitations of clumsy stone and brick, and weak, flammable wood. The total amount of architectural activity shot up, with ordinary working-class people getting more living space, new mod cons, new educational opportunities and new health facilities, each housed in new buildings. They travelled more, using upgraded roads, updated railways and new airports;

they had more leisure time to spend in the increasingly diverse facilities built to entertain them.[3]

Cheap energy made concrete and steel available in quantity, and engineers' understanding of reinforced concrete developed rapidly. For the first time in history the weight of very large structures did not need to travel down in vertical walls and columns, or follow the inflexible lines of arches and vaults. Architects could slide the constituent parts of their buildings around at will, massively increasing the range of ways they could arrange rooms and routes, bringing outdoor space to any part of the building they chose, escaping the architectural restrictions of ground-level the way sci-fi fans hoped rocket-packs would one day enable pedestrians to do, and opening up completely new shapes of building to the designer.[4]

Cheap energy also reconfigured Brutalist architects' attitudes to the design of interiors. To be a comfortable temperature in winter, British buildings had always needed to be divided into cellular rooms small enough to reduce drafts, each with its fireplace to warm it, served by thick clusters of chimney-flues. Daylight was the best and cheapest illumination, requiring relatively thin buildings so that light could penetrate to the back of each room, and higher ceilings for tall windows. If artificial lighting was needed it came with noxious gasses until the advent of electric lighting, and from then with the surplus heat of incandescent bulbs. In the 1950s and '60s all this changed. With cheap, cool electric lighting, mechanical ventilation, central heating, and the versatility of concrete structure, rooms could be whatever size and shape was needed. The building could fit round the functions rather than the functions having to accommodate themselves to the normal restrictions of buildings.

It is easy to see why this complete rewriting of the rules was a hugely exciting stimulus to architects to reconsider everything they had been taught, and rethink everything everyone had always taken for granted. Architecture in the post-war period exploded into new shapes, new ideas of what buildings could and should be, and new aspirations for cities and society. Architects felt no sentimental or apologetic need to disguise this thrilling progress behind ill-fitting simulacra of the architecture of older, poorer, more cruelly hierarchical periods in human history.

There may be those who feel that comparing 1960s architecture with earlier periods is unfair: the technologies available made it easy for the Brutalists. In fact, though, it is striking how primitive were many of the circumstances from which these great concrete monuments arose. The drawings for all the buildings in this book were produced by human beings sitting at drawing boards with pencils, pens, paper, and low-tech drawing instruments like compasses and set squares. The main new design technology compared with previous centuries was the ability to produce copies of drawings by primitive photocopying techniques as opposed to employing draughtsmen to copy them. Today's architectural design, with extensive catalogues of ready-made components, and computers to help sew it all together, is unrecognisably more technically advanced. The buildings discussed here were designed almost entirely from scratch, with even the door handles and signage often being drawn and made for each individual project. They now call such one-off designs 'bespoke'. In the 1960s they just called it 'architecture'.

The engineering of Brutalist structures had advanced much more: it could draw upon vastly greater mathematical understanding of physics than in earlier centuries. Yet the technology on the engineer's desk again remained simple. Until the end of the 1960s they did all the critical and fiendishly complicated calculations of structural requirements without the aid of computers.[5]

Nor were the building sites of the 1960s the orderly mechanised environments to which Modernism aspired. Petrol-driven machinery massively increased the productivity of labourers, but some of the craft which produced the buildings in this book, notably the expert carpentry required to make moulds to pour the concrete into, would have been recognisable to ancient labourers. Other techniques would have been unfamiliar, but the amount of knowledge, skill and care which went into making good concrete was immense. The concrete-workers of the 1960s could justifiably claim their place amongst the great craft traditions of masons, carpenters and plasterers, with intense pride in the quality of their work and gleeful competition between teams on rival projects.[6]

The architects were even more fiercely competitive, and as in the cathedrals of Medieval France or the paintings of the Italian Renaissance, rivalry fostered remarkable heights of ambition and achievement. The quantity of competitors in British Brutalist architecture was vastly greater than the number of artists in fifteenth-century Florence, and the amount and speed of construction by any British local authority dwarfed the cathedral-building boom of twelfth-century France. The result of these invigorating and unprecedented conditions was a brief but peerless flowering of architectural activity, made yet more fervid by the stimulus of a fast-moving international architectural press. From the grandest scale of public projects through to housing for the poor, the 1960s saw teams of obsessive, committed architects trying to find new improved conditions for human life, exploiting the vastly improved technologies and opportunities of their moment, and revelling in the wealth of new options then becoming available to designers.

ii: The Surprising Triumph of Modernism

The energy wealth of Britain in the 1960s was always likely to support a major building boom. Thirty years earlier, however, few would have guessed that the style of that boom would have been such a triumphantly Modernist one.

Modernism had been slow to catch on in Britain.[7] British architects in the 1920s and '30s, buoyed by the confidence that they and their clients derived from Britain's industrial power and its vast empire, had mostly felt uninterested in copying the European Modernist innovations of Le Corbusier or the Bauhaus with their white boxes shorn of ornament and teetering on skinny legs. Stone-faced classicism seemed better to represent the timelessness of empire and the stolid grandeur of world-power status. By the later 1930s, architectural schools were becoming increasingly speckled with enthusiastic Modernists, but the built work was largely confined (with a few very interesting exceptions) to the houses of arty left-wingers in wealthy suburbs.[8] The servants' bedrooms in many of them, whilst normal for upper-middle-income houses of the period, hint at the limits to the socialist utopian ambitions of the clients.

It was the Second World War that shook things up and allowed Modernism to sweep in as the dominant style. The wartime experience of mass-mechanisation, of the quick erection and sustained use of utilitarian structures, and above all of huge united effort from civilians and soldiers alike, set the scene for a dramatically different post-war atmosphere.[9] Whilst there had been plenty of disgust at the condition of industrial slums before the war, bombing and neglected maintenance during the six years of conflict pushed the position to obvious crisis. Already by the early 1940s a huge post-war effort was starting to be planned: to provide replacement housing not only for the bombed but also for the ill-housed; to improve and reform road networks; to separate housing from industrial areas, and to divide both from civic buildings.[10] For many, the spirit of self-denying common purpose which had become a habit during the war continued after the victory, the atmosphere of national emergency heightened by the continuing rationing of both building materials and some foods until 1954.

Modernism came out of the war on top in part because, just as with temporary structures during the war, decorating buildings with historical motifs was, in the immediate rush of emergency reconstruction, one of so many luxuries which must be forgone in order to get the country 'back on its feet.' Modernism could present itself as being unadorned and utilitarian, and so win the stylistic argument by default. Modernist architects rushed to take on urgent projects in service of the country's most pressing needs. Many were newly demobilised from military service during which they had been singled out for organisational or engineering roles, inducting them to the pragmatism, the teamwork, and the emphasis on efficiency which many would use in their peacetime architectural practice.[11]

Much of Britain's architecture in the 1940s and early 1950s focused on meeting urgent requirements for new housing, and extra schools made necessary by the baby boom that followed the return home of the troops. With circumstances almost as pressured as during the war itself, architectural aesthetics were much less important than speed and economy. Ingenious prefabricated schools were manufactured by former aircraft factories.[12] Vast numbers of decent but not very exciting houses were put up in a cheap simplification of traditional houses, the style given an unconvincing veneer of intellectual substance by the tag 'the New Humanism'.[13]

For the young architects who found this worthy self-restraint tedious, neither the kit-built schools nor the council housing were easy to attack: each tried to meet self-evidently pressing human needs with as little expenditure of hard-pressed resources as possible. When their rebellion did come it came as an incoherent roar – less like a reasoned rival manifesto, and more like bored teenagers smashing up the village bus stop.

The leader of the yobs was a charismatic young architectural journalist named Peter Reyner Banham, who gathered around him a group committed to correcting the failings of current British architecture. To indicate that they were taking the fight to the newly constituted Modernist establishment with its spirit of self-effacing social service, they parodied the tag 'New Humanism' by calling their own movement 'the New Brutalism'. The name rolled into one strong slogan the toughness and primitivism of their architectural expression, the nickname 'Brutus' by which one of the leading young Brutalists, Peter Smithson, was known, and an association with the French term for exposed concrete, 'béton brut'.[14]

Banham and his rebels, most notably Peter and Alison Smithson, gave the New Brutalism weight by harvesting theoretical snippets from a bewildering range of intellectual fields: advanced Modernist art theory, theoretical maths, the emerging discipline of sociology, and renaissance ideals of symmetry and proportion.[15] Beneath all its highbrow pretensions, this movement also served as de facto defence of the old role of the private architectural practice as the creative heart of architecture, attacking the work of many of the public-sector design offices and proposing radical alternatives from private practitioners.

At a time of national shortage the lofty statements of the Smithsons and their circle could easily have been lampooned as self-indulgent and luxurious. Perhaps as a pre-emptive defence against these accusations, the young gravitated towards a visual style tougher and more aggressively stripped-down than that of the economising older generation: it would be hard to attack them for self-indulgent aestheticism if their buildings looked *more* austere than those of their critics.

The Smithsons won an architectural competition of 1950 for a secondary modern school at Hunstanton, and produced a building of utter restraint: steel, brick and concrete are each clearly expressed, and even the plumbing marches its way proudly across the walls. This use of materials 'as found' called to mind the *objets trouvés* beloved of the art world. Alongside this ostentatiously gritty basicness, the architects highlighted the building's Palladian proportions and symmetry. Simultaneously intimidatingly intellectual and frighteningly tough-looking, the Smithsons' architecture was thrilling to many of the younger generation, and discussion raged about the merits or demerits of the New Brutalism.[16]

Wherever young, art-minded architects gathered, most notably in the gigantic Architect's Department of the London County

Hunstanton Secondary Modern School, Norfolk

Council (a stopping-off point and hothouse for many promising youngsters between architecture school and setting up their own practices), the New Brutalism was debated and its ideas elaborated. The catchy name served as a rallying point for younger architects wanting to produce something more aesthetically ambitious than their soft-Modern elders.[17] From the later 1950s an increasing number of hard-looking buildings started to spring up as blocks of council flats and school buildings, and then as the 1960s got underway the tough younger architects expanded to the better budgets and larger sites of the fast-growing universities. What had begun as the fight-back of art architecture under conditions of post-war poverty and shortages then grew into the fruitful summer of Brutalism under the increasing wealth and ever-cheaper energy of the 1960s.

The term 'Brutalism' could easily have died with the discussions of the 1950s: many architects had no time for theoretical writing amidst the busy years of the 1960s building boom. It was the

1966 book by Reyner Banham, *The New Brutalism: Ethic or Aesthetic*, which secured its continuing life, not as the rallying point for 1950s radicals wanting a change, but as a stylistic term for any large, concretey building from the 1960s or '70s.

In many ways the story of this meaning of Brutalism is the story of architects daring to come increasingly close to imitating the great Swiss-French Modernist Le Corbusier's post-war work. Having been one of the leaders of the skinny-columned white Cubism of the 1920s and '30s, Le Corbusier rebelled against his own influence in the 1940s and '50s, turning to a use of concrete so gloriously messy and primitive-looking that one sometimes worries the buildings may not be structurally stable. His post-war work, and particularly his block of flats at Marseille, which he called a *Unité d'habitation*, gave the biggest impetus to Brutalism internationally.

British architects seem to have been tentative about imitating Le Corbusier's outrageous primitivist freedom, playing a kind of grandmother's footsteps in which those who dared too much too soon were cut down by the criticism that they were being self-indulgent and wasteful.[18] The taut restraint of Hunstanton School's steel and brick gave way to increasingly chunky, sculptural abstraction in concrete, with necessary elements like rooftop water tanks and fire stairs becoming powerful pieces of art. As Brutalism became more expressive it got even tougher, perhaps to keep facing down potential allegations of artiness, or perhaps just because the designers liked that aesthetic. Architects became ever more interested in the effect of their buildings on viewers. Starting in the 1940s with the comparative modesty of the 'Townscape' movement, which exhorted architects to produce exciting and agreeable spaces between their buildings, by the late 1960s Brutalist architects internationally were building structures which had the thrilling, horror-film dominance captured two centuries earlier by the famous fantasy images of Piranesi, the great artist of the sublime.[19]

As Modernist architecture developed in courage in the 1960s, its range of clients also increased. British Brutalism has been widely seen as the architectural style of the Welfare State – a cheap way of building quickly, on a large scale, for housing, hospitals, comprehensive schools, and massive university expansion. Yet the period cannot in reality be neatly encompassed by an account of architects and clients united in a zealous desire to sweep away the old order and build afresh for a new one. Motivations behind building included – alongside genuine social progressiveness – electoral pressure, scene-dressing to disguise lack of change with apparent modernisation, and the usual edifice complex of the powerful (for which Brutalism's portentousness was ideally suited).[20] More surprising motives uncovered below for the ways some Brutalist projects were built include social conservatism, and personal or familial aristocratic patronage pursued with public money.

Wide disparities of motivation and indeed wide disparities of budget were rendered less conspicuous by superficial similarities in architectural expression. The apparent political consensus in the post-war years – on the need to subdue extravagance in favour of modestly benefiting everybody – is reflected by a visual workmanlikeness in the architecture. Rich and poor projects can look superficially alike, and superficially utilitarian. However, the usual range was present once you get your eye in: expensive and cheap, conservative and progressive, aestheticising as well as functional, grandiose as well as basic.

Uniting Brutalism in the face of this swirling complexity is an architectural style with its own momentum like that of any stylistic movement. Some of the tendencies of Brutalism, like its gesture towards egalitarianism, accorded well with the institutional and political priorities of the day. Others did not. The awareness of a fast-changing world led clients and architects to talk a lot about flexibility, and planning for future change foreseeable and unforeseeable.[21] Yet the cast-in-place reinforced concrete beloved of most

Brutalist architects is almost as inflexible a material as has ever existed.

Concrete, and the Brutalist style, acquired their own momentum in which an international spread of architects increasingly (but without acknowledging it openly) competed to produce the most stunning-looking building, sublime in scale and robust in detail. Once one recognises it as self-conscious, self-confident, hugely celebratory high art, one can see much more clearly why it was done the way it was. One can stop trying to project materials shortages of the 1940s onto buildings of the 1960s, and instead throw oneself into admiring and enjoying the spectacular outburst of architectural creativity which Britain saw in the years from around 1958 to 1975 – high Brutalism. That is what this book aims to capture: the architecture which celebrated the triumph of the period's achievement in conquering human sufferings (ill health, cold, and lack of space) which had been the experience of almost everyone since humanity came north to Europe.

It was a period of big commissions, intense competition and extraordinary technical progress. The most gifted architects of the period produced designs which may never be equalled in their glorious self-confidence, integrity and originality.

Brutalist architects were deeply proud of the forward-looking achievements of their moment, and could not imagine anyone ever feeling otherwise. Surely no one could ever be blind to the astounding accomplishments of modernity, bringing every single person in Britain improved material circumstances and the chance of a longer, healthier, better-educated life with better housing and working conditions.

iii: Concrete Carbuncles

Such a pinnacle of optimistic hyperactivity could not last. The 1970s oil crisis, and the failure of nuclear stations to continue the expected cheapening of energy, brought to an end two centuries of almost exponential growth in available power.[22] The past three decades have seen an increasingly urgent realisation that our dependency on oil, coal and gas is generating potentially devastating climate change. Whilst we are still building more than we can afford in environmental terms, new buildings are now built within the tight restrictions of energy conservation, trying to use less fuel in construction, and to require less for heating, lighting and cooling when in service. These restrictions rein in the experimental creativity of today's architects almost as surely as absolute energy poverty restricted their pre-modern predecessors. Alone of all architectural periods, Brutalism had massive energy wealth without being haunted by guilt, and the 1960s building boom was an orgiastic celebration of these exceptional conditions.

It is hardly surprising that so much strong, unfamiliar new architecture, and the destruction of familiar cityscapes which it required, should have produced a proportionately substantial backlash when fashion turned against it. As the Brutalist building boom died away into controversy and recrimination, the optimistic vigour of the 1960s soured to vehement loathing in the 1970s and '80s. Architecture was suddenly perceived as an allegory for, and the source of, social evils on an unprecedented scale.

'Later, as he sat on his balcony eating the dog, Dr Robert Laing reflected on the unusual events that had taken place within this huge apartment building during the previous three months.' So begins J. G. Ballard's celebrated 1975 novel, *High-Rise*. The tall concrete housing block in which the protagonist lives has spiralled into a level of social failure and near-war so rough that middle-class professionals have ended up murdering each other and eating dog. The rest of the novel retraces the steps by which things got this bad. The ever-present anti-hero of the book is the building, whose tough Brutalist architecture, faulty technologies and alienating scale promote the horrors of increasingly murderous social discontent.

Both fictional and factual writing about 1960s architecture in the 1970s and '80s seemed to suggest that its architects had been either mad or evil, with a consistent tone of conspiracy theory, whether the Prince of Wales's sense that the National Theatre seemed like 'a clever way of building a nuclear power station in the middle of London without anyone objecting', or Ballard's haughty architect watching with interest as his flats drive their residents to bestial disorder.[23]

These decades of recrimination are ending, and in the last ten years British Brutalism has seen a dramatic revival in interest and even popularity. Much of this has been from left-wing commentators holding up the post-war Welfare State as an attractive alternative to the current direction of austerity rhetoric and a shrinking public sector. The buildings of the 1960s are used to embody the optimism and ambition of Britain's social-democratic past.[24]

*

The following chapters will not take Brutalist architecture as a proxy for anything, either blame-worthy or admirable, nor as a set of clever ideas on drawing boards. They do not set out a linear history of a style developing, but instead form a rather personal greatest hits of British Brutalism: a series of real, individual buildings, hammered and poured into being in the mess of 1960s and '70s building sites, and then subjected to decades of wear and tear, modification and abuse. I discovered these buildings not through the pristine photographs of them when new, but through going to them, and coming to love them in all their neglected or hacked-around shabbiness, all their accumulated dirt and unsympathetic later clutter. Prince Charles famously felt that the facade of the National Gallery had about it something of the loved familiarity of the face of an old friend.[25] My own architectural old friends are a rougher-looking bunch, and have acquired more broken noses and scars in their half-century than the National Gallery has picked up in nearly four times as long. Nevertheless I love them just as they are, magnificent in their courage and confidence and, once you give them a chance, beautiful.

Chapter One

The Seduction of Concrete
Hermit's Castle, Achmelvich

(barnabascalder.org/rc1/)

i

For the love of concrete, I spent the night of my thirty-second birthday on the floor of an Inverness youth hostel day-room. On the pool tables above me slept two large Bavarians who arrived and left in lederhosen and Alpine hats. Other sundry travellers were distributed round the floor and benches. Below me a night club boomed, its flashing sign shedding furiously bright, changing colours into our curtainless room. The crowds leaving or smoking outside kept up a roar which made sleep unthinkable until about four a.m. I was back up at eight to catch a three-hour bus to the most remote north-western corner of the Scottish Highlands in search of a concrete castle.

At the time I was living in Glasgow, but had recently accepted a job in Liverpool, and was determined to make the pilgrimage before I left, and before the dramatically shorter days and colder nights of winter set in. I had been monitoring the forecasts for the north-west of Scotland closely for several weeks, waiting for the sun to allow me to take photographs of this humble dwelling in light which would bring out its various shapes and textures. The clear, rainless day came on my birthday, so I half-ran from my celebratory lunch to the station for the uncomfortable, expensive, seventeen-hour trip.

I got off the bus in the pretty harbour village of Lochinver, overlooking its quiet water. From there I set off past straggling holiday or retirement houses and into the coastal countryside. The path of stone and mud wound its way around the contours of the undulating headlands over scrubby ground, inlets of the sea visible to one side or the other, grey rock poking out from the tussocky grass and heather. The landscape changed quickly from minute to minute: here grass and drystone walls, there a stream flanked by spindly trees. After the pleasant six-kilometre walk, the village of Achmelvich itself seemed to consist only of a small handful of houses and a campsite. Beyond the campsite the path gave out, and I wove haphazardly over an undulating peninsula of rocks and wind-short grass towards where I thought – and hoped – the building I had come to see might be.

I knew little of the concrete castle's origins, and nothing of its creator, having stumbled upon it by blind luck in an obscure corner of the Internet: a few bleak and intriguingly titled photographs posted many years before. The castle – a building with no purpose, miles from anywhere – was a mystery. My only pre-visit research consisted of staring at overmagnified low-res Google satellite images of the coastline, trying to distinguish the six or eight pixels of grey hut from the hundreds of thousands of pixels of grey rock. I was determined I would find it.

From the few pictures, I had assumed I would see the object of my journey from a distance, but in the end it took me by surprise. Cresting the top of a small hill, I found myself looking down on a beautiful cove in which stood the goal of all this inconvenience, discomfort and expense: a small concrete hut, the 'Hermit's Castle'. From where I stood I could see that the glass in the hut's poky little windows had all been smashed. The interior could not be very well lit, and was open for the free use of any wild animals or odd humans seeking shelter. Yet, sitting in its lonely coastal location, it was – and remains – one of the most evocative and beautiful buildings I had ever seen.

ii

Fifteen years earlier I had been one of those who believed fervently that architecture had become steadily worse since the eighteenth century until its nadir in the 1960s, a time when architects had clearly given up all interest in the potential beauty of buildings in favour of cheapness, speed, and raw size. Concrete, in particular, aroused my sense of wary hostility: why could they not have made the bit of extra effort to use decent materials? Concrete seemed to me a representation in one material of human technology's harmful conflict with nature. The invariably pejorative tone of phrases like 'concrete jungle', or 'concreting over' of the countryside, suggest that I was not alone in my hostility.[1] Concrete was the material most associated with the rapid and massively sweeping change in Britain's cities in the 1960s and '70s, a cheap, hasty, nasty material easily associated with the neglected housing and alienating raised or sunken motorways which sliced wide swathes through cities, blighting the areas around.

Yet by the time of my visit to Achmelvich I had overcome my sense of alienation and evolved into a proper Brutalist pilgrim, willing to suffer chastening discomfort on the devotional journey to a remote concrete shrine. An architect at a conference once warned me that I risked becoming 'a concrete-sniffing wanker'. As I set out for this distant hut I was probably living up to his prediction.

My conversion had started with an aesthetic response to the sheer size and drama of the best Brutalist buildings, but had over the following decade become increasingly all-encompassing. I learned to love the subtle details of different concrete finishes, to decode from the surface appearance how buildings had been made, and to appreciate the considerable ingenuity and brio of the structural engineers who had made it all stand up. And the more I found out, the more I came to recognise the boundless potential and infinite variation and subtlety present in that often-denigrated material, raw concrete.

Concrete is made by mixing industrially produced cement (a mixture of clay and limestone cooked at very high temperatures) with water, sand (fine aggregate) and gravel (coarse aggregate). Its chemical composition and its aggregate can be varied to produce different technical properties – stronger, more weatherproof, lighter, or faster-setting according to the job it is doing. This variability has been exploited since concrete's early days in ancient Rome, when a volcanic ash found in deposits under Rome itself was employed as a very effective naturally occurring cement. Roman concrete was used extensively in engineering projects including the Pantheon where, to construct the vast forty-three-metre span of its dome, it was necessary to make the concrete as light as possible, and so lightweight brick, tufa stone and, near the top, pumice-like volcanic stone filled with air cavities, were used as aggregate. In the foundations, where strong ballast was required to resist the outward thrust of the dome, the aggregate was robust, heavy travertine.[2] The Pantheon's concrete dome has lasted 1,900 years so far.

After the fall of Rome, concrete was neglected as a material for one and a half millennia. Lime mortars similar to cement were used in European construction throughout, and a clear account of concrete survived in the only architectural treatise to make it from the ancient world to the Renaissance and beyond, Vitruvius' *Ten Books on Architecture*.[3] Renaissance architects and scholars examined and discussed Vitruvius' text in considerable detail, and meticulously measured and drew the Pantheon and other ancient concrete monuments, but they did not themselves build in concrete. The Pantheon remained the world's largest column-free span until the metal-and-glass roofs of the 1800s. The reason for this neglect of concrete was almost certainly that it takes a great deal of heat to make limestone and clay into cement. It could take up to a week of burning a lime kiln at 1,000 degrees Celsius for one batch of lime (the precursor to cement), with immense quantities of high-energy fuel like nut husks having to be shovelled in and the ashes raked out.[4] This made concrete an unfeasibly luxurious material until the nineteenth century, when the cheap heat of coal made cement production affordable.

Concrete's modern life began in the most unglamorous building sector: cheap, utilitarian rural buildings. If tamped down hard enough between robust vertical boards, some types of soil will produce quite a serviceable wall if you can keep the rain off it. In the 1800s builders began to add lime cement to the rammed earth to increase its durability. It could scarcely be further from the architectural world's highbrow discussions of Classical proportion and aesthetics. The English word 'concrete' reflects the noble Roman tradition of '*opus concretum*', but the German and French words for concrete ('*beton*' and '*béton*') are from a humbler root, the Middle French '*betum*' meaning rubble, rubbish or dirt.[5]

From this agricultural lowliness concrete graduated into a material for the fireproofing of warehouses and factories – an increasingly prominent preoccupation of the steam-driven and gas-lit Industrial Revolution. The extraordinary coincidence that, unlike most metals, steel happens to expand and contract almost exactly the same amount as concrete when it changes temperature, meant that concrete could be used to encase steel and prevent it from softening and collapsing in a fire.

Concrete on its own is a sludgy liquid with, once set, similar engineering properties to stone: it is very strong in compression but prone to snap or shatter when pulled or twisted. Once building contractors thought to put steel into the concrete, however, it became an extraordinarily useful composite material. Reinforced concrete has the strength of its steel when twisted or pulled, and the strength of stone when compressed. It is considerably more fire-resistant than steel alone, and is composed largely of cheap sand, gravel and water. Add to these virtues the fact that it can be built adequately by unskilled (and therefore cheaply non-unionised) labour and it is unsurprising that by the later twentieth century it became the second most used material on the planet (by weight) after water.[6]

The ways in which concrete can be used are hugely varied. It needs to be cast in a mould (though there have been challenging experiments in spraying it on to wire mesh reinforcement), but it can be made either in the final location of the building (known as 'in situ' concrete) or elsewhere as pieces in a factory (known as 'pre-cast' concrete), trucked and craned into position like a giant toy construction kit. It can be treated like steel as a structural frame to which cladding and floors are then added, or it can be made entirely structural like an all-plastic chair, the walls and floors forming a single piece with weight distributed through all of it to the ground. If the ground is marshy or difficult to put foundations into, concrete enables buildings to be built as self-contained rafts without deep foundations. Concrete can be any shape that you can make moulds for it, boxy or sculptural, rational-looking or expressionistic.

The complexity and rapid development of concrete engineering called into being the 'consultant engineer', who worked neither for the architect nor the building contractor, and could therefore give disinterested technical advice to both.[7] Yet despite the real sophistication required by concrete engineering, one of the major appeals of concrete to architects since 1945 has been almost the opposite: that it frees them to a large extent from worrying about engineering calculations whilst they design. Where Gothic masons had to design engineering and architecture as one, according to the engineering requirements of stone, concrete architects can design the spaces and shapes they want using broad rule-of-thumb or intuitive bases for their assumptions on what will stand up, secure in the knowledge that if the spans turn out to be demandingly long, the engineers will be able to tell the builders to put more steel into the concrete.[8] This freedom is exploited at every level: architecture students who have not thought through their structures properly mumble 'concrete' when asked how their proposed building would stand up, whilst at the other end of the professional spectrum leading Modernist architects were liberated to play compositional games with columns rather than worrying about where the load would most logically and economically fall. Once the building was designed in outline they could then turn their attention to the textures and surface treatments of the concrete.

Whatever the excitement Modernist architects felt about its engineering possibilities and its aesthetics, concrete is seen by some as having the most generic-looking and uninteresting of finishes. Words which come up again and again are 'oppressive', 'grey', 'streaky', 'ugly'. It is certainly true that Brutalist architects tended to avoid adding colourful pigments to their concrete, but once you get your eye in you start to see a huge range of textures, tones and colours – a level of variety almost comparable to that of building stone, which is rarely attacked for its monotony. The buildings I found myself particularly drawn to as I started to get interested in Brutalism boasted a pretty good spread of concrete finishes, from carefully emphasised marks of the moulds into which the concrete was cast, through to techniques for exposing stone aggregate on the surface of the concrete, allowing the colours and textures of the natural stone to blend with that of the cement in the final effect.

Concrete can be one of the cheapest options for getting something solid built at speed, or can be a highly refined craft material, and can often be beautiful in either capacity, from the heroic roughness of the unreinforced-concrete Glenfinnan Viaduct in Scotland (1897–1901), made internationally famous by Harry Potter's trip to school, to the impeccable refinement of the National Theatre in London

(1969–76).* Sometimes it is handled to seem like the last word in high-technology modernity; sometimes it is used for primitivist experiments which seem to recall the first caves in which our anthropoid ancestors once perhaps found a sense of home.

Of the many moods and textures of the material, perhaps the rarest in Britain's concrete architecture is genuine roughness of construction. In this, Britain's modern architects departed from their Swiss-French hero, Le Corbusier. They absorbed every Le Corbusier drawing or photograph they could lay their hands on, and cycled or hitch-hiked their way fanatically across France to see each building in person, yet they did not tend closely to imitate his joyfully clumsy construction techniques. The roughness of Le Corbusier's monastery of La Tourette – built partly by its own monks and showing in some horrendously crude execution that they had a lot to learn about making shuttering and pouring concrete – was certainly too much for most clients, so architects avoided it. For example, the greatest British exponent of exposed concrete, Denys Lasdun, was so eager to dissociate himself from the monastery, despite its clear influence on his glazing at the National Theatre, that when asked for a list of his influences he specified 'Le Corbusier [. . .] (not La Tourette).'[9] By the end of the 1950s the British building industry was becoming highly competent with concrete, and, pushed as we shall see by perfectionist architects, by 1970 it had raised it to a construction craft as sophisticated as any in architectural history.

The many tendencies and virtues of concrete are rarely clearly distinct from each other, and seldom all thought through in any single project. Brutalist architects chose concrete and its textures sometimes at the last minute, sometimes by default, sometimes with loving care and attention, sometimes modified to please planners or clients, and sometimes for the engineering qualities of the

---

* Both projects were built by the contractors McAlpine, whose founder was nicknamed 'concrete Bob'.

material. In almost all its states and uses it fitted well into the late Modernist preoccupation with architectural honesty, allowing buildings to show simultaneously how they were built, what they were made of and how they stood up.

What is repeatedly clear, through all its variations, is that concrete was anything but an unfortunate necessity for most of these architects, most of the time. In fact, it was typically at least as expensive as brick, and was chosen as an active preference. In mid-century, energy-rich Britain, concrete joined cars, easy international travel, central heating and universal healthcare as a new, life-changing luxury for all.

iii

In the decades after 1945, economic growth and the rapid expansion of the Welfare State called for new building on an epic scale. Concrete gave architects a whole new palette with which to supply the need. Now buildings could be sculpted into whatever shape suited their function and site, with gardens on the roofs, open space or parking underneath, and pedestrian walkways snaking effortlessly through space to join neighbouring buildings and get people clear of the danger, noise and dirt of cars below. Each floor could at will be stepped back from the one beneath so that every room had its own outdoor terrace, or if space was tight a building could soar thirty storeys into the sky without needing walls so thick that the rooms at the bottom became small and dark. How could architects *not* have been fantastically excited and stimulated by such a remarkable new range of possibilities? Whatever the budget, whatever the client, many Brutalist architects were mesmerised by what Denys Lasdun was to describe with careful poetry as 'a muddy mixture of marl, clay, lime, sand, gravel, water, heavily laced with steel'.[10]

If post-war concrete was more carefully crafted than its reputation, another later myth also needs dispelling: although their buildings do not attempt to look like earlier buildings, Brutalist architects were in most cases strongly interested in architectural history as the longer context of their work, and as a major inspiration. They also took lessons from the existing city around their projects, and used their new historical engagement to differentiate themselves from the older generation of Modernist architects. Early Modernism had proclaimed its exciting novelty in part by reacting strongly against the historically inspired styles which had for centuries characterised architecture in Europe. Much Modernist architecture of the 1920s and '30s explicitly or implicitly suggested that it was the start of a programme to tear down the dirty, class-ridden, dilapidated Victorian city and rebuild it anew – white, spacious, well-planted, clean, and with large, efficient roads. There can be something shrill or insecure-seeming about buildings from these early years of Modernism: they appear to shout their allegiance to the new, terrified of any accusation of being old-fashioned. If your buildings obeyed the stylistic rules you were part of the club; if they deviated you were out – other aspects of design were secondary to the question of which side you were on.

Post-war Modernism may scarcely have been more pluralist, but it was certainly more confident. In Britain Modernism was so dominant after 1945 that architects had greater freedom to experiment without their Modernist credentials coming into question. Brutalism, for all its exaggerated toughness and aesthetic unfamiliarity, was led by architects who were very interested in architectural history and not ashamed to admit it. For one thing, Modernism itself had by the 1950s been around for long enough to have its own history. The person who did most to push the name and the early ideas of Brutalism, Reyner Banham, was himself a historian of Modernism rather than an architect. Banham's PhD research (supervised by the great cataloguer of English architecture, Nikolaus Pevsner) on the early years of Modernism hugely enriched the architectural vocabularies firstly of those immediately around him, then through articles in the *Architectural Review* – the dominant journal of the 1950s – the wider architectural world. Banham unearthed the technological fantasies and social experiments of Constructivist Communist architects in revolutionary Russia, and their right-wing counterparts, the Futurist dreams of some of the founders of Fascism in Italy. Oddities of pre-war Modernism – like the wonderful, bonkers Gut Garkau farm, built north of Lübeck in the early 1920s by Hugo Häring – were brought by Banham to the attention of a younger generation bored with the white boxes of the 1930s and angrily hostile to the pretty softness of the Swedish-inspired decorative design that was coming to replace them.[11] The rawness of Garkau's materials and its strange, unfamiliar, organic-looking shapes thrilled the young and gave them a sense of how much artistic experimentation might be possible still under the banner of Modernism.

Behind the Brutalists' enthusiasm for Banham's new additions to the Modernist canon lay a longer sweep of history. Almost all the major Modernist architects were educated in architecture schools which had at the time either not yet adopted Modernist curricula at all, or had not done so to the point of eradicating their emphasis on the history of 'Western' architecture since ancient Egypt or Greece. Even as they established their Modernist credentials, therefore, these architects had a lifelong visual lexicon of ancient Athens and Rome, Egyptian temples and Baroque churches and palaces, Christopher Wren and John Soane.

These historical references are very rarely explicit in Brutalist architecture, which accepted uniformly the Modernist ban on ornament and historical quotation. However, the work of many architects of the 1950s to 1970s is discernibly underpinned by a classically trained sense of the axis, the vista, and the architectural set piece. From the later 1950s a strange pairing began: Modernist architects like Alison and Peter Smithson and Denys Lasdun began to take a serious interest in fitting their buildings well into an existing urban context at the same time as momentum gathered behind the Comprehensive Development Plan demolitions of huge swathes of Victorian and Georgian city.[12]

iv

A small concrete hut in a far corner of the Scottish coast may seem a funny place to go looking for evidence either of Brutalism's deep commitment to concrete craft, or of its interest in the subtle reworking of historical precedents. Yet in fact the building is free to show up the true preoccupations of its architect better than any other in the book: the same man was client, designer and builder. He had no one to please but himself.

My editor, when I told him of the mystery of this little masterpiece on its remote coastal promontory, set to work tracking down the architect but got there just too late. He had sadly died a few months earlier.[13]

David Scott was born in the east of England into a family of architects. In 1955, in his early twenties, heavily bearded and newly qualified as an architect himself, he set off for an extended trip to Scotland, eventually winding up in Achmelvich. There it seems he befriended a local crofter, who gave him permission to construct a temporary shelter on the rocky coast, and a more permanent one if he so wished. Scott set to work, built a sturdy turf hut, a mattress of rushes 'from the field up the road', and began to plan his project.

For around six months, Scott worked on the castle. His building operation, though low-tech, was by no means chaotic, with a walkway of planks running down to the beach so that he could push sand and pebbles up in a wheelbarrow to mix them with his cement. Yet whilst he was purposeful about his task he was clearly determined to disengage from the concerns of his normal life. Margaret MacLeod, the crofter's daughter, remembered: 'He took his watch off when he moved into his hut and he never ever wore it or looked at it again until the day he left.'

She recalled her father saying that the architect repeatedly attempted to add to the concrete hut after it reached its completion, but each time abandoned the additions in dissatisfaction. The idea that he was reluctant to acknowledge that the construction process was finished paints a picture of someone for whom building in concrete was in itself a therapeutic act. The original turf hut survived for a couple of years after the completion of the concrete one, before being butted out of existence by the croft's bull.[14] If it objected equally to the concrete one, the bull made little impression on it.

Scott spoke little about his building in later years, and it has never received much attention. In the decades since he left it has served as an occasional bothy (a free, primitive shelter for walkers), but otherwise has just sat there, through harsh winters and blustery summers, sun, rain and snow. Arriving there nearly six decades after Scott left, I saw something which cannot have changed much in the intervening years.

After the anxiety of whether I would find it, and my prolonged travel, arriving at the hut was a huge relief. As I stood above it, taking in my first view, it was, if anything, even smaller than I had expected. Its little chimney jutted above it like a child's drawing, and its lumpy division into different parts gave it a mysterious, defensive appearance. The few very small square empty windows did not make the abstract shapes any more domestic or welcoming. As I moved towards it, the mystery deepened rather than being solved: each angle revealed new shapes and elements, suggesting but not making clear how the inside might be arranged. The building combined with charming individuality an inscrutable irregularity of shape and an overwhelming consistency of material: every part of it is built of concrete. The limited range of colours, and the lack of distraction or softening that might have been produced by prettier materials, forced my concentration on to shape and texture.

I hurried to it, and round to the entrance, which gave me pause. With my substantial rucksack on I could not get through the narrow doorway, teetering above a fairly steep fall into a cove. Even with the rucksack off it was a squeeze, and there was definitely something uninviting about the unknown darkness of the interior, approached through a trap-like entrance, stooped and twisting to get in. The slops of cement down the concrete walls looked at first sight ominously faecal, but I was determined to stay inside the hut if I could. I was steeling myself for a really revolting clear-up operation if the interior turned out to be full of detritus. Or if it was infested I was getting ready to remind myself repeatedly that the most dangerous insect life in Scotland is the tick, whatever the crawling feelings on my nocturnally over-sensitive skin. I experienced a huge surge of pleasure on finding that aside from a single beer-bottle cap the interior was immaculately clean and free of fauna. I find it hard not to romanticise the remoter parts of Scotland, with the touching feeling they give me of universal honesty and goodwill. The spotless condition of the hut contributed to my elation at arriving.

With my rucksack declaring the hut to be mine for the night, I was able to relax, roam around and explore the various views of Hermit's Castle from the ground around it, enjoying its pale glow in the watery sunshine. The hut is on a rocky spit which shelters on one side a waveless cove (waveless, at least, in mild summer weather); it stands above the cove atop a bleakly beautiful wall of rock which shelves down steeply into the water at high tide. Over the hours the water ebbs away slowly to uncover black-stained boulders, seaweed and pebbles. It would be hard to imagine a more beautiful place to build. Those who like their nature completely raw and with no sign of human proximity might feel a sympathy for the 1960s architect Peter Moro's witty, if somewhat unfair, attack on Frank Lloyd Wright's most famous house, Fallingwater: 'if you block out the buildings, it's even better'.[15] Yet the west coast of Scotland is rich in beautiful, rocky coastline, and for me the artistic intervention in it here by a gifted architect heightens the beauty of both the building and the natural surroundings.

Margaret MacLeod recalls that after David Scott's departure the windows were smashed and the locked door broken in using tools which Scott had left outside it.[16] If this is right it seems to have been done with delicacy – the glass is gone, but the frames have been carefully missed by whoever smashed the windows, and the door frame survives the removal of the door itself. The impression I had was that the intervention had been an adaptation rather than vandalism. If the interior was becoming damp, fusty or infested, opening it to the air has certainly cured it.

The hut has not been thrown up but designed, and does not take its appearance from any one source. If the surrounding rocks are a clear inspiration, there is also in its rough concrete, and the way its assertive little T-shaped chimney enlivens its roofline, something of the post-war work of Le Corbusier, coarse in craft and hugely expressive in shape. There are older precedents here too, perhaps including an implicit meditation on the original basic human shelter about which – as the presumed origin of architecture – architectural theorists have speculated since at least the eighteenth century.

On its south front the hut meets the ground in a series of zigzagging pyramids which seem a miniaturisation of the angular bastions which defended the seventeenth-century fortresses of Sébastien de Vauban. The confidence with which Hermit's Castle perches on a clifftop perhaps has echoes of the Parthenon on the rocky mass of the Athenian Acropolis, or nearer at hand the castles of Edinburgh or Stirling. A small-windowed concrete structure on a coastline also calls to mind the defensive pillboxes and bunkers of the Second World War.

Below the hut, on the edge of the cove, a large shelf of stone makes a sheltered suntrap, and a particularly comfortable place to lie looking back at the building. I spent much of my stay doing just that, watching the waveless tide come in and go out and the sun work its way round the sky, changing the composition of the shadows and highlights on the complex shapes of the hut. I suspect

that David Scott spent time on just the same rock, because his design looks particularly good from there, and it is from this lower angle that the extent of the building's specificity to the site is most apparent. A natural, heavily weathered fault in the rock below the hut has created over millennia a deep, dark vertical crack running down almost to the water. The doorway of the hut – narrower than is practical, and taller than is necessary – continues this vertical line into the architecture, uniting hut and stone.

From other angles, too, the architecture appears to accommodate itself closely to the outcrops amongst which it sits. Like them it has a blocky, irregular, cubist composition. It is in a similar colour tone to the rocks on which it sits, and into the concrete have been pushed small boulders from the vicinity to pick up the bursts of black, pink and yellow which seem to shine out from the weathered stone of the area in some lights. Yet whilst the hut takes clear inspiration from its surroundings, it is not uniformly self-effacing. If it almost disappears into the surroundings from some angles, from others it stands on the skyline with the pride, ostentation and apparent robustness of a monument.

These resonances with a long history, and relationship to the eternal bedrock and water of the site, are expressed with potential incongruity in the archetypal material of modernity: concrete. The architect was free to produce a hut of wood or stone if he wished – enough wood must have been transported to the site as shuttering and as construction ramps down to the beach to build a pretty decent shed, and the site is surrounded by loose stones of all sizes and shapes. He *did* produce and live in a hut of turf, which makes it all the clearer that the concrete one was built for building's sake, not to provide shelter. In its smallness and simplicity, Achmelvich does not explore the advanced engineering potential of concrete, but in some ways its simplicity and the crudity of its construction craft show up the 1950s architect's love affair with the material and with history even more clearly.

If concrete is generally held as the opposite of nature, suspiciously technological and homogenising, at Achmelvich it is anything but. Apart from the cement, which makes up perhaps 20 per cent of the material of the hut, everything else in it is as local as it possibly could be. The sand is the bright, white sand of the local beach, and you can see shells and shell fragments scooped up with the sand and embedded in the walls. These show through on the seaward side of the hut, where the harsh weather has scoured away the surface of the concrete to reveal its constituent aggregates. The coarse aggregate consists of pebbles from the same beach, within ten metres of the hut. The fact that the hut is made of the rocks and sands on which it sits explains why it tones in so well with its surroundings.

The cement, though industrially produced and alien to the site, is not in the least industrial in its expression. If Hermit's Castle was indeed built in 1955, it is one of the earliest expressions in Britain of the full rawness of Le Corbusier's post-war concrete. Cement has slopped through gaps in the moulds in which it was cast, running in grey-brown, viscous drips down the concrete below and pooling by the entrance door, filtered of its aggregate by the narrowness of the hole in the shuttering through which it escaped. It looked disconcertingly organic, but certainly not incongruously industrial.

Not only the constituent elements of the concrete are made clear at the hut; the way in which it was built is equally evident. The method of concrete construction used at Achmelvich involves producing moulds which are a negative image of the lower levels of the building, then pouring in the concrete in situ. You then wait for the concrete to harden before repeating the process for the next stage up. Here the moulds, known as formwork, were made with rough-textured planks of wood. You can see this from the wood-grain patterns which they have left in the finished concrete. The successive lifts (sessions of pouring) are unmistakable because the joins between different days' work are messy, and concrete often dribbles through beneath the new day's formwork.

The windows were industrially produced glass bricks which were bought already set into concrete frames – the crofter's daughter reports that they were imported from France. These must have been pushed into the in situ concrete once the building reached their level. The roof was also cast into wooden boards, but whereas during the construction of the walls some slopping-through of cement was permitted and enjoyed, it has been prevented in the roof. The board-marking of the roof is thus less clear than that of the walls, but instead the texture records the well-rounded wrinkles in the tarpaulin or plastic sack which must have been used to line the mould. The concrete ceiling has then been given a lick of white paint which increases the amount of light reflected into the living area.

The thoughtfulness of the overall design meets very satisfactorily with the romantic primitiveness of the construction methods. On the rocks around the base of the hut there are various dribbles of concrete – drips and slops produced wetly in the 1950s but quickly almost as solid as the stone on to which they fell. They and the walls paint a picture of a building site on which the architect struggled to bring the heavy materials up through the rocks, nailed together planks into crude formwork, and splattered the concrete around as he mixed and poured it, enjoying the physicality of the material and its extraordinary ability to transform itself from manipulable sludge to unbudgeable rock literally overnight. The man who made it is dead, but tiny incidental details of his day-to-day work sixty years ago have been immortalised in the hut's surfaces – where he knocked nails into the formwork to hold it in place; where he was rough or approximate in his work; how the planks aligned to make the tray for the roof to be poured on to, and where the waterproof lining wrinkled.

Stone, water and cement are all immensely heavy, and it must have been exhaustingly hard work lugging the local materials up from the beach and the cement bags from the car at least two or three hundred metres away over rough ground. The building process itself must have been gratifying and acutely sensual, fighting with the escape attempts of the weighty concrete amidst the mess and dust of crude woodwork and concrete mixed presumably in a large bucket or a very basic concrete mixer. It sounds like a superb way of escaping from a stressful moment: the rest at the end of each physically hard day, the visible progress, and the growing skill and fitness that Scott must have acquired over the months; freedom from the criticisms of collaborators or teachers, from the weight of family expectation, from the daily routines of city life and from the never-completed to-do list.

If my account of Hermit's Castle seems hopelessly poetic, there is evidence that I am not alone in responding strongly to it. The shamelessly romantic name it has ended up with shows in its self-contradiction (hermits did not as a rule live in castles) the resonances of meditative solitude from its single-sleeper interior, and the apparent fortification of the exterior. Both words also evoke a period vaguely but vastly earlier than 1955.

On the afternoon of my arrival my somnolent watching was punctuated by a constant succession of visitors from the campsite. The most frequent were parents bringing children on what were manifestly repeat visits. With some I got talking. Others came and went without noticing me sitting a little way away amongst the rocks. The children's excitement at the building was evident, and the parents, too, asked eager questions, in particular about what it was built for.

As the long August day reached sunset the sky became a deep blue overlaid with a lacework of pink clouds. The families were back at their campsite, but now some older children appeared, trying not to show that they were a little put out that there was a strange man sitting outside the hut which was presumably the usual centre of their games.

They left me to my watch, and I sat out in the cooling air, weighing against the beginnings of chilliness the specialness of the fading light over the sea, and letting the view win. A distant lighthouse flashed, and the beacons of a ship passed along the horizon with the consistent but imperceptible progress of a clock's second hand, whilst pink turned to blue and then black. I shuffled back into my hut. Inside, by torchlight, perhaps the strongest echo of older architecture emerged. The hut has a hard, mineral interior, made entirely from concrete except where the rocks beneath emerge through the concrete floor. Within it, all formed from concrete, are the bed space, some basic seating, a fireplace and a set of shelves in a hearth area. These, and even the scale of the hut, call to mind the 5,000-year-old Neolithic houses unearthed a century earlier and a hundred miles away at Skara Brae on Orkney. The Skara Brae huts, too, have a cosy tightness of planning, a single central space approached through narrow tunnels like the antechamber of the Achmelvich hut, and built-in furniture, though of course Skara Brae's beds and cupboards are of stone rather than concrete.

The inbuilt furniture in the Achmelvich hut brings together Skara Brae with a post-war architectural preoccupation with designing very closely around function. Where other periods of architecture might have produced an empty hut to be temporarily furnished by residents, the post-war designer thought through the living functions of the hut and built them in, from concrete. Thus there are shelves, a fireplace, a bed encased with hard walls like a sarcophagus, and in the remaining floor space a series of raised triangles on which to sit or place objects. It is characteristic of this degree of functional specificity that it can be overprescriptive and limiting: although there would be room for three or four sleeping bags in a structure that size, the seating triangles cut into the floor space to the point that if two people wish to visit Achmelvich together, one of them will need a tent. It was designed to sleep one, and it only sleeps one.

I wriggled into the welcome warmth of my sleeping bag, wearing all my clothes apart from my boots and waterproof – I had brought only a light sleeping bag to offset the weight of camera, tripod and (in case the hut had turned out to be uncleanably revolting, or occupied by someone else) tent. My sleeping mat was a good fit for the bed coffin, and lying in pretty much the only position the bed allows, flat on my back, I looked up into the absolute darkness and felt utterly relaxed, drinking in the clichéd but genuine pleasures of being briefly out of all contact with phone and email, the deeply relaxing day I had had, and the primitive cosiness of the hut.

In the night the weather changed, and I was woken by the deep whistle of blustery wind booming irregularly through the broken windows, its gusts shaking the windward walls with dull thuds. Rain was spitting through the window openings, pattering harmlessly but loudly against my orange survival bag (a body-sized, thick bin bag carried by winter hill walkers in the hope that they might see morning if they sprain an ankle). I dug through my rucksack for the earplugs which one of the Bavarians from the youth hostel had kindly given me the previous morning when I had complained how little sleep I had got. With them in I got back to sleep easily, enjoying all the more in these basic and isolated surroundings that atavistic pleasure in being warm and dry when it is wet and cold outside.

One more time I woke during the night, this time for a pee on a nearby rock. The rain was still spitting, but the early dawn light was a stunning yellow which I knew at the time I would regret not trying to photograph, as I looked at it for a bleary minute and then staggered back to bed.

In the morning I stood my little Trangia camping stove on the hearth and boiled the water for a cup of camomile tea. I was very sorry to have to leave for my bus, though the sadness at leaving the hut behind me was considerably mitigated by the fact that the walk back has ever-shifting distant views of one of Scotland's most dramatic groups of mountains, each hill isolated from its neighbours right down to the valley, as in a child's drawing of mountains, and all the more dramatic for it. Waiting for the bus I had my first hot food for twenty-four hours, a burger from a roadside van, eaten sitting on the rock-built coastal defences of the harbour.

As for David Scott himself, after living there for six months during the construction he apparently only returned once, for a single weekend. Perhaps something about the hut disappointed him, but I would prefer to think that it had fulfilled its purpose in liberating him, through the isolation and the focus on building, from the weight of his young man's anxieties. It certainly relaxed me far more than you might expect in just a twenty-four-hour visit, and I will return again one day.

I have very frequently thought of Hermit's Castle since, and indeed I have a favourite picture of it as the background image on my phone. I delete apps in order to keep it visible. I would take David Scott's inspired coarseness and artistic haphazardness every time over the highly crafted perfection of a building like Mies van der Rohe's Farnsworth House – the last word in rationalistic steel-and-glass order, perfect in its geometries and slender in its structure. Remarkable, and in its way stirring, as Mies's achievement was, I respond so much more to the contingent wildness of Brutalism than to the chilly perfection of Miesian steel Modernism.

Peerlessly dramatic as is the setting and design of Hermit's Castle, it is by no means the only place where I have experienced the highest elation and pleasure from the raw concrete power of the best Brutalist architecture. For me, the cave-like magnificence of the National Theatre's foyers, or the external landscape of cliffs and gulches created by the Barbican Estate's huge buildings, are as overwhelming as any natural landscape. And for me, the great Brutalist landscapes are made more interesting, not less so, by the fact that they were brought about not through the arbitrary swilling of lava or water but through the determined pushing of clients, architects, engineers and builders, striving to fulfil everyday human needs and wishes, and to add to them something more. The best Brutalist architecture turns necessity into the sublime.

Chapter Two

Monuments to the People
Trellick Tower and Balfron Tower

(barnabascalder.org/rc2/)

i

Just after I turned twenty, I begrudgingly allowed a friend to take me on a tour of Trellick Tower, thirty-one storeys of concrete council housing in West London. When we arrived, I am ashamed to say that I found myself a little scared. It was not from the pleasurable aesthetic frisson of a huge weight of concrete towering over me, but from the altogether more cowardly and absurd fear that someone might mug me. Having grown up through the 1980s and '90s I had a luridly ill-informed perception of Brutalist housing, pieced together from media portrayals of council estates plagued by gang wars so vicious that the police did not dare enter.

I felt that we could scarcely be more conspicuously out of place: wearing the wrong clothes, talking loudly about architecture in the wrong accents, standing still and gazing up, rather than walking purposefully to or from somewhere. I was accustomed to a clear separation between the public street and the private front garden, and the walkways of the estate did not seem to fit either of my narrow categories: residents might have a legitimate grievance against

MONUMENTS TO THE PEOPLE

me for intruding. I was also acutely aware that the walkway we were on was high-walled and narrow; it offered no escape if someone decided they did not like us.

Despite being busy concealing my deeply uncool collywobbles, I could see my friend's arguments for the architectural excellence of the building in front of us. He pointed out qualities from the overall impressiveness of its scale down to the tiny details: a concrete pyramid beneath a gutter gargoyle on one of the outbuildings of the estate – a wonderfully self-indulgent touch allowing the passage of time to be recorded by the medium-term accumulation of water-staining and the long-term erosion of the pyramid under decades of drips. I had no idea about the differences between concrete construction techniques or finishes, and little sense of how to read on the exterior the engineering and internal disposition. Trellick Tower was simply a mysterious aesthetic object, overlaid with broadly negative associations, but all the more exotic and thrilling for them.

Built in 1968–72 by the architect Ernö Goldfinger, Trellick Tower forms the spectacular landmark of the predominantly low-rise Edenham Street Estate, sandwiched between the Great Western Railway and the Regent's Canal, as they pass north of Westbourne Park in West London. On an earlier estate in Poplar, ten miles to the east, is the unmistakable older sibling of Trellick Tower, commissioned in 1962, built in 1965–67, and named Balfron Tower because of historic Scottish connections in the area.[1] This older estate, Rowlett Street, has more high-rise blocks than Edenham, but Balfron Tower nevertheless bulks there with nearly as awesome a clarity as Trellick dominates in Westbourne Park. Though the two towers are strikingly similar, Trellick is slightly taller, slightly more complicated in its planning and elevations, and its contradictory characters of brittle-looking slenderness and invulnerable-looking weight are even more pronounced. They are too spectacular to be regarded as typical of anything much, but together they are one of the great achievements of the post-war Welfare State housing programme, and have come recently to be widely discussed flashpoints in the debates about the past merits, the present policies and the future prospects of social housing in the UK.

ii

Housing reflects social and economic change with extraordinary clarity, whether in the sudden Georgian explosion of London into new squares and streets for the solid merchants who thrived in abundance during the expansion of the British Empire, or in the Victorian industrial cities where in a matter of years the surrounding villas and farms vanished into countless terraces of tight little houses for the workers in docks, mills and warehouses. The twentieth century's British council-housing programme was equally sweeping, and equally closely related to developing social patterns. The legacy of nineteenth-century population explosion and over-rapid city growth was, it was generally agreed, polluted, crowded, slum-blighted cities. In the nineteenth century, people moving to towns drawn by the Industrial Revolution's seemingly limitless demand for new urban workers had been housed almost entirely by private speculative builders. Over the course of the century local authorities had taken increasingly interventionist measures to raise standards of health and hygiene, but it was 1890 before the London County Council's Boundary Estate set an example in directly providing housing for lower-income groups, replacing a notorious slum, and following the lead of the philanthropic Peabody Trust. After the First World War, local-authority housing provision picked up pace, with around a million flats and houses (about 30 per cent of the total new supply) being built by councils between the wars.[2]

This movement gained further momentum after the Second World War. Six years of total war had made central coordination the default solution to national problems, and no one could deny that the state of much British housing constituted a serious and urgent problem. In the first place there was a substantial rise in demand for housing in many areas, with soldiers returning from active service and young wartime couples seeking married homes. This demand was ill met by the existing housing stock. Bombing had destroyed or rendered uninhabitable 450,000 houses, and with much of the workforce away at war, and industrial activity and labour diverted to military purposes, standards of maintenance and updating had been woefully inadequate even in houses that had emerged otherwise unscathed.[3] Overcrowding was rife in poor areas, coal fires (the main source of domestic heat) kept everything constantly sooty, damp led to health-ruining mould, polluting industry and transport were slammed up against homes, and cars were making the streets where children played increasingly dangerous. As usual, poor housing became associated at least in people's minds with poor health, poor education, and poor social outcomes.[4] It was easy to condemn whole swathes of a city as irrecoverable slums. It followed irresistibly that they ought urgently to be demolished and replaced.

Despite the tendency since the 1980s to paint the boom in council housing as a left-wing moment, at the time it was barely possible to distinguish socialist motivations from the ongoing right-wing tradition of benevolent paternalism, forgotten subsequently in the Thatcherite project of associating Conservatism with small-state politics. It was clear to those of any political stripe that the conditions of the poor were unacceptable, and state action seemed to almost everyone the self-evident mechanism to fight the new war which William Beveridge, in his formative 1942 report, had called for.[5] Both Labour and Conservative governments presided over the huge council-housing boom of the post-war period up to 1969, which saw four million council properties built – 59 per cent of all housing production.[6]

There were, however, shades of difference within the council-housing movement. Many on the left wanted public housing to become a standard option for middle-income people, whereas the right wing of the Conservative Party was opposed to the provision of council housing for any but those who could not afford to buy their own or rent at an economically viable rate. Despite dissenting voices, the total proportion of publicly owned housing rose from 18 per cent to 27 per cent over the Tory-dominated decade from 1950 to 1960.[7]

This national tendency to expanding state provision was in large part administered and driven by local councils, which enjoyed considerable independence in directing their own housing policies, resulting in considerable differences in policy and architecture from area to area.[8] Not only did councils respond to changes in legislation and subsidy through which Parliament sought to shape local housing provision, they also campaigned for the central government measures they thought would help them in their housing programmes.[9]

The largest quantity of new council housing nationally remained on the inter-war pattern of so-called 'cottage' estates of suburban low-density houses with gardens – statistically important, but without much to offer to the seeker after Brutalist sublimity. Inner-city 'slum clearance' areas were most often rebuilt at higher densities than the cottage estates, but here too the most common type was generally limited to five storeys, a height where money could be saved by providing few or no lifts and avoiding the structural challenges and wind-pressure that come with taller buildings.[10]

Despite the considerable extra difficulty of building high, from the mid-1950s high-rise towers or tall slab-blocks became more and more common, often dotted amidst lower blocks, or standing in large open areas to keep densities down to the new recommended figures, and to avoid cutting out sunlight from each other or neighbouring housing. Local authorities were proud to be providing new housing, and it seems likely that most were pleased to have it marked clearly on the horizon to remind the electorate that they were achieving up-to-date housing improvements as fast as they could.

In most developments, whatever their height, the single biggest motivation tended to be quantity of supply – the desire to bring down housing waiting lists and to be able to boast of the number of units completed.[11] The second-biggest priority was standards, in particular in the provision of facilities which had previously been confined to the homes of the rich: fitted kitchens, central heating, and dedicated bathrooms with hot water on tap and flushable indoor lavatories.

The huge quantity of high-rise produced in the 1950s and '60s all over Britain has given rise to a widespread perception that it must have been a cheap option. There has been a ceaseless repetition in subsequent decades of claims that many tower blocks were 'shoddily built'. When, in 1968, a gas explosion from a botched cooker installation pushed the walls of Ronan Point apart, a whole corner of the building collapsed, killing four and spreading doubts about the safety of high-rise buildings.[12] But it was a solitary case. Despite the understandable anxiety caused by such a prominent disaster, most tall blocks were structurally sound, and very rarely the cheapest option. Building high always cost more than building low, and under UK regulations on daylight and density, tall blocks did not house substantially more people than lower-rise estates. They were high-rise through choice, not compulsion or corner-cutting.[13]

As the 1960s high-rise boom gathered pace, many councils negotiated deals with construction companies like Wimpey or Crudens to design and build a given number of units on a given number of acres of land to be provided by the council.[14] Others had in-house architects working with their officers, and some even did the building work in-house as well, setting up their own substantial direct-labour building concerns. You might loosely call some of this output Brutalist – there is usually at least some exposed concrete, and they are certainly free of decoration – but it tends not to be particularly visually exciting. Only a few councils let architects of real creativity loose on something as politically sensitive and expensive as large housing programmes.

After an inauspicious start, by far the most notable exception to the low-key, almost utilitarian norm was the London County Council (LCC). From the end of the war until 1949, London's public housing provision was placed in the hands of the LCC Valuer, an administrative role previously concerned only with acquiring and managing sites. This department took on the huge task of meeting vast and urgent housing requirements on a very tight budget.[15] Many blocks of red-brick 1940s flats in poorer inner suburbs like Lambeth bear witness to this unglamorous building boom.[16]

In 1949 the LCC Architect, Robert Matthew, managed to take control of housing from the Valuer.[17] This turned out to be far more than departmental empire-building. Once Matthew, and his deputy Leslie Martin, gained control of housing they set out to make the LCC's housing estates world-beating in their quality, diversity and innovativeness. Resisting the temptation to make economies of scale from large-scale repetition of the same housing blocks, the LCC Architect's Department organised its designers into smallish teams and gave them considerable autonomy to develop and execute their own ideas under the benevolent supervision of Martin and Matthew.[18] This, and the lack of private work available before building materials ceased to be rationed in 1954, made the LCC hugely attractive to the best young designers emerging from the nation's architecture schools. It rapidly became the world's largest architectural grouping and one of the best anywhere, the more so because both Matthew and Martin had remarkably sure eyes for spotting promising young talents.

Even an office of this size and quality was not adequate to the task of designing all of London's immense building-boom of housing and schools, and certain schemes were accordingly offered out to the council's approved list of private practitioners, further increasing the quality and variety of the LCC's architectural patronage. Trellick Tower and Balfron Tower and their estates were two of those projects.

Ernö Goldfinger had worked during the war as a member of the team which produced the hugely influential *County of London Plan* drawn up for the LCC. Now that there was building to do he was on the list of approved private architects, and had shown his abilities in working to Welfare State budgets designing Brandlehow School, Putney, for the LCC in 1950, using a clever prefabrication system he had devised to speed up and cheapen the building of decent school buildings.[19] Having demonstrated competence and quality in smaller schemes, Goldfinger was rewarded with first the Rowlett Street Estate and then, as it moved towards a successful conclusion, the Edenham Street Estate.

iii

When Goldfinger was awarded the commission for Rowlett Street he was an imposing sixty-year-old, six foot two and very well built, with a reputation for being face-whiteningly intimidating in person and manner. It is perhaps a tribute to Ian Fleming's courage that he dared to borrow the architect's striking surname for his famous villain. When the publishers agreed under pressure from Ernö Goldfinger to make it clear that the fictional Auric Goldfinger was in no way connected to him, Fleming was angry, proposing instead an erratum slip in each copy of the novel changing the name throughout to 'Goldprick', and explaining why. After the release of the film, the Goldfingers were repeatedly woken by idiots calling in the night, pretending to be James Bond.[20]

Goldfinger's accent and demeanour might in fact have made him a good Cold War Bond villain. He was an upper-class Hungarian by birth, whose parents' marriage had united the forestry and industrial interests of two families. His father had duelling scars, and Ernö Goldfinger appears to have retained an *ancien régime* sense of his own importance and of entitlement throughout his life. As a student he had had a number of fights, one of which came close to a duel of his own.[21]

As a young man in the 1920s, Goldfinger had studied at the École des Beaux-Arts, whose pre-eminent place in the world of architecture had been beyond dispute for decades. Goldfinger was one of a group of students there who challenged the institution from within. They decided that they would like a studio master more contemporary and innovative than the selection of classical architects then on offer. They petitioned Le Corbusier, but he had been noisily using the school as a shorthand for all that was wrong with architecture, and turned them down. Instead he recommended Auguste Perret, under whom he had himself worked a few years earlier. Perret jumped at the chance to display his legitimacy by teaching at the heart of the French architectural world.[22] He was to be a huge influence on Goldfinger.

Perret, a member of a family of building contractors, understood the technical and building-craft aspects of concrete better than most. His perpetual dapperness – Poirot-ishly comical to today's eyes – may have been a response to insecurity about this artisan background. He never looked as if he had just stepped off a building site. Perhaps for similar reasons he felt a passionate desire to establish the intellectual and architectural respectability of the material in which his family specialised, concrete. To do so Perret drew on the then-dominant classical language of architecture drawn ultimately from ancient Greece and Rome. His work, though often claimed as an early flowering of Modernism, was in fact concerned with creating a new variant of Classical architecture which expressed the realities of concrete engineering just as a major strand of French architectural theory felt that classical architecture had originated from the expression of first wooden, then stone, construction techniques. Perret replaced the mouldings which had been evolved in ancient Greek and Roman temples with new ones of his own devising, which reflected the practicalities of concrete casting and finishing. He derived new column shapes from the structural requirements of all-in-one-piece concrete structures rather than stone resting on stone.

Perret's profound understanding of reinforced concrete, both in engineering terms and in terms of the challenging building craft required to produce high-quality exposed concrete surfaces, evidently made its mark on Goldfinger, who treated the material with similar deep respect, and with a comparable level of technical skill.

Goldfinger emerged from his architectural training with a lifelong conviction as to the importance of architecture, and was convinced too of his own ability to produce it: 'There are good and bad architects. I am a good architect.'[23]

His career began with some comparatively modest commissions, amidst the exciting bohemian art world of pre-war Paris. When he met his wife Ursula Blackwell (of Crosse & Blackwell, the food manufacturers) he was living with an artist in Paris, and continued to do so as he and Ursula became lovers.[24] He is widely rumoured to have continued to sleep around throughout his life, perhaps suggesting a view of relationships with women which combined old-fashioned, upper-class caddishness with an art-world refusal to accept bourgeois constraints.

Ursula and Ernö moved to London in the early 1930s, living at first in Berthold Lubetkin's Highpoint flats before Goldfinger built his own brick-fronted Modernist house overlooking Hampstead Heath.[25] There, in 1942, he held an impressive art sale. Artist friends and contacts who exhibited included Augustus John, Barbara Hepworth, John Piper, Fernand Leger, Joan Miró, Henry Moore, Ben Nicholson and Kurt Schwitters. Goldfinger was a lifelong Marxist, and the charitable cause for which they were raising money was the Soviet Red Army.[26]

After the war Goldfinger gained a steady stream of commissions, mostly of medium scale, with the substantial exception of Alexander Fleming House, a complex of Ministry of Health offices and a cinema on the Elephant and Castle roundabout in South London.[27] It is the two tall blocks of council housing, however, that really represented the flowering of his decades of experience.

Both Balfron Tower and Trellick Tower are classic Brutalism at its best. Each shows Goldfinger and his team developing ideas from Le Corbusier's *Unité d'habitation* at Marseille, the founding monument of Brutalism. This influence was seen not just in their exposed concrete finish but in their complex section which gives access to three storeys of housing from each corridor, cutting down on the amount of circulation space, and allowing most flats and maisonettes to run the whole depth of the block with windows on each facade; and with no walkways overshadowing the windows or allowing passers-by to peer in.[28]

In each Goldfinger block, the overall shape arises from the functional disposition of flats, access to them, and provision of the necessary servicing and lifts, but the expression of each of these is heightened to produce not just a lift and boiler tower but a sculpture about lifts and boilers. To twenty-first-century eyes these objects might seem oddly banal subjects of architectural expression. However, most of the first generation of tenants moved in from low-rise terraces heated with grubby coal fires which required recurrent tending. Their awkward cooking arrangements had provided at best coal-fired stoves, and in some cases just the heating fire on which to cook food. They had bathed in a tin tub by the fire, and shivered in the outdoor privy every winter. Balfron Tower and Trellick Tower exploited the rapidly dropping energy prices of the 1960s to offer life-changing improvements in facilities: the new flats were amongst the first generations of LCC housing to be centrally heated (earlier post-war flats mostly still had fireplaces in order not to lumber tenants with the higher bills of central heating, but by the mid-1960s it was affordable). They had easy-to-clean kitchens and bathrooms, with hot and cold water constantly on tap, electricity, double glazing and built-in storage. Until very recently many of these facilities had been confined largely to the houses of the most up-to-date rich, but now they could be provided as standard to ordinary people. These working-class tenants had views over the whole of London, opened up by the height made

possible by electric lifts. Why *wouldn't* the architects celebrate this extraordinarily substantial and sudden rise in standards of living? Why shouldn't the highest point in the borough be the boiler house which provided this new comfort to existing residents, and offered the promise of comparable luxuries to those not yet rehoused? Balfron and Trellick are hymns to the energy wealth of the 1960s.

In parallel with this excitement at the democratisation of new technologies, Goldfinger's architecture also drew on older architectural traditions, including a somewhat mysticist belief in proportional systems. As far back as one can trace, many masons and architects have favoured certain proportions of rectangle over others in their designs, admiring in particular those whose mathematical or geometric properties single them out as remarkable. One proportion favoured by, amongst others, ancient Roman architects and Gothic masons was the Golden Ratio, a rectangle proportioned so that if you cut a square off one end of it you end up with a remaining shape in the same proportions as the original rectangle. In architecture this can be practically useful, but another strong attraction must have been the uniqueness and perfection of such a proportion.

The main elevations of both Balfron Tower and Trellick Tower can be divided up into series of squares and Golden Ratio rectangles, their underlying geometry giving discipline and order to the tight grid of flats.[29]

At Balfron Tower and Trellick Tower, then, Ernö Goldfinger was combining contemporary and timeless architectural preoccupations with the confidence and skill of an architect whose extensive experience had not dulled his focused commitment to design. And throughout both projects the concrete work is the worthy successor to the accomplished perfectionism of Goldfinger's teacher Perret.

Plain grey cement is the finest powder in concrete and accordingly comes to the front of the formwork during casting, producing an even grey surface textured by the shuttering against which it set. At Trellick and Balfron the concrete was cast thicker than was required, with the reinforcing steel deeper beneath the surface, in order that this grey outer layer of cement could be removed. Once the concrete had thoroughly set, the contractors ran over the surface with a heavy, mechanical bush-hammer (a pneumatic drill with a broad steel head shaped like several Toblerone bars set side by side). This smashed off the smooth grey surface, revealing the pebbles within and allowing their colour and texture to form the surface. The pebbles weather more evenly and with less change of colour than does a surface of smooth cement. Perret, who used bush-hammering extensively, may also have enjoyed the way in which it heightened the prominence of the stone pebbles within the cement: stone being a material with a flawless classical lineage, its visibility helped to legitimise concrete as its successor material.

This violent smashing-away of the surface achieves a well-controlled rough texture over a flat wall. When it comes to the corners, however, the reaction of the concrete is less predictable. A right-angled corner does not bush-hammer evenly, but produces a crumbly looking, irregular edge. Given the importance of edges to the appearance of a building – a wiggly silhouette gives an entirely different impression from a crisply orthogonal one – this would not have been acceptable to Goldfinger. Perret had solved this problem by putting wooden fillets into the corners of the formwork, meaning that the edge would be recessed behind the main surface of the concrete which was to be bush-hammered. Once the wall surfaces are hammered away this leaves a neat, wood-shuttered corner, framing the textured, bush-hammered walls on each side. At both Balfron and Trellick Towers this refined concrete detail was executed with great skill by the contractors, R. G. Minter Ltd, as shown on the rain gargoyle on the front page of this chapter. And the joy which Goldfinger and his team felt in this elegant detail can be seen by the discreet flourishes which they include in the design, like the cutaway at the bottom of an escape stair in front of Balfron Tower. The cut-away parapet is functionally absolutely

An escape stair in front of Balfron Tower

unnecessary, but just below twenty-six storeys of Brutalist tower block it is elegant, charming and curiously delicate.

Goldfinger's perfectionism is nowhere clearer than in the specification documents in which he indicated to the contractors the extent and nature of the work. A draft specification for Balfron Tower contains forty-one pages of detailed instructions on the concrete, starting with the need to stockpile all the gravel aggregate from the start of the project, to ensure they would not change source and therefore colour some way up the building, and carrying on through every stage of the process right through to strength-testing the concrete, and checking the details of shuttering, which must each time be approved by the architect (one assumes a more junior site architect rather than Goldfinger himself every time) before the concrete is poured, and on into a discussion of the dangers of staining from the oil that enables the shuttering to come smoothly off the finished concrete.[30]

iv

Such high quality came at a price: Goldfinger bullied everyone he felt he needed to in order to get the perfection he sought in his buildings. In the macho world of 1960s architecture, he used his size and physical strength to contribute to his dominance within his office: he would insist on hole-punching several sheets of card at a time – a method only he was strong enough to implement. His biographer Nigel Warburton records that he was celebrated for firing people with abandon and lost twenty-six employees in 1954–55 from a small office, either because he sacked them or because they left in anger or distress at his behaviour. Stories abound of Goldfinger's rages, including his attempt to sack a man who didn't even work for him, because the visitor was not getting on with work.[31]

As the architect John Winter, who worked for him, recalled, 'Goldfinger was a difficult man, explosively impatient of any shortcoming, and the mood in the office was often uneasy but the standard was never allowed to falter and respect for the art of architecture and the quality of construction was absolute.'[32]

His assistants worked hard on every detail, and Goldfinger monitored them closely and personally, tearing up drawings of which he disapproved, but extracting – from those who could tolerate his intimidating manner for more than a few days – the highest standards. Contractors, too, were bullied into their best endeavours by his authoritarianism and his expert awareness of defects in their work. At Balfron Tower, for example, Goldfinger discovered that a detail designed to carry rainwater away from the face of the wall and thus slow down weathering had been left out by the builders:

'Both Garage entrances and the bridges near the Garage and all the bridges have this ½" drip omitted. This is a scandalous state of affairs. Draw all the group leaders' attention to it, so that this sort of thing shall not happen again.'[33]

On budgets comparable to those of his contemporaries his buildings tend to be better detailed and better built than almost anyone's. The suffering of individuals has passed, the buildings are mostly still there, and – when not overhauled wrong-headedly for reasons of fashion – wearing well. Goldfinger's imperious hauteur, his pre-occupation with architectural art, and his sense of what was due to him, might suggest that the powerful, distinctive architectural statements made by his blocks were precisely the abstract artistic expressions of political dogma, or arrogant, self-glorifying tributes to the architect himself, which Postmodernist critiques of Modernism tended to find everywhere. There is overwhelming evidence to the contrary.

v

The quality of living conditions which Goldfinger secured for what he saw as 'his' residents was impressive on the tight budgets of the period. The sound insulation between flats, for instance, is anecdotally better than in almost any block of their time. This is expensive and difficult to get right, and easily sacrificed to limitations of budget or materials. The room proportions, too, are attractive and liveable. Many blocks of double-aspect flats followed the example of Le Corbusier's *Unités d'habitation* in being designed in the most structurally efficient manner, which is achieved by making each flat as deep and narrow as possible. This can result in corridor-like spaces which are hard to furnish – more like a train carriage than a living room. The closeness of the flanking walls can make the architecture overwhelm residents' attempts to customise and personalise their flats. Goldfinger, uncompromising as ever, ensured that living rooms and kitchens are close to square in plan. They are delightful rooms with ample windows, those higher up the blocks profiting from stunning views across London.

Nor did Goldfinger's dedication to the residents' comfort remain at the safe distance of the drawing board. When Balfron Tower was completed he and his wife rented for two months a top-storey flat in order to experience the living conditions he and his team had created. This was excellent publicity for Goldfinger and for the Greater London Council (the successor from 1965 of the London County Council), and was exploited as such. The GLC's press release was, for example, eager to clarify that the Goldfingers were not sponging on the ratepayer even for those two months:

> Mr Goldfinger will pay approximately £11 10s a week rent, exclusive of rates, but including central heating. This is the cost without any subsidy from the ratepayer or taxpayer. The subsidised rent for the flat will be £4 15s 6d, including heating, but exclusive of rates.[34]

Although it was undoubtedly exploited for publicity purposes, the archive shows that this stay was more than just an exercise in public relations. Ursula Goldfinger's notebook recording her life there is a charmingly human diary of her experiences and observations, focusing on the practicalities of the architecture. She documented everything from the stiffness of the entrance doors when struggling with shopping or a pram, to post-installation glitches with the lighting system. Here and elsewhere the spelling and punctuation seem to suggest that Goldfinger's perfectionism did not extend to the written word, and that whoever typed up Ursula's notes was not a distinguished typist:

> There are many complaints that the lights on landings passages and escape stairs are out at night [. . .] This is not only disagreeable but I would say unsafe. On one occasion our

front door bell rang at 11.30 at night. There was a rather drunk very large man who suggested I might like to see him throw himself off the building. I gathered he had walked up the stairs [to their twenty-sixth-floor flat], he did'nt even know there was a lift, and after some conversation which convinced me he did not intend to throw himself off the building, I shut the door and telephoned the caretaker.[35]

Ernö, too, seems to have taken his personal experience of Balfron Tower seriously. An article he wrote at the conclusion of his stay has a tone which seems far from the Goldfinger of legend – it is modest, self-analytical, practical and balanced:

Thresholds for the front doors were not originally provided and cold winds blew into the flats. This has been remedied by the provisions of a threshold for each flat. Windows have a copper gasket which proved satisfactory from the point of view of thermal insulation and sound insulation. Unfortunately, in certain high winds these copper gaskets vibrate, and, although they do not let the air through, create a trumpeting noise in flats at high levels. These have now been redesigned. Also being redesigned is the so-called permanent ventilation [an open vent causing a constant loss of heat], which is required by the London Building Acts. Tenants very wisely blocked this up as soon as they moved into the flats.

Even where his architecture is compromised by the tenants his tone remains civilised:

No door bells were provided, the letter box plates forming knockers. The result of this economy was that many tenants fixed electric door bells in odd places, with wires trailing inside the flats. This was a pity, after so much thought had gone into avoiding surface wiring.

Along with details of defects and teething problems – none of them particularly substantial for such a major building project – the Goldfingers recorded residents' responses to their new flats. Ursula reported that:

> I have talked to a number of tenants mainly in the lift or walking to the shop. They frequently started the conversation asking how long I had been in and if I liked the flats, bar the complaints of draughts from some windows, heating that did'nt work they all said the flats were lovely, those I have been into are beautifully kept, people are going to a lot of trouble to install them mostly with outragiously terrible furniture carpets, curtains and ornaments, though I dont think the designs of fabrics are much worse than those I see currently displayed at the Design Centre [a part-shop, part-exhibition intended as a national showcase of good Modernist design]. I have never heard anybody express regret for the terrace houses they have mostly come from.
>
> Some people complain of the size of the bedrooms. On enquiry this generally seems to be because they are trying to use single bedrooms as double ones, plus the fact that they have too much unsuitable furniture in those I have seen, but as one tenant said to me 'some people are never satisfied she's always been a grumbler and I happen to know she's never been in anything bigger than a one room dwelling all her life'.[36]

After a Tenants' Association meeting, Ernö transcribed a conversation he had had with Mrs Macdonald, a resident of a flat on the twenty-fourth floor:

> 'Mrs M: "I'm perfectly happy here I wouldn'nt change it for all the world, the people are very nice and my flat is beautiful I dont need to have the electric light on at all because the place is beautifully light. In fact I wish I'd had the chance to come here many years ago, had it been built."

E. G.: "How do you like the view Mrs Macdonald?"

Mrs M: "Absolutely marvelous, I really and truly pray for the evenings so that I can stand on my balcony and look at the beautiful lights."

E. G. "Do you like your balcony or do you find it to windy?"

Mrs M: "No – of course it can be windy which I suppose it would be in high buildings but this is really wonderful the winds don't worry me at all."

E. G. "Do you have any whistling noises in the living room and the windows?".

Mrs M. "Well occasionally but not a lot to grumble about. I'dont find no fault with the place at all".

E. G.: "Thats to kind Mrs. Macdonald"

Mrs. M.: "No I'm noted for being straight forward. I'm perfectly happy here and I would'nt change it for the Queen's own Buckingham Palace. I was born here and I know everybody and any body that I know in these flats says that they are perfectly happy here. There's nothing to find fault with, it's beautiful."

E. G.: "But do you find that there's less friendleness here"

Mrs. M: "No we're all friendly everyone you speak to is ever so nice, No we're all a friendly lot of people. [. . .] Everyone is sociable and that is God's truth." '[37]

The things residents would say to the architect and his wife (whose incognito status, if any, must have been pretty ineffectual in their expensive clothes, striking physical presence, and distinctive accents) might have been overgenerous through intimidation or politeness. The records of Tenants' Association meetings, however, also show a general atmosphere of satisfaction and pleasure at their new homes.[38]

One final document in Goldfinger's archive, a handwritten breakdown of the employment status of every head of household in the block, helps to give context to these early days in Balfron Tower, completed a few crucial years earlier than Trellick. When Balfron Tower was first inhabited, of all the heads of household only one was unemployed, and only one was recorded as being a 'housewife' – presumably indicating a woman with no job living without an earning partner. Ten were pensioners. All the rest were employed: fifteen were white-collar workers in jobs described as 'clerk', 'telegraphist' etc.; thirty-two were service-workers including drivers, 'char ladies', dustmen or tradespeople; fourteen worked in the nearby docks; fourteen in construction, decoration, or as 'labourers'; and the remaining forty in a wide range of industrial, blue-collar jobs.[39] Completed in 1968, Balfron Tower was occupied at the tail end of a period of high employment, and as the comments of tenants show, new council housing was regarded as a privilege for which to be grateful. In many estates things were soon to change.

Getting an accurate national overview of the declining fortunes which some social housing experienced from the 1970s is essentially impossible – anecdote and politically charged myth-making have trampled out the fragile evidence like the police in a Sherlock Holmes story. One pattern which is repeatedly attested, however, is the spiral of decline within which a small minority of antisocial tenants in a given block made flats there less attractive to new residents. In turn this would mean that tenants with the least choice over where they lived would be placed in vacant flats, and this sufficiently often included people with their own serious social problems: as a result a block could go in fairly short order from being functional and pleasant to being horribly intimidating and dogged by various bizarre trends for high-rise vandalism, including fouling and breaking lifts, discharging fire hydrants, and throwing ever more dangerously massive objects (live cats, televisions, motorbikes, etc.) from high floors.[40] Too often, high-rise estates became the storage places for society's most troublesome and vulnerable individuals, producing inevitable horror stories which in turn made high-rises less attractive, and gave the vicious circle an onwards shove.

Goldfinger's post-occupancy interest in the precise details of what worked and what did not at Balfron Tower must have been sharpened by the fact that Trellick Tower was in its final design stages at the time. There is every indication that Goldfinger truly wished to learn the lessons of Balfron Tower in time to implement them in Trellick Tower, which shows a number of developments from Balfron, ranging from its even more expressive silhouette and more variegated facade rhythms to the closer relationship between the entrance and the street on which it sits. This scientific-minded Modernist belief in improvement through experimentation and iteration was surprisingly rarely followed through with any rigour or consistency in public housing. Trends would often change before the previous fashion had had time to be built and tested, sweeping away both the good and the bad of the previous trend. One of the great lost opportunities of the nation's vast social housing boom was that no consistent effort was made by any central authority to follow up the outcomes of different housing types in order to discover what actually worked and under what circumstances.

vi

On the completion of Trellick Tower, Goldfinger again demonstrated his faith and enduring interest in his own designs by moving his office into one of the commercial units along the road front of the estate, where he worked until his retirement in 1977. This, sadly, gave him a front-row seat to observe the social problems which Trellick Tower rapidly experienced. These seem to have been overwhelmingly linked to management rather than being intrinsic to the architecture: the block is easy to superintend by a single concierge, but the council resisted the expense and left the corridors and stairwells open to all, as sheltered and heated lurking spaces ideal for the most unattractive activities of a city in the 1970s. This included devastating vandalism like the opening of fire hydrants in the main stairwell in late December 1972, putting out not only lifts but all power throughout the block for Christmas.[41]

Prostitution, the increasing drug-dealing and -taking of the 1970s, and the new concept of 'mugging' – a word borrowed from America as the crime became a media preoccupation in that decade – made the corridors alarming places to be. Some horrible sexual offences committed there contributed to the prominence of Trellick Tower as the 'Tower of Terror'. It is reputed to have been an inspiration for J. G. Ballard's dystopian *High-Rise*.[42]

The provision of a concierge, initiated in 1987, greatly improved the liveability of the block.[43] By the 1990s it was starting to become architecturally appreciated by a small minority who saw its remarkable visual strength as a positive thing. Some began to attempt to buy flats in the block.[44] The return of vigorous, initially minoritarian interest in the project from the later 1990s tracks the more recent history of Brutalism. This revival was characterised by a sense that the Welfare State was a worthwhile project, but more acutely by visual excitement at the excessive power, ruggedness and exoticism of buildings like this. These phenomena are experienced most often by generations who were not born when Trellick was first finished, and who, like me, have discovered the architecture as young adults, often as the thrilling antithesis of the pleasant suburbia in which so many of us grew up. Trellick Tower has become visual shorthand for this tendency. Flickr has a seemingly inexhaustible supply of dramatic photos of it dominating its surroundings or thrusting angularly into the sky. It has featured in numerous adverts (including for the 2012 Olympics), and in music videos as shorthand for urban grit. Its distinctive silhouette appears on plates and tea towels, as a bookend and even in simplified silhouette as a diamond ring. A student of mine did a wonderful study on the building's appearances on Twitter and Flickr, finding that the cult of Trellick Tower is largely a matter of external imagery, taking it as a graphic shorthand for Brutalism.[45]

To architects, too, Trellick and its contemporaries have a particular glamour and attraction: they were solidly built from robust, legible materials as opposed to the many layers of plastic bag, insulating foam, cladding and dry-wall which make up most of today's new buildings.

Even for the most devoted fan of Brutalism, being close up to Trellick Tower now is a mixed experience. The demolition of the car park and playground has left a scarred hole where once was refined concrete-work, and despite having gained heritage protection at the high level of Grade II* the building continues to feel mutilated and neglected. Trellick Tower is at present most architecturally exciting from a bit further away, but even from there clumsy changes are apparent, with the awkwardness of the boiler house's replacement uPVC double glazing visible from half a mile away. The original balustrade which capped the flats has gone, leaving the ends of the parapet sticking up to the original height, no longer joined by the high concrete beam underlined by a sliver of sky. As with so many tall Modernist buildings, the highest point wears an ad-hoc crown of thorns made up of irregular mobile-phone masts, awkwardly attached.

Trellick's landscaping is so mutilated that you cannot get much sense of how its ground levels should be. You can see this at Balfron, where the tower retains its architect-designed landscape of concrete and grass, hard to read from ground level, but a revelation when seen from the flats above. From this vantage point it becomes a kind of Modernist bas-relief, featuring in particular a playground nicknamed from early on 'the bear pit', and furnished with a range of concrete children's resources including a concrete slide, now missing the metal chute.[46]

vii

Fifteen years after my first timorous visit to Trellick Tower, attitudes to this architecture were strikingly different: the National Trust was doing tours of Balfron. Last time I was at Balfron I found myself once again standing on the concrete walkway outside a Goldfinger tower, discussing its architecture. This time my interlocutor was an artist who had lived in the block, and my sense that a man was lurking and watching us was not merely nervous unfamiliarity with my surroundings. The lurker came up and introduced himself – he was another artist also working with Brutalist buildings as his inspiration, and was there to make a rubbing of the concrete texture, a sort of latter-day brass rubbing.

The entrance to Balfron Tower

We also got hostile glares from an unfriendly resident, but again she was a world away from the dark fantasies of my first encounter with a Goldfinger tower: her disapproval was of the fact that we were yet another party of gawpers with cameras, come to stare in admiration at the block in which she lived.

The fame of Balfron has now contributed to a new phenomenon. With London housing prices rising and rising, the Thatcherite Right to Buy has made a considerable number of former council flats and houses available to the free market. Whilst this has produced a temporary social mixing that has its attractive sides, with first-time-buyer professionals living alongside less well-off tenants, over time it is reducing the amount of social housing available. This has more recently been hugely accelerated by housing associations selling off entire blocks to private developers in order to raise money to subsidise their other housing provision.[47] Balfron Tower has become the most celebrated of such sales, arousing the fury of those who were housed there before, and other housing campaigners, who feel understandably bitter.[48] For decades high-rise council housing was seen as inhuman and failing, but inhabited throughout by tenants. Yet as soon as it became widely recognised that Balfron Tower was excellent housing it seemed immediately as though it was too good for social tenants, and has been sold off to developers to house the better-off.

The developers have been very effective in raising the public profile of the block, holding events and talks, working with the National Trust to provide tours and open a flat furnished as an exhibition of 1960s design. They have given artists the chance to live and work in Balfron Tower on short-notice tenancies whilst the remaining tenants have been 'decanted' from the block before refurbishment. Opponents have coined the term 'artwashing' for this process, and refer to the systematic removal of poorer tenants from London housing as 'social cleansing'.[49] Meanwhile, Wayne Hemingway, the high-profile designer of the National Trust's Balfron Tower exhibition flat, has fought back, appearing to show total indifference to the experience of those who, having lived in an area for a long time, find that gentrification is pushing the shops and restaurants out of their budget:

> Don't get me started about the accusation that all this leads to gentrification. Why is gentrification a dirty word? Many people say that East London has gentrified because it's all cafés and interesting little shops. Well, if that's gentrification, bring it on. It's better than betting shops that just encourage folk who can't afford to gamble, to gamble! And what's better? A greasy kebab shop on every corner or a nice café that happens to have a man with a beard serving you decent hot chocolate and healthy bites?[50]

The gentrification of good 1960s housing is threatening to split Brutalism's fan base between those who are fundamentally above all else enthusiasts for the concrete, and those who prioritise more highly the social ideals of the Welfare State. To keep buildings like Balfron Tower viable as housing association properties there is a limit to the additional cost that they can impose over the maintenance budget for normal, unlisted flats. Refurbishment for sale on the open market generates more than enough money to conduct the work to a very high heritage standard (though the early glimpses of the Balfron scheme at the time of going to press fill me with anxious gloom). Potentially, therefore, the interests of those who want the buildings to be looked after well as 'heritage' will start to separate from those who want them to continue to serve their original purpose, housing non-rich people.

What is clear is that, within the current legislation, each actor is doing what is rational for them: the housing association is avoiding the cost of refurbishing a listed building, and is instead getting money from the developers which it can spend on its other housing; the developer is buying property that it is confident it can sell for a profit even after a substantial refurbishment; artists are accepting comparatively affordable live-work studios and the media attention and community of artists that the scheme brings. It would be odd if each group did not do what it is doing. There is undoubtedly something very ugly, and easily turned into a political sign of the times, about the fact that social housing ends up effectively being sold off because it has not failed enough. However, this is likely to be dwarfed by the wider problems of social housing at present, with housing associations coming under such financial pressure from government-imposed rent reduction that many will be unable to afford to build new stock or maintain the costlier existing buildings.[51] This is likely to make the gentrification of one very good block look like a detail (albeit a photogenic one) against the nationwide housing problems that lie ahead.

Whilst they remain shabby and rough around the edges, Balfron and Trellick represent the classic Welfare State Brutalist project at its clearest and most socially engaged. Many of my favourite Brutalist buildings point to exceptions and greater diversity than is generally acknowledged within the movement's client base and its outputs, but this is not to deny the seriousness of many 1960s architects and clients in their commitment to providing better facilities and better conditions for the poorer people in society, and real efforts were made by left-wing councils to reduce the gap between rich and poor.

Some of the most high-profile and widely admired architectural projects of the 1950s and '60s were social housing, including Park Hill in Sheffield, the Alton Estate in suburban London, and the Queen Elizabeth Flats in Glasgow. Whatever mistakes were made by those commissioning, designing and building some of these blocks, and however difficult the following decades were for many such projects, real effort and thought went into producing good living environments and a sense of community for people who were not well off. Whatever else Brutalist architects and clients may have been up to, this baseline of serious social endeavour should be taken as a constant background.

Trellick Tower and Balfron Tower perhaps set out better than any other project the archetype of the most architecturally exciting buildings of the post-war Welfare State. They were built in a spirit of optimism, with a confident faith in continuous progress in the provision of improved housing for all. Their architecture was the product of considerable earnest effort, with a brio and energy which reflected both the confidence of the designers in the value of social housing, and the 1960s spirit that the new and exciting were better than the old and familiar.

Chapter Three

The Bankers' Commune
The Barbican

(barnabascalder.org/rc3/)

i

If Trellick Tower gave me my first intimation that housing could be turned into a monument, another complex of buildings, some six miles east, showed me just how far this could be pushed.

The Barbican Estate is a landscape of gigantic concrete buildings and walkways, inhumanly vast in scale and hard in texture: the ultimate Brutalist council estate. So convincingly does it resemble Welfare State housing that it took me years to notice that its rugged, vandal-proof surfaces have always been the durable containers not for the needy working classes, rehoused from slums, but for the rich workers of the City of London, peppered with such architects and creative types as can afford the high prices.

I first became enthralled by the Barbican in 2001, when I was reading for an MA in medieval architectural history at the Courtauld Institute. I had been noisily enthusiastic about visiting churches from fairly early childhood, initially at least partly as a child's niche-seeking self-promotion. From my early teens, however, my enthusiasm had gathered its own momentum, after a very knowledgeable friend showed me round Salisbury Cathedral, thrilling me with the amount of information that could be decoded from its stones. I think I also admired – and dreamed of one day emulating – his profound and apparently effortless expertise.

As an undergraduate I had broadened my interests so far as to spend a summer holiday driving round English Baroque country houses with two good friends, enjoying the sound of my own voice echoing round one or other palatial interior as I dismissed the later intrusion of a Wyatt ceiling or enthused over the sublimity of a Hawksmoor–Vanbrugh entrance hall. Now, for my MA, I was back with the Gothic, studying under a generous-minded, enthusiastic professor with a group of very clever, entertainingly eccentric fellow students.

We spent longish days in the Courtauld library, competitively preparing our next seminar paper on the iconography or architecture of Westminster Abbey or one of the Île-de-France cathedrals, and longer evenings drinking alongside some of the Strand's least chic population in a neighbouring pub where slightly sulphurous pints were still available for less than £2 each.

One morning, after a party at a friend's flat in Dalston where most of us had slept over, I was coming back across town when, on a whim, I got off the bus, bought a large polystyrene cup of scorchingly hot black coffee, and wandered with it into the Barbican Estate on the northern edge of the City of London. It was a bright, cloudy day, just on the edges of being too cold, and the combination of excesses was delightful: a mellow, self-satisfied afterglow of the previous night's drinks, the cool of the air and the heat of the coffee. Above all, though, there was the intensity with which I suddenly appreciated the architecture. I sat on a bench, dwarfed by seven storeys of flats all around, punctuated by three much taller towers. The towers are triangular, and their chunky, curvaceous balconies come to points of apparently unbelievable sharpness,

THE BANKERS' COMMUNE

threateningly jagged like a cruel saw from a horror film, amidst the primitive-looking solidity of the rest of the estate.

In the way that a twenty-one-year-old will, I sat looking at the buildings and feeling as though my pleasure in them was in some way profound. Undoubtedly I also enjoyed the sensation that I was appreciating in the Barbican a beauty to which most of the people I knew would be blind. I never had a tattoo or a vomit-rich, neighbour-scandalising party in my parents' house, but suddenly I could feel that I had detached myself from my suburb. The Barbican was my intellectual eyebrow-piercing. It was with the Barbican Estate that my interest in Brutalist architecture blossomed into love.

And once I had myself 'discovered' the Barbican, I felt the need to proselytise it to my friends, to the point where they started calling it after me: 'the Barnican'. I cannot now reconstruct how many kind friends allowed themselves to be dragged the three-mile round trip across the centre of London from the Courtauld to the Barnican. An international and artistically sophisticated bunch, several disappointed my new-convert fervour by reacting with the more reserved enthusiasm of people who knew there was plenty of other good post-war Modernism all round the world.

For me, though, the Barbican was a revelation, and bore comparison with all my existing architectural favourites: it was far bigger than Blenheim Palace, its towers as tall as the spire of Salisbury Cathedral, and its chunky concrete as bombastic, powerful and magnificently bleak as Hawksmoor's stone-clad churches of the early eighteenth century.

As I got to know it better, my love only deepened. Undoubtedly it helps a great deal that the Barbican is finished – here, unusually for Modernist schemes of its scale and ambition, you do not have to imagine the missing 70 per cent of the original master plan, nor think away later additions, messed-up windows or beige paint on the concrete. The local council which commissioned it, the Corporation of the City of London, is very unusual in its structure, with much greater stability and continuity of intention than councils subject to the customary electoral swings and the constant cycle of arriving and departing elected representatives. Nor did the project of such a wealthy client suffer budget cuts with each tremor in central government funding. Equally remarkably, the architects themselves heroically ignored changing fashions, not redesigning later stages to meet newer architectural trends, but sticking loyally to their 1950s conception refined in 1961–63. As a result, you can see the Barbican pretty much as the architects intended, with only the occasional regrettable addition like a woefully kitsch pair of dancing bronze dolphins added beneath Shakespeare Tower in the 1980s by someone who must have stood beneath more than forty storeys of jaggedly upswept balconies, refusing to look up, and thought, 'This needs some sculpture.' The Barbican's architecture is exceptionally consistent for a project planned and erected over, by modern standards, such a long period (1955–82), and its maintenance and management have been effective throughout at preventing it from slumping into the kind of serious problems that require radical modifications when repair eventually comes.

At the time of my Damascene conversion to concrete Modernism there, I had no idea what had gone into the Barbican in the way of building craft. I did not know that almost all its exposed concrete had been carefully hammered to produce the handsomely rugged finishes. I did not even know that it was well built. What I responded to was its size, its rough textures, and its strong shapes. I do not think I asked myself much about the reasons it had been brought into being, accepting large concrete housing estates as a natural part of London. Yet for all their architectural comparability, the Barbican was not at all the same kind of project as other council-built housing. Balfron Tower's residents paid only £4 15s 6d in rent (including heating but excluding local government taxation – 'rates'), with government subsidy covering the remaining 58 per cent, whereas Barbican residents paid the full price of £12, despite the immense wealth of the Corporation of the City of London, their local council.[1] Goldfinger's towers for the London County Council were intended to raise housing standards for lower-income people and their dependants. The Barbican, for all its architectural similarities to the best Welfare State council housing, and erected by the same legal mechanisms, was built to establish a substantial colony of middle- and upper-income residents on the northern edge of the City of London. The school and community centre of early schemes were to mushroom into world-class facilities for expensive high culture, poles apart from the modest community facilities on even the best other council estates. Adverts for the flats (in the resolutely middle-class *Sunday Times*) talked mainly of the mod cons, but finished with a boast of 'uniformed porters'.[2]

The City of London Corporation was in striking contrast to other urban local authorities of the period. As against the explicitly politicised councils which reshaped many major British cities, the Corporation of the City of London was – and remains – largely without party-political alignment. It is a highly unusual local authority, with a residential electorate in the immediate post-war years of only around 5,000, substantially outnumbered by non-residential business votes.[3] These non-residential voters are people who work in the City but live elsewhere. A quota is allocated to each business in the City in proportion to the number of employees it has, and the business itself can then choose them from amongst their partners or staff. Elections for aldermen tended in the 1950s and '60s to be uncontested. Other figures in the Corporation are elected exclusively by senior members of Livery Companies. The structure is, in other words, closer to a medieval civic authority than any other in Britain, having dodged electoral reforms of the nineteenth and twentieth centuries, and overwhelmingly represents the interests of financial and commercial enterprises. As one historian of planning put it, 'from a democratic point of view the City is a rotten borough, which survives only by performing a specialized support role [. . .] for London's financial services sector'.[4]

The reason the Corporation decided to build housing at all – earlier ideas for the bombed-out and disused fabric warehouses of that part of the city proposed more office buildings – was that central government was contemplating legislation which would make the size of residential electorates increasingly important. It might leave a depopulated City of London vulnerable to a forced merger with the much larger (and by this date unshakeably Labour-dominated) LCC.[5] The provision of housing in the Barbican area would increase the residential vote, and the decision not to subsidise it would bring the higher tax revenue and reduced social needs which come with a higher-income population. Perhaps it would also reduce the risk of a left-wing councillor being returned, to participate in, observe and potentially publicise or disrupt the opaque local government procedures of the City.

In other words, whereas most social housing was built in order to bring improved conditions to lower-income groups, and to reduce historic inequalities between rich and poor, the Barbican was built in order to preserve the privileged autonomy of the City. The names of its buildings reflect this: where one of Lubetkin's schemes came within an ace of being called 'Lenin Court', the Barbican takes the names of safely remote historical figures, mostly from the 1500s: Shakespeare, Marlowe, Ben Jonson, Thomas More, Lancelot Andrewes (a sixteenth-century bishop), and so on.

ii

The Barbican arose from a need for housing that was conservative rather than progressive. But the architecture is absolutely contemporary, and could easily be mistaken for a project seeking to create an egalitarian utopia. Why would this self-consciously archaic and conservative council commission an estate which equalled the most avant-garde Modernist designs of the socialist LCC, and beat the LCC's architects to it in implementing on a large scale the great new planning ideas of the 1950s?[6]

Where the LCC spent the war planning to implement radical modernisation in the forthcoming post-war reconstruction, the City took the conservative route you might expect from its structural bias towards protecting business interests. This is clear in the 1944 plan drawn up by the Corporation's engineer, in response to the need to rebuild approximately one third of the City which had been destroyed in the Blitz. In order to avoid disturbing existing assets like sewers, waterpipes and cables under the streets, the engineer proposed that the existing road network should be reinstated in post-war construction. Bucking all the Modernist trends of its moment, his report proposed that new buildings should be regulated by restricted facade heights and building lines, with compulsory setbacks above a given height to allow more light down to the street.[7] This sort of planning framework was hugely outmoded by the 1940s, with most new plans preferring the more up-to-date plot ratios, where the planning authority specified the maximum amount of new accommodation which could be provided on a given site expressed as a ratio to the size of the site. Thus if the council dictated a plot ratio of 1:4, the developer could have a four-storey building covering the entire site or an eight-storey building covering half the site, with parking or open space over the rest; or (subject to the architects satisfying the planners that it would not steal too much daylight from existing buildings around) you could develop a twenty-storey building on a fifth of the site.

Where the older style of planning restriction, through maximum heights, building lines and light setbacks, had essentially dictated (in areas with high enough land values to guarantee maximum development) the shape of the resulting buildings, the plot ratio enabled architects to propose much greater variety of shape, height and open space. At the negative end this is partly responsible for the many second-rate projects of the 1960s and '70s in which the disposition of the buildings produces awkward leftover spaces (attractive gardens or plazas in the architects' minds, but in reality too often sterile gaps in the city). These unexplained openings in the wall of a nineteenth-century corridor-like street can seem like broken teeth in an otherwise regular smile. At its best, on the other hand, plot-ratio planning freed architects from the creative restraints represented by a fixed shape of building – restraints which Modernist architects felt had reduced their predecessors to stylists, taking the preordained shape of the building and icing it with their choice of modish facade ornamentation.

Both central government and the London County Council objected to the conservatism of the City's 1944 plan. They forced the City to draw up a comprehensive plan for reconstruction in the area around St Paul's, but the City quietly sabotaged its implementation by selling off the new plots piecemeal to speculative developers rather than rebuilding them in the integrated manner that the planners had prescribed.[8]

The Barbican was carried through with much greater vigour, though it also began partly from impositions by the LCC. As the overall planning authority for London, the LCC was able to intervene in City of London road planning, and did so in the case of one of the major new bypass roads, Route 11 or London Wall. The LCC used their road-planning powers to impose on the northern end of the City a system of raised pedestrian walkways. Ironically this was the first place that the LCC managed to carry this through, despite the conservatism of the Corporation, and it was these walkways which formed one of the major starting points for the excitingly Modernist planning of the Barbican.[9]

As for the architectural practice from whom the Barbican was commissioned, Chamberlin Powell & Bon (CPB), they might seem the most improbable choices for the bowler-hatted City men: all three partners were bohemian, left-wing and uncompromisingly aesthetically progressive in their architecture. Their first contact with the City came before the Barbican idea had got started. In 1951, wanting to provide nearby housing for the white-collar and blue-collar support workers whose labour was crucial to the running of the City, the Corporation acquired land just over the border in the London Borough of Finsbury, where it was cheaper, and promoted an architectural competition for a council housing estate there. The RIBA appointed Donald McMorran, a gifted non-Modernist architect, to judge the competition.[10] The estate was to be called after a poetically named street on the site, 'Golden Lane'.

Coming so soon after the war, when most architectural activity was still urgent and unglamorously impoverished post-war reconstruction, the Golden Lane competition attracted huge amounts of attention. Alison and Peter Smithson's rejected scheme was the one which made the biggest splash. In it they spread a single block across the whole site, a slab which bifurcated in two places, but in which the whole giant building was to be socially united by access balconies which ran uninterrupted round the entire estate. The Smithsons were amongst those who thought that the working-class street had a sociological value which had been largely ignored by earlier Modernist estates. If their sociology was humane, however, the Smithsons' aesthetic was remorselessly robust. Under the influence of their pop-art contacts in the art world, their ostentatiously cool publication images of the scheme included collaged images of Marilyn Monroe with Joe DiMaggio, Gérard Philipe looking young and tough, and other up-to-the-minute references to popular culture.[11]

The winner, however (and it is a tribute to McMorran that he selected a victor on planning merit without imposing his own classical stylistic preferences – a courtesy seldom later extended to his own practice by Modernists in positions of power or influence), was Geoffry Powell, at the time a thirty-year-old design tutor at Kingston Polytechnic. He, Christof Bon and Peter Chamberlin, always called 'Joe', all teaching at Kingston, had each entered the competition individually on the understanding that should one of them win they would together form a partnership to execute the winning scheme.

Once Golden Lane was under way, Chamberlin Powell & Bon were handed the Barbican without competition by a City Corporation which clearly trusted them to handle such a large scheme. The three partners were as spirited and remarkable a group of men as you might guess from the spectacular aesthetics and awesomely confident scale of their estate. They were quintessential 1960s architects. Although there were increasing numbers of successful architects emerging from less privileged backgrounds in this period, an unrepresentative proportion of big names then (and now) were middle or upper-middle class, and these three were no exception. Joe Chamberlin and Geoffry Powell were both sons of army officers based overseas; Christof Bon the child of wealthy Swiss restaurateurs, trained in architecture in Zurich. Rebelling elegantly against their pukka backgrounds, the three architectural partners were uninhibited, trendy bohemians with an enthusiastic zest for the enjoyable. In 1967 they bought together a holiday house near Uzès, in southern France, the culmination of holidays they had been taking regularly in Italy and Mediterranean France since the early 1950s. This familiarity with the exotic south of Europe was

the height of cool – only in 1950, after all, had Elizabeth David popularised the use of olive oil for cooking.[12] Back at home the trio drove magnificent cars. Powell's 1928 open-top green Lagonda was a particular highlight, and Elain Harwood in her superb monograph on CPB records that he drove it until it fell apart – the final straw coming when some Barbican drawings disappeared through a hole in its floor whilst he was driving.[13] Bon lived with Chamberlin and his wife, favouring cars 'with bench front seats where they could squeeze together'.[14]

These pleasure-loving, enthusiastic young men had, even by the standards of their period, an exceptional grandeur of vision. It is typical that when they proposed a design for one of three new colleges in northern Cambridge, they suggested redesigning the entire area of all three so that they effectively formed a single immense unified project.[15] On that occasion they were thwarted, but at the Barbican they found a canvas for their art that was big enough for them to really show what they could do: over 2,100 flats, maisonettes and houses, underground parking for 2,500 cars, towers of up to 44 storeys, a substantial arts centre, a girls' school, a school of music and drama, a lake, and gardens, all threaded through by a road and a Tube line. The designs developed from first discussions in 1955 to a near-final master plan in 1959. Construction started three years later.

iii

Each design, as it emerged, was proudly contemporary and clearly Corbusian in its inspirations. CPB's handling of their client throughout the design process appears to have been extraordinarily effective, and it is striking how much more successfully they were able to keep the Corporation engaged with their scheme than the earlier planners had been in their attempts to secure coherent development of the area round St Paul's.[16] Setting aside the leftist rhetoric more normal to Modernist grand plans, CPB's proposals

Aerial view of the Barbican Estate. Photograph: Neil Perry (neilperryphoto.com)

compared each aspect of the Barbican to historical examples whose safe poshness and unrevolutionary grandeur made them easy to swallow for the City men: the flats were likened not to the social housing they actually resembled so closely, but to the luxury 1930s Dolphin Square development near the Houses of Parliament; the notion of a circulation deck with building above and below was compared not to the 1950s university project by Alison and Peter Smithson from which it probably came, but to the 1820s Carlton House Terrace, on the Mall – safe John Nash classicism, and one of London's most snobby addresses. CPB's vaulted roof structures were not ascribed to the influence of Le Corbusier's 1950s schemes – his chapel at Ronchamp or his Maisons Jaoul – but to pre-modern Mediterranean churches. A covered road they were forced to include in one scheme through the centre of the Barbican was given the historical referent of an arched viaduct.[17] Without their skill in selling radical architecture to conservative clients, it is hard to imagine the Barbican getting built in such confidently contemporary style. To drive the point home they took leading members of the Corporation on agreeable research trips to the great historic buildings of Europe, selling them dreams of past and future grandeur. It is characteristic that their research visit to support separate circulation systems for vehicles and pedestrians was to Venice, where canals rather than roads make up the vehicular routes.[18]

The Barbican's terrifying combination of scale, complexity and perversely designed perfectionism made for an exceptionally difficult construction project, as a recent oral-history project recalls through fascinating testimony of those involved.[19] Such a large project as the forty-acre Barbican Estate would potentially have challenged the capabilities of any single building contractor, and over the course of the construction four different contractors were to be involved on the site, often simultaneously, operating across a number of separately let, phased contracts.[20] The project started with the clearing of 150,000 cubic yards of rubble and ruins from wartime bombing, a job made comparatively straightforward by

McAlpine's use of heavy clearing equipment.[21] Once the first three phases of flats, school and other works got under way, the building site had up to 1,000 people working on it. The conditions on the site were pretty basic – ubiquitous mud, only chemical lavatories, and extensive ad-libbing amongst the contractors to work out how to build unusual structural and servicing details to the required standards. There could be substantial differences in how very similar designs were put up by different contractors on different parts of the site, with those from one firm waiting for their slow cranes, having plenty of time to watch in bored dismay as the much faster cranes on the neighbouring contract shot up and down the tower doubling the speed of work.[22]

Recollections of workers on the site have about them something of the confidently adversarial energy of schoolchildren rebelling against a weak teacher. Unhappy with the chemical lavatories, the workers on one contract decided to protest by forming a constant procession to walk over a mile in round trips to the public lavatories at St Paul's Cathedral, so that at any time a substantial proportion of the workforce was missing from the site.[23] Or in another incident, the night before the topping-out ceremony for one part of the structure (the celebration held when the structural work reached roof height), the Union flag was removed from the summit of the building and replaced by the Irish tricolour, a humorously antagonistic reminder that much of the concrete work had been done by Irishmen.[24]

The extent of Britain's 1960s building boom drew in labour from all over Britain, Ireland, Eastern Europe and parts of the British Empire and Commonwealth.[25] If much of the shuttering was by Irish workers, Sikh carpenters were also well represented in it, and generally respected for the quality of their work.[26] The building site was by no means a happy melting pot, though, with the little-questioned racism of the period ensuring that 'about half a dozen coloured guys' got the worst job going: hammer-texturing the massive area of exposed concrete of the Barbican Estate and

Arts Centre. The concrete had to be 'cured' for twenty-eight days first until it was fully hardened, after which the six or so black workers on whom the job was dumped would go over every inch with heavy mechanical hammers – either bush-hammers with flat heads to produce an even texture, or pick hammers pointed like chisels to give the pitted texture which predominates at the Barbican. This was unappealing work. Apart from the noise and dirt, and the all-day weight of the heavy machines held up at right angles to the concrete surfaces, the vibration caused nerve damage known as 'white finger'.[27]

Even amongst the higher-status jobs on the site, the safety arrangements were scarcely advanced from the famous images of workers wandering around on the steel frames of the Empire State Building thirty-something years earlier. Cranes fell over, large pieces of shuttering fell off because it had been deemed unnecessary to bolt them on, and a workman was decapitated by the descending counterweight of a lift whilst peering down to see if the lift itself was arriving. Without safety harnesses or systematic safety routines, a young Irishman fell off a scaffold to his death in a way which had been happening on construction sites since medieval times.[28] Asbestos sat in dusty piles, and when the builders, by the 1970s knowing its dangers, asked for it to be removed, they were told they would be fine if they hosed the area down before sweeping up.[29] Of the many strikes that delayed the progress of the building site, quite a few were for these kinds of important questions of health and safety, and conditions of work. Whilst there are now loudly publicised claims of cases where 'health and safety' is used as an excuse for managerial joy-killing, the improvements which have occurred on building sites since the 1960s – through trade-union pressure, litigation and legislation – seem to me to be worth any amount of over-precautionary form-filling for office workers.

Not all of the industrial action was so clearly derived from urgent needs. The curious political position of the Barbican, as a protection for the autonomy and opacity of Britain's leading financial district, appears to have been recognised at the time within the more politically militant end of the trade-union movement. Far-left activists selected the scheme as a high-profile target for strike action. Whilst the motives for targeting the Barbican were never made explicit, some of the industrial disputes which it witnessed had the appearance of something larger than specific site disagreements. Having tendered low for the contract, one of the contracting firms was struggling to keep the job on time and on budget. When a small-scale strike took place on its site it chose to lock out its entire workforce, possibly in order to be able to blame industrial action for the delays and overspend on the contract. The situation was promptly exploited by a charismatic Communist, Lou Lewis, who had, according to contemporaries, smuggled himself on to the site in defiance of his blacklisting, dressed as a harmless-looking elderly worker. In 1966–67, Lewis and his group held a strike of over a year, against the noisy denunciations not only of the employers but also of the unions themselves to which the workers belonged.[30] The unauthorised strike saw scenes of violence when buses carrying scab labour were stoned and attacked. When the strike was finally broken the site was very heavily policed by authorities anxious about another such high-profile, expensive industrial dispute. It was 1982, twenty years after the clearance of the site had begun, before the Barbican Arts Centre was finally complete, the last part of the massive project to come into use.

iv

The same architects putting up similar-looking housing over a forty-acre site could so easily be dull – look at the rather remorseless uniformity of Halle-Neustadt or so many other town extensions from the Soviet bloc. Yet with the support of their clients, Chamberlin Powell & Bon had the creativity and the budget to turn the various constituents of the Barbican Estate into a magnificent urban set-piece – a whole new district of London, dense, distinctive and coherently set out. There is a strong unity to the architecture:

blocks of flats come in two types, the seven-storey slab blocks and the forty-three- and forty-four-storey towers. The towers are indeed to very similar designs: three flats per floor around the triangular plan, with three-storey penthouses on top with roof gardens. The unified appearance of the slab blocks, however, disguises considerable variety within. Behind near-identical balconies are a range of sizes of flat from studios to many-bedroomed maisonettes. Most are approached by staircases or lifts, with the flats in pairs to each side of them, but some are off internal corridors. There is, in a sense, no 'typical' Barbican flat. Of all the flats I have been in there, each feels distinctive not only in its layout, but in its individual views of the landscape and architecture. The balance of unity of architectural elevation and variety of living experience is remarkable.

The chief unifying factor, the balcony front, is not merely a powerful visual element throughout the estate, it is also doing structural work as a beam, helping to support the floors of the flats along with the load-bearing walls which keep each dwelling soundproofed and fireproofed from its neighbours.[31]

The integration of road and rail within the scheme is exemplary. The road runs under the broad raised walkway to the north of the site, avoiding the need for the extensive structure which would have been required if many storeys of housing had been heaped on top of the roadway. By boxing the entire road in underneath a new ground level, the peace of the estate is safeguarded. As for the rail, its position is harder to spot; it runs wherever possible under the central open spaces of the Barbican. The rails were laid on rubber footings in order to minimise noisy vibrations from the trains. The piling beneath the towers was in places driven sixty feet below ground level to support the height and wind-load of the forty-four storeys above.[32]

As if the existing complexities of the project were not prohibitive enough, the brief changed more than once even after construction had begun. Many of the flats had a lavatory in a separate room

from the rest of the bathroom, without its own sink. Building regulations changed to require a handbasin in every lavatory room, but the design was too tight to fit one in and still be able to open the door. The architects worked with a sanitary manufacturer, Twyfords, to design a basin which could be partially recessed into the wall, and only project 150 millimetres into the room. It is still in production and widely used.

Much more challenging than squeezing a basin into a small bathroom was squeezing hugely expanded facilities into the space left for the Arts Centre. When first proposed, this was to be comparatively modest, serving the Guildhall School of Music and Drama and the residents. In 1964 the plan changed in order to make the Barbican's theatre the London home of the Royal Shakespeare Company, and this was then joined by a full-sized international-standard concert hall as the home of the London Symphony Orchestra.[33] The new scale of the Arts Centre was spectacular: a concert hall for almost 2,000, three cinemas, two theatres, two art galleries, a good-sized public library, and attendant foyers, restaurants, bars, cloakrooms, lavatories (still in elegant condition, unlike so many which have been cheaply 'cheered up'), shops, and administrative and backstage facilities.

Adding all this to the brief posed huge difficulties. Some of the housing around had already been built, as had the Underground line and road, which meant that the footprint of the Arts Centre could not be increased. Instead, redesigning it to its ambitious new brief in 1968, the architects had to make the Arts Centre a tall cuboid, its lower levels pushed deep into the ground and the theatre's fly tower at its top projecting up high above the top walkways of the upper part of the estate. From outside you might not guess it, but the section of the Arts Centre is a tremendously complex three-dimensional jigsaw, fitting the large performance spaces in around each other, and winding dressing rooms, foyers and other more flexible rooms through the gaps left over. The Art Gallery on the top overhangs the pavement far below, partly because this allows it to be excitingly sculptural, but mostly in order not to have columns landing on the fragile roof of the Underground line which lies just in front of the Arts Centre.

Added to the challenges posed by the brief and the late changes to it, the architects gave themselves other difficulties which would have been more in their power to avoid. The detailing of the Barbican is an exploration of architecture as a Modernist visual art. As at Trellick and Balfron Towers, where the architecture took necessary services and celebrated them as expressive compositional elements, so does the detailing at the Barbican. This is clearest in the Arts Centre, where necessary extras like lighting and speakers, rather than being screwed into the walls after completion with trailing cables, were neurotically pre-planned to emerge from the raw concrete free of visible ducting. It was an unappetising challenge for the architects to foresee and accommodate all these elements in a building of such immense size and complexity, and the magnificent achievement it represents is fundamentally quixotic: a plastered or veneered building can be made to look good at the last minute by plasterer or carpenter, covering the mess of contingent pipes and wiring in a cosmetic coat. It is much harder to service a building where the raw concrete which supports it is visible throughout. As one of the quantity surveyors on the Arts Centre ruefully remembered, this requirement to integrate services in such remorseless exposed concrete presented considerable difficulties. Before you started building the formwork for the lift tower you had to know what size and shape the lift buttons were, and where their wiring would need to emerge – these would generally have been different design stages in earlier buildings, where overall structure could start going up whilst the architects thrashed out room finishes on the drawing board.[34] One way CPB managed the massive design effort was by running a large office of low-paid, high-quality assistants, many of whom came from all over the world to have a couple of years' experience there. They worked them hard, and a great deal of design effort went into each building.[35]

Not only services, but surfaces also needed to be impeccable. The architectural world imagined that hammering off the outer surface of concrete was a way of reducing the demands on the formwork carpenters, as the imprint of any imperfections would be removed. However, if there were leaks in the shuttering of the sort seen at Hermit's Castle, the aggregate within the concrete would flow into patterns around the leak, visible once the surface was hammered off. Thus the formwork needed to be first-rate and the surface pretty good, so it was a high-quality finish which was then removed. A civil engineer from the job recalled that he felt it was 'a crying shame because you went to enormous lengths to make sure you produced a beautiful fair-faced bit of concrete and then you ruined it'.[36]

It was an attractive idea for architects to have one material being at once structure and aesthetic, but it placed a lot of pressure on the concrete-shuttering and pouring craftsmen. In the past their heavy work had been tidied up by the cosmeticians of the building industry – plasterers, carpenters and painters – once all the heavy machinery and clunking scaffolding was safely out of the way, but now the heavy structural concrete itself had to be presentable. Furthermore, the meeting of elements built off-site (like windows and doors) with concrete cast in situ might have seemed like a modern and Modernist way of moving production off the messy building site into efficient factories, but in practice required very precise dimensions to be achieved on the concrete work in order that the inflexibly sized pieces made elsewhere would be able to fit, whereas traditional carpentry could be adapted round irregularities on the hoof.[37]

The kind of concrete that CPB sought at the Barbican Arts Centre was, then, an expensive art finish chosen for aesthetic and theoretical qualities rather than easy construction. Since the architects needed to think about services and fittings early on anyway, they made a virtue of it, and the major aesthetic elements in the Arts Centre are accordingly these necessary fixtures turned into art. Where there are speakers, lift buttons or fire hoses, they are received and acknowledged by the walls in which they sit by smooth niches amidst the roughness of the main surface. With their space-age, rounded-off rectangles they give the cave-like primitivism of the complex as a whole an exhilarating futuristic note.

This architecture, responding artistically to building technologies whilst in fact becoming less practical to build, is a recurrent tendency in much Modernism. Architects were (and are) educated in studios and lecture theatres far detached from the practicalities of the building site, and they typically completed their training guiltily insecure about the realities of construction, but with higher professional status than their builders. This made too often for poor or non-existent relations between builders and designers. This gulf was widened by overtones of class conflict – architects suspected construction workers of dishonesty or laziness, whilst the builders suspected the designers and their clients of exploitativeness or ignorance. Whilst major projects generally had permanent supervision from within the architectural practice, this job was often given to young, newly qualified practitioners, partly to blood them and partly because no one else wanted to do it. This cannot have helped: the young site architects' paper authority transparently lacked the experience to back it up, whilst older, more knowledgeable men were expected to obey their orders because of the younger designers' educational qualifications and, generally, higher social status. At the Barbican, once construction was under way, this powder keg of political tension exploded.

V

The twenty-year construction process of the Barbican may have been deeply bruising for many of those involved, but it resulted in an extraordinary complex of buildings. On my early visits to the Barbican I knew little else about it beyond its aesthetic effect on me. I found its peacefulness and wide spaces awe-inspiringly tranquil amidst the cluttered, traffic-blighted, narrow streets of the City – streets too busy during work hours and eerily deserted at weekends. I found the consistency and strength of the Barbican's architectural expression at once restful and thrillingly crushing amidst the endless patchwork of medium-scale Victorian and Edwardian street architecture which makes up so much of London. Standing beneath one of the towers I would feel that strange release which comes with being dwarfed by natural or man-made immenseness; what some feel on contemplating the immensity of the universe, others of us get from the more aesthetically perceptible immensity of the Barbican. It can be paradoxically comforting to be given a direct aesthetic experience of one's own smallness and the corresponding triviality of one's worries and ambitions.

My most frequent approach, from Barbican Underground station, is, I think, one of the best ways to experience it. A staircase within the station leads up to a bridge over the busy road straight into the estate's uppermost public pedestrian level. As you cross the bridge you can see the three towers lined up in front of you, intimidatingly vast, and, with their curiously primitive-looking humped tops, much less technological in their imagery than the glassy office blocks of the City beyond. To your right is what looks like a defensive structure: behind a curving brick wall is a deep, dark, sinister-looking undercroft, and spiralling upwards above this a concrete fort, complete with arrow slits and a vaulted roof. In fact, when you get round the other side, this magnificent defence turns out to be only a pedestrian ramp on to the walkway system, but its aggressive and excluding appearance is surely the architects' reference to the location of the estate on the line of the historical city wall of London, as well as a nod to the name of the estate, a 'barbican' being a fortified, defensive outwork in a medieval structure.

As you walk around the estate the consistent appearance of the flats themselves never comes close to monotony. Each time you pass under a block you are presented with a substantial variation.

Now you are looking at a brick-paved piazza at your own level; next, without having changed level yourself, you are peering down over a parapet as solid-looking as an anti-tank defence, overlooking a grassy garden with mature trees, tantalisingly inaccessible to non-residents and singingly green after the purplish bricks and brownish concrete of the previous courtyard. Further along the same walkway a lake opens up, oxygenised by fountains and flanked by a terrace café, the girls' school, and an oddly congruous (though not especially pretty) medieval church. One walkway runs parallel to a stretch of excavated wall, much patched, but originating in the early second century AD as a Roman fort.[38] Another runs as a slender bridge over the lake, hanging between the double line of columns which supports the flats above, and offering views through the estate, powerfully framed by the dark weight of the concrete slab overhead. Down below it, in the lake, round planters with brick benches are sunk beneath the level of the water so that one can sit in them perfectly dry and safe, with the pleasantly unreal sight of water lapping just inches away.[39]

At the Barbican the exceptional aspects of the design lie in the very large scale and the fairly small scale: the overall layout of the estate and the detailing. The architecture in between is simple, and at its best when it is not doing too much or trying too hard – as in the simplicity of the seven-storey blocks at the Barbican, whose plainness allows materials, details and overall planning to speak for themselves. Most of the estate is composed of these slab blocks with seven storeys of flats and maisonettes generally standing on columns above a podium. The uninterrupted, thick concrete stripes of the floor decks give them a horizontality which would be overwhelming in a less robust setting. Here, though, this horizontality is offset by the strong verticality of the massive columns beneath, and the towers which repeatedly stab up from behind or between the slabs, jagged and threatening. The windows of terraced houses built into the podium echo in downward curves the barrel vault over the uppermost storey of the slab blocks above, producing a suggestion of continuous vertical shapes.

Of the estate's large outdoor spaces, some seem formal – immense reworkings of the Georgian London square – others more dynamically irregular, in particular the long one at the north of the estate where the irregular shape of the site leads to a splendidly theatrical meeting of the right-angular blocks of the majority of the estate and the clashing geometry of the northern boundary. Along this disruptive line the three giant towers soar, each one triangular and, whilst they are almost identical in planning, rotated to three different angles which means that they present constantly changing profiles against the sky.

In the heart of the estate is the Arts Centre. The multiple levels of pedestrian circulation, each feeling like ground level, mean that no one who does not know it well has ever found it easy to locate the Arts Centre when arriving from outside, but for those who see the quality of the architecture this is like complaining that an E-type Jaguar needs a lot of cleaning and polishing: it may be true, but it is a trivial price for such beauty. The architects themselves defended the complexity of the Barbican's layout by pointing out that it was a new area of London, and that older areas of London do not have clearly marked entrances.[40]

I like the kind of architecture where a single stone colour runs throughout the entire exterior, or ideally where grey concrete and grey sky make it impossible to see whether a photo is in colour until you notice a pigeon's pink feet or the glaring red of a discarded crisp packet. For me the colourfulness of the nearby Golden Lane seems compromising and needy – a cry for affection. By contrast, the Barbican's magnificently glum palette shows a hugely confident indifference to the opinions of the uninformed, making it much more attractive to those who do love it: Heathcliff in concrete.

The Arts Centre's foyers are a favourite place of mine in which to work or read. They are not as spatially sophisticated as the outdoor areas of the Barbican – they are detectably carved out of the volumes left over after the auditoria and library have been slotted into place – but what they lack in overall shape they make up in architectural language. Concrete dominates, mightily. The rough textures of the outside of the building are brought indoors where their toughness becomes even more striking, and the lightness and remoteness of sky is substituted for a heavy-looking concrete waffle grid pressing down towards one. The immensity of the square columns which carry the services and hold up the building seems hugely excessive for the scale of the space around them. With its overhanging facade the Piranesian crepuscule of the foyers is rarely intruded on by alien sunlight, and even when busy and loud the architecture seems to retain a sense of dignified dominance over the frothy throngs of concert-goers, conference delegates or graduands.

The art gallery on the top two floors is double-height, its upper storey divided into room-like spaces breaking out from a circulation balcony overlooking the lower level. From outside one realises suddenly that these windowless bays are the white-tiled protrusions which bulk unexplained over the facades of the Arts Centre – a typical piece of Brutalist planning in that it is an 'honest' expression of internal disposition, but you only know that once you have been round the interior, or looked for some time at cross-sectional drawings.

For me the best interior of the Arts Centre is the theatre, buried deep inside it. Its remarkable achievement is to get a sense of celebratory festiveness comparable with the great playhouses of the years around 1900, without compromising the Modernist restraint and elegance of its elements. The way in which it is lit contributes, but the absolute highlight is the moment at the start of each production when the many Peruvian walnut side-doors (one at each end of every row of seating) all shut smoothly, quietly, and in exact synchrony into the roughened concrete wall.[41]

Emerging from the top of the Arts Centre one finds oneself in a crescent of flats, their balconies screened by adjustable louvred shutters whose different angles give random variation to the facades. The brick paving of the crescent was intended as an outdoor sculpture display area.[42] At the mid-point of the crescent is a pair of grandiose stairs arranged in a symmetrical splay, like those of a Baroque palace. Yet here they are enclosed in raw concrete, turning them into heavy-looking monoliths, lightened by joyously vigorous planting on their roofs. To one side of the square a conservatory wraps round the fly tower of the theatre, its gloriously exotic plants creeping over the rough concrete like trees round an Aztec ruin.

Over many visits I have rarely been to the Barbican without finding something new to notice and admire. On one occasion I was taking round a group of students when an inhabitant of the estate, hearing us talking about the architecture, offered to let us into the residents-only gardens, surprisingly delicate and pretty beneath the magnificence of their surroundings, and – more surprisingly – not at all incongruous despite their appearance of fragility. Seeing our great enthusiasm, he then showed us round his flat, and as the supreme highlight ushered us past the concierge of one of the towers to take the lift up to the triangular lift lobby of the penthouse level.[43] The lift call buttons are mounted on a free-standing steel column in the centre, an effect like a sci-fi film set for a climactic scene, the buttons representing an opportunity for salvation or the threat of apocalypse. From there we peered excitedly out of vertically elongated porthole windows to London far below, and looked down the spectacular fire stairs which gave me one of the most elating surges of sublime vertigo that I have ever experienced: flight after flight of stairs spiral jaggedly round a triangular well which appears from the top to recede almost infinitely, offering at its most extreme the terrifying seduction of the question, 'What would it feel like if I jumped?'

The Barbican's flats are, as in many 1960s schemes, heated through the floors, avoiding inflexible, inelegant and space-consuming

THE BANKERS' COMMUNE

radiators. They have some wonderful sci-fi features, surviving in many flats partly thanks to an enlightened pooling system in which people throwing out original fittings offer them to a collective scrapyard from which others who wish to retain theirs can scavenge replacement parts.[44] The sleek fitted kitchens were the height of 1960s cool, with high-technology-looking controls and plenty of stamped steel to prevent cracks in which dirt could fester. A Garchey waste-disposal system sucks your wet and dry kitchen rubbish away through a fitting in the sink. Perhaps the most exciting detail, though, is the operation of the doors to the balconies: to open them, rather than simply release a catch, you push down a large heavy lever, lifting the entire door a few centimetres, clearing the frame and allowing it to swing open. It is the kind of enjoyably innovative fitting which could have gone catastrophically wrong, but at the Barbican it was so sturdily made that the doors tend to work well after fifty years of use and weather. The number of different flat types, different orientations and different views at the Barbican makes it the antithesis of the anti-Modernist allegation that the flats are oppressively identical. There is in the faintly haphazard division of roof gardens and the ample circulation space something of the cool *savoir vivre* of the architects themselves.

This is not to suggest that these architects suffered no strain from their huge obligations. Joe Chamberlin's premature death in 1978 was ascribed, by some at least, to the anxiety and overwork occasioned by the Barbican.[45]

Yet the personal price which some of these architects paid for the strain of their great projects was not without some recompense. The legacy left behind by a partnership like Chamberlin Powell & Bon would be hard to match in most professions. The Barbican is a whole area of London, bearing faithfully so many years later the extraordinary artistic vision of its creators, and – robustly built, widely loved, and now granted listing – with a very good chance of continuing to do so for centuries.

The Barbican – unsubsidised council housing for the well off, built by a council determined to remain unlike any other, and chosen as a target for hard-left, high-publicity strike action – is on the face of it typical of very little. I fell in love with its architectural quality, scale and consistency, but at the social level it makes a very important point too; it is perhaps the closest that the UK has ever come to a perfect Brutalist housing estate – well built, well maintained, richly supplied with social facilities and conspicuously free of social problems. It is called on as a key example of these virtues by some advocates both of social housing and of concrete architecture. The fact that it does not actually meet the social criterion of improving the housing or economic opportunities of the less well off is generally not emphasised by its fans, yet for me this seems to be one of the central facts about it: as with examples throughout this book the reality of Brutalist architecture when looked at in detail tends to be much more chaotic and complex than some of its admirers would like to admit. There is in Brutalism – as in most styles before and since – a fairly strong correlation between the most exciting aesthetic achievements, and 'prestige' clients willing and able to spend more to get buildings which stand out. In the 1960s as in most other decades, these clients tended to be not the politically radical but the Establishment, and in the case of the Barbican the most firmly capitalist end of it.

This argument could be pushed even further: Brutalism at some times and in some projects was socially conservative in its effects, helping to camouflage the continuity of established privilege. Its origins may have lain in a backlash by aesthetically driven younger architects against an older generation whose preoccupations were primarily political, but it looked like a radical and progressive style. It is harder to criticise for social or political conservatism a project which is being admired for its wholehearted implementation of a radical set of planning ideas and an advanced aesthetic. There may have been those within the Corporation for whom the thrilling architecture of the Barbican, and its uncompromising concrete, were welcome not only for their own sakes, but as smokescreens for the City of London's self-protecting conservatism.

Whatever the political resonances of the Barbican then and now, it has established its high place in the architectural pantheon of British Modernism. It followed me through my MA year, not only in my frequent visits but also in glimpses every day on the skyline from Waterloo Bridge during my commute – a walk that was to begin another concrete obsession, one that would prompt me to move city, and to have my first experience of actually living in concrete housing rather than gazing longingly at it from outside.

Chapter Four

'Preponderately Precinctual in Intention'
New Court, Christ's College, Cambridge

(barnabascalder.org/rc4/)

i

'THOSE WHO WANT TO LIST BRUTALIST BUILDINGS SHOULD TRY LIVING IN ONE', blared the title of a recent piece of anti-concrete invective in *The Times*.[1] The argument is not new. For many people, concrete housing evokes television-drama depictions of murderous hellholes with leaky roofs, crumbling rust-streaked walls, sinister windswept walkways and a complete absence of charm or greenery. The perception was for a long time widespread that only those too poor and powerless to choose would end up living in such buildings. But the truth is very different indeed.

I had, by the end of my time at the Courtauld, spent hours staring longingly at the Barbican and other Brutalist housing estates, gazing up from their walkways like an architectural stalker. I ached to have my own key to Trellick Tower, my own balcony in Balfron, my own concrete . . . anything, really, more muscular than the Edwardian brick low-rise in which I had grown up. But by 2002 there was already no possibility of my affording a flat in any of the estates I loved in London. My own slice of a Brutalist masterpiece appeared to be an unrealisable dream. I would have to keep on staring in from outside.

During my MA, the building which had taken the strongest hold on me was Sir Denys Lasdun's National Theatre. Lasdun was perhaps the most internationally influential and admired British practitioner of heavy-concrete late Modernism, but I knew next to nothing about him when I first started to fall for his building on the South Bank of the Thames.[2] The more enthusiastic I became, the more puzzled I was by the fact that so few people seemed to share my enthusiasm. I began to feel the zeal of the convert, and the convert to a tiny and oppressed religion at that. The sense that there were battles to be fought for this wonderful building persuaded me that the thing I most wanted to do was spend the next few years researching the object of my new obsession, and its creator. After a bit of digging, I discovered that the academic whom I would like to supervise my doctoral research on post-war architecture was based at Cambridge. He explained to me that I would need to apply to become a member of a college, which immediately turned my thoughts to the question of which college had the best Brutalist architecture.

My answer to this question was New Court, a block of student accommodation in Christ's College. It had the added benefit that its architect was the very man I would be studying, Denys Lasdun. I applied to Christ's simply to get near it: New Court was normally reserved for undergraduates, and term was about to start, so I thought my chances of living in the block were pretty slim. But if there might be any possibility whatsoever, I knew I had to give it a try. Only once my application had been accepted did I summon up the courage to call the college. I rang the Fellow in charge of accommodation, and with considerable nervousness set out to him my interest in Lasdun's architecture, and my eagerness to live in the block. He seemed a little baffled, but said that yes, they had one remaining room, and he could not see why it should not be mine. The college's attitude to its concrete masterpiece was not at the time very enthusiastic, and I suspect either that he was too surprised to say no, or that he felt it would be salutary for me to suffer the realities of modern architecture for a year. Whatever the reason I will always be grateful to him. Within days I was moving into my new home: one of dozens of neat little pigeonhole student rooms near the top of a great hillside of glistening white precast concrete.

ii

I have never had a very clear sense of where Denys Lasdun's level of energetic passion about architecture came from. Born in 1914, he was still young when his father died, and his mother appears to have lived a rather rootless life, mostly in London but with some time in New York, mixing with an interesting musical and artistic set. Lasdun went to Rugby School, where his favourite subject was art. From there, in the manner of so many upper-middle-class architects then and since, he probably went on to study architecture as it was the nearest respectable, professional counterpart to the art lessons he loved.[3]

From 1932 Lasdun studied at the Architectural Association.[4] Whilst his growing interest in Le Corbusier was tolerated by the school, his education still involved plenty of measured drawings of Classical architecture, formal composition of complex programmes around symmetrical axes, and other training projects derived closely from the Parisian art and architecture school, the École des Beaux-Arts, whose international pre-eminence has seen its name used for the whole late-Classical style, 'Beaux-Arts'.[5]

Lasdun visited Paris in the early 1930s and, by his own recollection, was hugely excited by Le Corbusier's recent buildings there. He left the Architectural Association early to work first for the Canadian-British Modernist architect Wells Coates, and then for the most sophisticated and remarkable of Britain's pre-war Modernist practices, Tecton, under its complex and deeply gifted head, Berthold Lubetkin. Lubetkin had an impressive Modernist CV: born in Georgia, he had witnessed the Russian Revolution first-hand, trained and worked across the leading institutions in Europe, including studying as Ernö Goldfinger did with Perret at the École des Beaux-Arts. Lubetkin and Tecton had built the wonderful Highpoint flats in Highgate, London, which Le Corbusier visited in person and praised highly.[6]

Lasdun appears to have learned an immense amount from Lubetkin, including how to run an effective practice whilst keeping personal artistic control of large, complex jobs. Lubetkin, like Lasdun after him, was exceptionally skilled at retaining, within the Modernist rhetoric of function and economy, an unashamed emphasis on architecture as an art.

Before the Second World War, Lasdun's independent commissions consisted of two private houses, both gained through personal and family contact with the clients, typically of early career work in an architectural profession which has always substantially over-represented the middle and upper classes.[7] In the Second World War, Lasdun laid out front-line airfields to service the Allied advance after D-Day. He surveyed the sites from the back of a stray horse which he had snaffled against regulations after it was left behind by the retreating enemy, until the horse put its head out of its transporter into the face of the Military Police and was confiscated.[8] Once demobilised, Lasdun went back to Tecton and was a partner there until its dissolution in 1949. Over the course of the 1950s he established a growing reputation, and effortlessly and self-consciously built up his own architectural style distinct from his work with Tecton.[9] By the early to mid-1960s he had emerged as one of the most skilled architects in Britain at producing a building which fitted attractively into its location, served its function well, produced exciting outdoor spaces, and used contemporary concrete technologies with both artistic and technical mastery.

Despite the importance of concrete to his architecture, Lasdun hated the term 'Brutalism'. My acceptance of it as an art-historical term like the originally derogatory 'Gothic' would have upset and enraged him. He felt the apparent thuggishness of the word ill represented the careful humanity of his design process and the thoughtfulness with which he tried to make enjoyable and beautiful public spaces around his buildings.

Lasdun's approach to designing a building involved repeated phases of redesign to refine the original outlines into something with a deep consistency running through every aspect of the finished building. His design process accordingly took longer than that of most architects, and limited the amount of work his practice could undertake, as he warned prospective clients like the Estates Officer of Liverpool University when he was first offered the commission for a sports centre there in December 1960: 'I regret very much that due to pressure of work at the moment I would be unable to undertake this commission, should it be offered to me, until September 1961. The practice in this office is that all design work is handled personally by the partners.'[10]

The bonus from this slower speed was a more considered building, in functional and artistic terms. He said in 1965 that 'our job is to give the client, on time and on cost, *not* what he wants but what he never dreamed he wanted and, when he gets it, he recognizes it as something he wanted all the time'.[11] The way he did this was to talk to and observe the client institution at some length, until their pattern of activities gave him not only a functional understanding of their needs, but also an artistic inspiration as to how his architecture could be shaped to enhance their life. As a result of this unusually intuitive investigation of his buildings' users, his projects offer a sort of portrait of his client institutions at the moment he was designing for them. In his New Court, Lasdun was to produce just such a portrait of Christ's College.

iii

The new building at Christ's College was commissioned in order to increase the proportion of students who could be housed within the college. In the 1960s Cambridge University was working hard to maintain the sense of community which comes from having a large proportion of the student population living, eating and going to chapel within the college itself. With an expansionist climate in higher education, they were fighting an increase in the proportion of students living out in privately rented accommodation.[12]

The northern end of Christ's College's site was at this time a scrappy jumble of squash courts and service buildings, nibbled into by the backs of shops facing out on to King Street beyond. The initial brief from the college was to add some new facilities for students and staff, and provide as many undergraduate study bedrooms as possible. It was later added that 'all College accommodation should be effectively soundproofed against the inevitable noise from King Street and from the new shops'.[13]

The climate of architectural appreciation in Christ's College in the decades before the commissioning of New Court was by no means uniformly avant-garde. The college had rejected a scheme by one of the great early leaders of the Modernist movement, Walter Gropius, in 1937, and instead had commissioned shortly after the war two blocks of safe, if elegantly restrained, neo-Georgian accommodation from Sir Albert Richardson. Correspondence in the college magazine in 1954 showed solid support for Richardson's work: 'I think most people will agree that the results of Professor Richardson's work are, and will be in a century, more satisfying than a monument of the transient phase which the Gropius design so typified.' The same writer's only criticism of the two new blocks was that 'possibly the Richardson design lacks gaiety. There is perhaps too little decoration.'[14] The scene hardly seems set for Denys Lasdun's magnificently bold concrete battleship, a building which makes even Gropius's scheme look tentative and traditional.

Perhaps unsurprisingly in the light of this cautious atmosphere, the choice of architect for the next new block was neither swiftly nor simply made. In 1956, only three years after the completion of their last building by Richardson, the college approached Casson

Conder & Partners, whose gently Picturesque Modernist campus for arts departments on the western edge of Cambridge had been designed in 1952 and was then going up – a scheme that at the time represented a major break with tradition.[15] Their design for Christ's broke the necessary accommodation and facilities into a series of pavilions which could be composed in careful relation to each other, unlike Lasdun's scheme which folded the whole brief into a single large object. Casson Conder & Partners proposed some 'physical encroachment' on the Fellows' Garden, which appears to have caused alarm to the college's governing body, and in July 1959 they dropped them.[16] The college consulted Cambridge's new Professor of Architecture, Sir Leslie Martin, on other architects they might talk to, and he recommended Mervyn Handley or David Roberts, from each of whom outline schemes were sought.[17]

The selection process morphed into an unofficial competition. As the Master said in his first letter to Lasdun in July 1960, four years after their opening discussions with Casson Conder & Partners, 'the College have already had some schemes submitted to them, and we feel that we should like to have one or two more before making our final choice'.[18] Participation in this would have got the architects into trouble with the RIBA if reported – the RIBA was entitled to regulate all architectural competitions, and tried to prevent the unprofitable work which resulted when clients shopped around for ideas from multiple architects before settling on a scheme. In March 1961 Leslie Martin was again consulted, this time on the three schemes under consideration, and he recommended dropping the Roberts design.[19] In May the college governing body voted for Lasdun's proposal, with only five out of twenty-seven against it. Lasdun was offered the appointment.[20]

iv

Lasdun's design developed considerably over the following eight years. In each of the schemes for which evidence survives, the

accommodation provided is a stepping hillside of student rooms, gently concave along its length so that the curve of the building embraces the green space in front. Each floor is set back by most of a room-length from the floor below. This gives the service parts of the block (showers, kitchens, storage etc.) claustrophobically low ceilings, but the living part of each room is comfortably higher. The roof of each unit offers a sun terrace to the room above, but even more importantly this tight vertical planning makes a seven-storey building a similar height to the four-storey Victorian building opposite, squeezing considerable extra accommodation into the maximum height permitted by planning restrictions on the shadow the building could cast on to the street behind.

The bottom of the building's seven floors seemed to sink comfortably into a soft cushion of grass, whilst at the mid-level a terrace of grass ran along in front of the upper rooms, before stairs and greenery cascaded down over a series of common rooms to ground level, running parallel to the outdoor stairs with their long landings and short flights to keep even the most studiously unsporty undergraduate in breath. The building as it stands is only the first of three proposed stages. It would have been nearly three times the length had it been completed – the same hillside of housing would have continued along to the edge of the college site – but after the prolonged delays in getting Stage 1 through planning the momentum had gone and the building budget went instead to a new library.[21]

The steep slope of the building's rooms is entirely artificial on a near-flat site, producing a substantial triangular wedge of space beneath it. Into this cavity the architects tessellated all the remaining functions which earlier or later architects, including Casson Conder & Partners, might have dotted around as subsidiary buildings: a row of street-facing shops, a service road behind them, a parking deck above with its access ramp, and in the bowels of the building squash courts and changing rooms, a photographic darkroom, performance and social spaces, a boiler house and so on. The building extends below ground level, with the squash courts so deep that there have occasionally been problems from the pressure of the city's drains pouring waste into them. It is as if the site had been laid out with a slender, seven-storey accommodation block, and a range of smaller buildings next to it, separated by a road, but then the accommodation block had been staggered into a slope to cover the entire site, making out of its bitty components a single, handsome piece of city.

This kind of stepped section was, like so many other design ideas, popularised amongst Brutalist architects by Le Corbusier in two unbuilt projects of the 1940s for housing on steep hillside sites.[22] An estate closely modelled on these was designed from 1955 and built in 1959–61, on the outskirts of Bern. A group of recently qualified young Swiss architects named Atelier 5 – as there were, initially, five of them – designed it for a developer who was willing to back a hunch.[23] The Siedlung Halen (aimed squarely at wealthy bohemians) was widely published in architecture journals, and warmly admired.

British architectural interest in the stepped section also began around 1960 with discussions at the Architectural Association

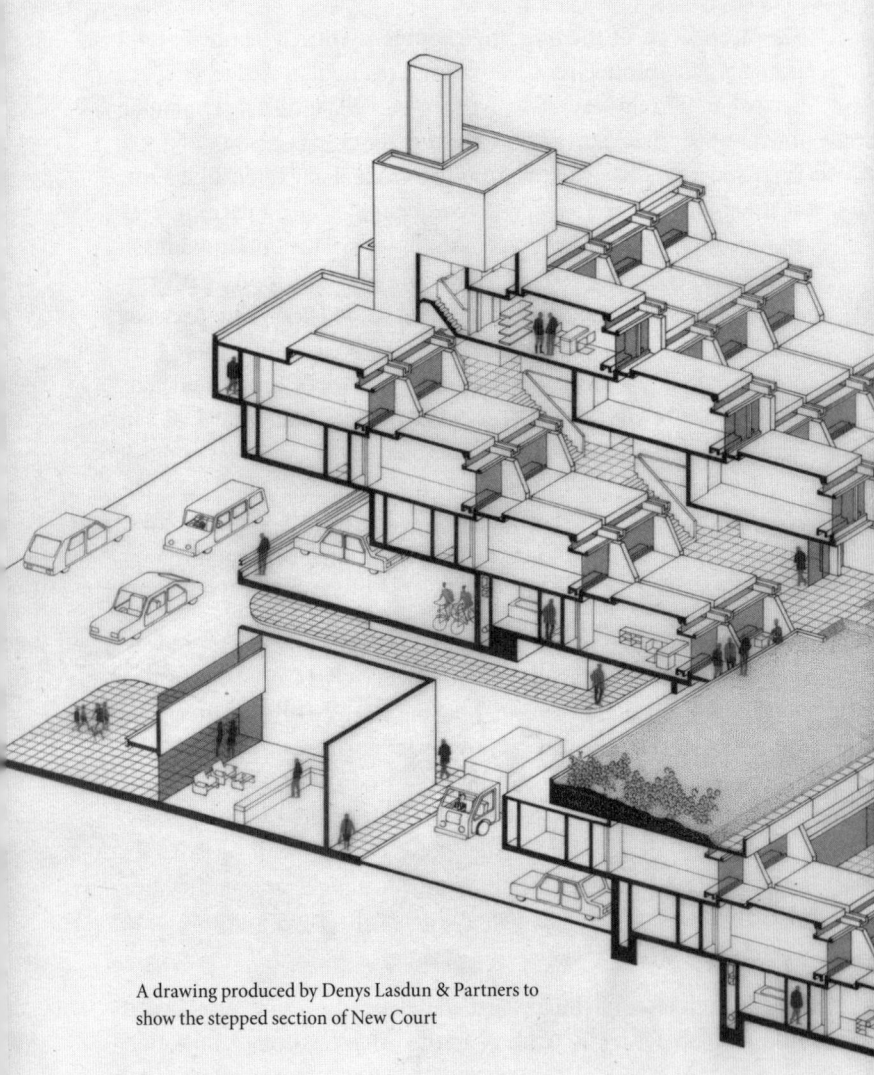

A drawing produced by Denys Lasdun & Partners to show the stepped section of New Court

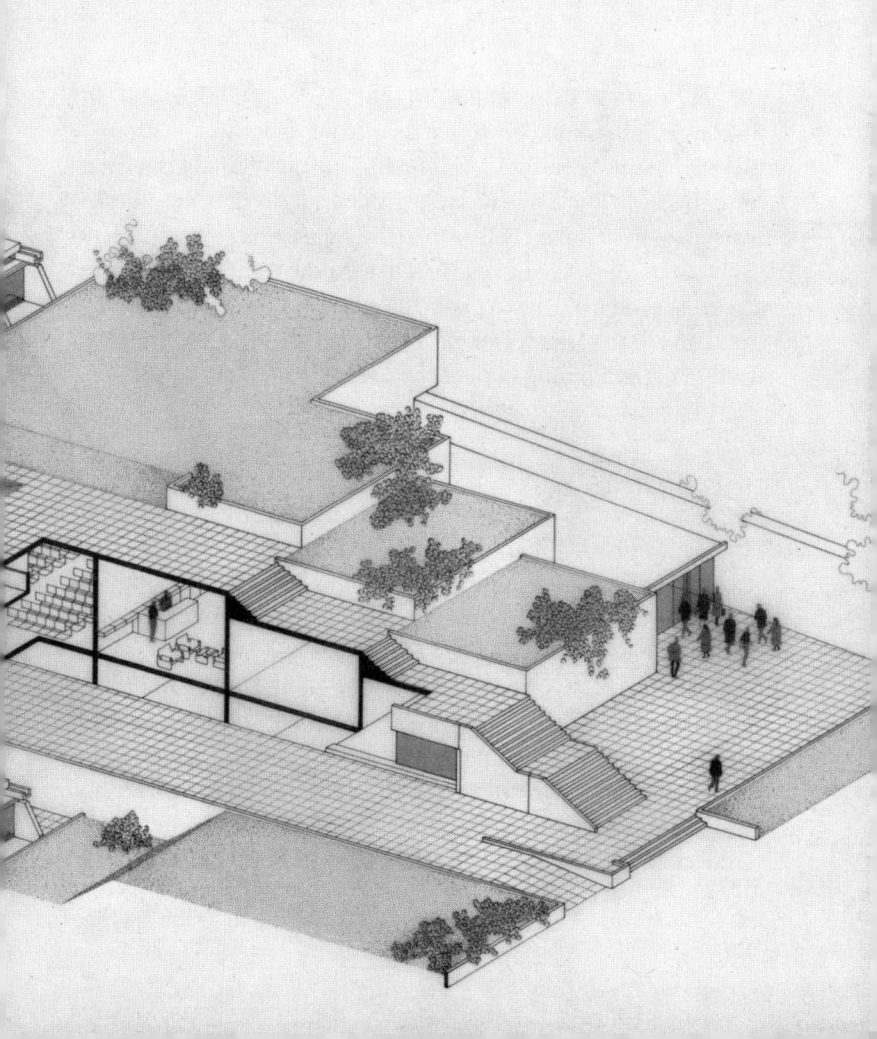

school of architecture (where Lasdun had briefly taught part-time five years earlier) about council-housing densities and the best ways of achieving them.[24] A young faction argued that the use of towers was socially alienating to residents accustomed to terraced housing.[25] A group around Leslie Martin at Cambridge in the 1960s explored the maths of this and concluded that indeed lower buildings could unexpectedly fit more inhabitants per acre than towers set in grassland – the long shadows the latter threw meant that they had to be quite widely spaced to meet building regulations on light.[26]

These British architects, including Lasdun, took the stepped section further than Atelier 5 did: Siedlung Halen and the Corbusian precedents on which it is based are dependent on naturally sloping sites. A Brutalist variant on this, which as far as I can determine began in England, saw these stepped housing schemes injected with ideas from Italian Futurism or the *immeuble à gradins* of Henri Sauvage in Paris just before the First World War.[27] These designs raised flats on a much steeper artificial slope than the natural hillside of Siedlung Halen, and placed lifts, access corridors and other facilities (a swimming pool in the case of the Parisian block) into the triangular void underneath.[28]

V

The delayed execution of Christ's – building work only began in 1969 – may have deprived it of some of its avant-gardism, but did give its architectural language a chance to profit from Lasdun's experience elsewhere. At Christ's, Lasdun and his team took the design of precast components as one of the most important methods of architectural expression, and each constituent part is clearly visible as a separate piece. The quantity of construction photos Lasdun kept of his earlier precast concrete buildings for the University of East Anglia (more than 200) suggests that he became seduced by the sight of his building at its Lego-kit stage, its giant, toy-like components being dropped into place by cranes on train tracks. At Christ's College, Lasdun's architecture does all it can to record the excitement of that construction stage in the completed building, with the separate fins, cross-beams, gutters and roof lids as clearly articulated in the finished building as in the construction photos. The building looks like the balsa component models with which it was designed. The gutter beams, for example, are not merely a functional and structural component; they seem to take on the numinous solidity of Aztec sculpture.

Because the basic student room in Lasdun's scheme repeats identically, it was relatively economical to design these room units to be built as a series of factory-made parts. The initial cost of setting up the moulds is comparatively expensive, so the more rooms you produce the cheaper that original cost gets per room. Actually, in a building like this – mid-sized and with a decent budget – prefabrication probably had more advantages of quality than of economy, allowing the construction to be carried out under the more rigorous controls of a factory rather than submitting it to the chance of weather conditions and craft skills on a potentially patchily supervised building site. The prefabricated parts of the building were grit-blasted in the factory to remove the outer layer of bland grey cement and to reveal instead the white, glinting quartz aggregate which the clients had selected from various possible finishes which they were shown by the architects.[29]

Above the hillside of prefabricated rooms stands a pair of service towers housing water tanks and in one case the boiler-house chimney. The concrete, now painted, was originally visibly different: darker, yellower, and all-of-a-piece, in situ work with the marks of its shuttering still visible on it. These towers, as well as their functional role and the compositional gesture they make of offsetting the horizontality of the rest of the building, serve to tell the architecturally aware viewer that the structure is not entirely of prefabricated kit parts, but stands on a rising deck of in situ concrete, topped by the in situ towers.

From the street side this monolithic underpinning was originally all the more obvious. Below a frosting of precast concrete at the two top levels the north-facing elevation of the block to King Street was entirely made of this darker, heavier-looking in situ concrete. The body of the building overhung the street like an immense cliff, its weight emphasised by huge beams and slab-columns whose absolutely simple rectangularity highlighted their bulk. Chamfered corners or other surface treatments might have diminished their apparent solidity and thickness, but as at the Baroque churches by Lasdun's hero Nicholas Hawksmoor in the East End of London, plain, overscaled, blocky volumes give the building a spectacular muscularity. At New Court a car park, the cars contained by rugged-looking girders, hovered ominously over a row of fragile-looking glassy shops, dwarfed by the magnificent concrete behemoth above.[30] New Court, magnificently aggressive, stood as a shocking interruption to a row of smaller, more homely looking older buildings.

Lasdun believed strongly in the importance of peace and architectural introspection for scholarly environments. He said of another project of his that 'a court defines in physical terms a scholastic body, inward looking and protected from traffic noise'.[31] And sure enough, almost all of his university and collegiate projects exaggeratedly shut out traffic and the world to create sanctums of green, peaceful space in which he hoped that scholars would think and discuss ideas. At Christ's this is particularly strongly articulated through the contrasts between the windowless, yellowish, shadowy overhang which confronts the street, and the white, sun-sparkling hillside rich in greenery and human-scaled windows which smiles into the college.

Why did a college which had regarded Richardson's 1950s buildings as rather daringly austere, only a few years later commission a design so startlingly avant-garde as Lasdun's stepped-section New Court? I suspect it was because the design did what Lasdun always

tried to do, and gave the client what they did not yet know they wanted, but then realised they had wanted all along.

Thus once one puts aside the fact that it is concrete, structurally exciting, and devoid of Gothic arches or Classical columns, New Court can be seen as an expression not of radical change but of institutional continuity. As the Master himself wrote, the building was intended to allow the institution 'to move forward, not by discarding our traditions but by refining and strengthening them [. . .] in the national interest'.[32] It may be expressed in the architectural style of the 1960s, but the college got what it wanted and needed, a building which fulfilled traditional collegiate functions. In the Master's words, 'this is far removed from a conventional college building yet it is a logical development of the staircase pattern of residential building in the idiom of the mid-twentieth century'.[33] The rooms are, in the customary Oxbridge manner, arranged round staircases rather than corridors. There is the usual grass outside, though democratised here by allowing students to walk on it, unlike in many college courts. To reflect Modernism's emphasis on south light, the two ranges of this court, rather than facing each other across open space, are vertically stacked, but the inward-facing curve of the rooms aims at a similar feeling of community to that produced by a four-sided court. The architectural ideas and concrete engineering of the 1960s allow the ancillary buildings which have often sat awkwardly within traditional collegiate court planning to disappear beneath the building. Concrete engineering also made viable a wholly new facility, cool and modern – the roof terrace outside each room. Overall, though, Cambridge norms were reinforced rather than challenged. It is characteristic of the continuing hierarchy that the egalitarianism of the block's identical-sized rooms does not extend to the Fellows' sets, which are not only substantially larger, but also stand out physically in front of the ordinary students' rooms in a way dictated at least partially by planning practicalities, but which gives them clear precedence.

'PREPONDERATELY PRECINCTUAL IN INTENTION'

In the design and furnishing of the rooms, too, the old patterns of social hierarchy sat surprisingly comfortably alongside the new Modernist practice of experimentation and mock-up. Living in typical recently built student rooms, with their tiny en-suite lavatories and showers, and nowhere to put one's things, one feels like an overstaying hotel guest. The rooms at New Court, characteristically of 1960s student accommodation, let one really live, study and socialise there, with space for a decent desk, bookshelves, storage shelves, a chair or two (besides the bed) to sit on, and a basin for tooth-cleaning and a surreptitious midnight pee.

The basin was perfectly circular, which produced mesmerising whirlpools when you drained it after washing up, and Lasdun's cupboards were lovely. Simple, white-painted doors and shelves made of robustly stocky wood or board not only provided as much storage as possible in a tight space, but by using full-height slits rather than handles they preserved some of the strong, solid character of his architecture, as well as being economical to build and maintain.

My room

Sadly, a Fellow of Christ's College vetoed in March 1968 Lasdun's original proposal for built-in concrete desks and bedheads.[34] They would indeed, as he warned, have made the room inflexible, in the overdetermined way of Hermit's Castle's built-in furnishings, but I would have loved them.

The practicality of the neat little rooms arose from Modernist experimentation. Once the bottom floor of the building was more or less complete, sample rooms were fitted out and furnished to demonstrate alternative options. Fellows and students came to see the rooms and gave their comments which, when summarised for Lasdun by the Bursar, were sometimes tantalisingly cryptic: 'The dimensions of the bookshelving were studied with growing astonishment and finally universally condemned.'[35]

This progressive attitude, consulting the students before equipping their rooms, and experimenting with alternatives, carried Modernist, science-influenced techniques and attitudes into the tradition-laden atmosphere of a Cambridge college, but in common with Modernism worldwide it also embodied unselfconscious continuation of attitudes to gender which now look positively Old Testament. The Fellows and students in 1969 were still all men, but the daily cleaners ('bed-makers') were typically women. Students were allowed to see and comment on the mocked-up rooms, but the bed-makers were represented by their boss, the College Manciple, and by some of the Fellows' wives, who lent their feminine expertise:

> The ladies who went through the motions of making these [beds] condemned them outright – a typical man's design. In theory the bed pulls out from the wall, leaving the drawer unit [beneath] in situ. In practice it is much too heavy for the average woman; if one tries to swivel it from one end, the heavy drawer unit moves with it, and unless you have the arms of a (female) gorilla, there is nothing to catch hold of at the side.[36]

Meanwhile the only comment on beds from the male undergraduates was that they must have bedheads for 'an important part of their lives – reading in bed'.[37] This picture of young, often socially privileged men reading in bed whilst older, working-class women cleaned up around them came a year after French students set off an international movement for socialist world revolution.

Another possible sign of ongoing class attitudes occurs in discussion of the minimal cooking arrangements and washing facilities.[38] The bath and showers shared a single large room, suggesting that users were intended to wash in front of each other, presumably a habit which they would have acquired at the boarding schools to which so many would have gone previously. Nevertheless, the spartan lavatory facilities were referred to by one of the 1969 consultees as 'lavish'.[39]

vi

Similar continuities are visible in the overall shape of the building. Though Lasdun's New Court was erected under the banner of national university expansion, in the detail of its eight-year planning battle far older collegiate patterns emerge. Most of the centre of Cambridge is owned in a complex patchwork of varying-sized plots by individual colleges, which have been important landlords in the city for centuries. The long history of collegiate expansion and consolidation has seen a half-millennium chess game of exchange and purchase between the colleges. New Court was another move in the game between Christ's College and Jesus College in which both sought to acquire as much of the area between the two as possible, ideally in big enough chunks to redevelop commercially or as additional college accommodation.

With Christ's College, Jesus College and Sidney Sussex College all developing new housing on King Street, and the city council considering street widening and new parking provision, Trollopian politicking was inevitable. Early in their own planning for King

Street, Jesus College approached Christ's to discuss the possibility of the two schemes being drawn up with a measure of cooperation between Lasdun and Ivor Smith, the architect of the Jesus block. The Bursar of Christ's, however, mistrusted the intentions of his counterpart, telling Lasdun, 'As you know, they were very anxious to land us in their net a year or two ago and so, I think we have to treat this rather carefully. [. . .] I just do not want to give the impression of being in too much haste to swallow their ideas!'[40]

Jesus College did not give up easily. A 1964 letter from the Bursar of Jesus College to the Bursar of Christ's sets out all the arguments and persuasions at his disposal. It hints, in characteristically diplomatic terms, at Jesus College being able to cause Lasdun's scheme potential problems with planning permission, lighting legislation and bad publicity, and it dangles the hope of Christ's College acquiring land owned by Jesus College in exchange for shrinking their scheme:

> Although we appreciate that your development is preponderately precinctual in intention, we hope that you will not regard the King Street frontage as merely the back of a College building [. . .], but will include in your considerations the impact that this building may have on all that lies to the north.
>
> It is not impossible that you may wish to consider whether this is a favourable opportunity to contemplate a collegiate building on the north side of King Street on land now in the ownership of this College.[41]

The Bursar of Christ's College rose to the hint of possible land deals, hoping to buy from Jesus College remaining properties along the perimeter of the Christ's site:

> Any such sales might very well help to reconcile my Governing Body to the loss of accommodation from a partial lowering in height of our proposed building.[42]

In other words, the Bursar might be willing to compromise Lasdun's scheme to gain other objectives. Hearing of this, Lasdun's associate Harry Pugh wrote to the Bursar of Christ's in January 1965 warning that if the college were to decide expediently to cut the height of the building,

> it would be necessary for the present scheme to be completely re-designed. You will appreciate that the removal of probably the top two floors would destroy the coherence of the design in itself, and also make it quite meaningless in relation to the rest of the College. In our view this aspect of it is of greater importance than the sacrifice of a number of rooms.[43]

Meanwhile the wrestling between the two colleges was further complicated by the input of the town planners. The City Architect proposed as early as 1963 that the scale of redevelopment proposed by Jesus College and Christ's College was such as to suggest treating it as a Comprehensive Development Area, which would bring with it a requirement for ministerial approval, and consultation with the Royal Fine Arts Commission, a committee of senior architects and other worthies who gave influential but not binding advice on important schemes.[44] The colleges seem to have had a combative attitude to the intervention of the city in what they saw as their affairs, and the architects may have picked up on this. As Harry Pugh recorded dismissively, 'Logie [the City Architect] is clearly pre-occupied with his traffic, parking and servicing problems.'[45]

The situation got messier still when the city council decided to widen King Street to increase traffic flow, telling Lasdun that his scheme must move several feet back from the existing building line, requiring alterations to the whole of the tightly planned design: in order for precast concrete moulds to work, the student rooms all had to be identical, so every part of the building had to be adjusted to the new limitation.[46] The college took the matter to a public inquiry but lost. Only by 1969 was the new scheme (as lightly revised as possible within the new building-line requirement) tendered for and under way.

The aggression of New Court's elevation to King Street may partly have been a matter of sound insulation against the proposed wider road. However, given Lasdun's tendency to draw architectural portraits of the institutions he built for, it reads as a curiously exact metaphor for the relations between college, town and neighbouring colleges. The Christ's College governing body had played a harshly competitive game with its neighbours about land ownership and scale of development, and in the end pushed through its hermetically introverted scheme most of a decade after Lasdun's initial proposals: the intimidating facade perhaps provided an unbreachable defence against the unreliability of neighbouring landowners and the council. Lasdun's handsome but forbidding scheme had met with the warm approval of the college governing body in March 1967. As the Bursar reported back to Lasdun, 'It is clearly well liked and if the applause at the end seemed subdued you should content yourself that it was the first applause ever heard at a College meeting within living memory.'[47]

The social controls of Cambridge colleges in the 1960s are also clear from the excluding back of the building. Students were still shut in at night in this period, and one of Lasdun's collaborators told me that the stepped-section residences designed by the practice for the University of East Anglia was a deliberate statement of democratic lack of nocturnal lock-in.[48] In 1960s Cambridge a culture of climbing buildings had long been well developed. It had originated with students breaking back into their own colleges after nights out in order to avoid fines. If you walk round the perimeters of many Oxbridge colleges you will see the lethal-looking spikes and barred windows which those pre-health-and-safety days regarded as a proportionate response to breaches of the rules. Starting as a necessary part of the high-spirited student social life, climbing buildings became for some an art in itself, the apogee of which was a number of successful nocturnal attempts on Kings College's immensely tall medieval chapel.[49] Lasdun's King Street facade, with its huge concrete overhang, looked like a serious defence against night climbers, for all the democratic climbability of its inward-facing side.

This same facade was also a spectacular statement of the division between 'town and gown' at the time. For all the aesthetic radicalism of Lasdun's design, the architectural exclusion of non-members ran contrary to the progressive mood of the decade. England's seven New Universities on their unfenced sites shared social and sporting facilities with their local towns; the Open University (under discussion from 1965) denied the need for any physical limitations; and international student rioting in 1968 was questioning authority in almost all its established forms. Yet in Cambridge Christ's College was making one of the clearest statements since the castle-like gatehouses of the sixteenth century of the separation between the noisy ordinariness of the town street and the peaceful, grassy enclosure of the college. For those privileged to be members of the latter there was a huge range of social and recreational facilities; for those outside there were only the shops, conspicuously dwarfed by the building above.

The irony is that, whilst colleges remain essentially introverted and private, Lasdun's Brutalistically candid display of the collegiate norm has long been taken amiss by the college itself. In the 1990s a new accommodation building was added along King Street, wedged into the former parking deck of New Court. It is contextual and neighbourly in its image, as Lasdun's never was. Access to its rooms, however, is just as firmly internalised to the college, and protected behind a robust steel gate hidden within the friendly looking miniature gatehouse. The institutional reality of an inward-looking college community – very un-1960s and very powerful in developing connections between members of the college – is remarkably little changed, but Lasdun's characteristically late-Modernist wish to express functional realities in strong architectural terms has been masked and equivocated away.

vii

Having begged myself a room in New Court I arrived full of excitement at the prospect of new studies, a new city, new friends to make, and – not the least elating – a year surrounded by my beloved Lasdun concrete. Knowing that this was such an important building, my first reaction to seeing it myself was, distressingly, disappointment. In the pictures of the building which Lasdun circulated, it peeps intriguingly round walls and bushes, or its sculptural quality is captured in powerful, semi-abstract photos of details, cropped in tightly. As you actually approach the building through the college it has rather less presence than one expects: because it steps back with each floor it does not seem tall, and with only just over a third of its intended length ever built it does feel truncated. Above all the context, carefully excluded from Lasdun's favoured photos, is an unprepossessing set of backs and sides of buildings. The main view from New Court's rooms is the red-brick back of the stone-fronted Victorian Stevenson Building, of which Casson Conder & Partners had warned that 'the frankly rude rear of the Stevenson block is the main hazard to the character of New Court'.[50]

Perhaps the real killer for my early impression of the building from within the college was that its profusion of outside space seemed to attract less sociable use than one might have hoped from a building full of first-year students. Christ's College when I was there had a reputation for spectacularly earnest academic endeavour. There was something peculiarly bleak about the sun beaming down on unoccupied, south-facing, sheltered, informal grass whilst the Midwich Cuckoo scholars slogged silently in the diligent solitude of their study-bedrooms.

The front of the building to King Street (probably the bit I would have found most exciting and beautiful, to judge from the few tantalisingly intimidating photos which record it) had essentially disappeared – vanished behind the building erected in the 1990s.[51] The Lasdun roofline can still be pointed out by an expert, like a medievalist identifying the traces of an earlier Roman wall, but below it are several storeys of yellow-brick Postmodernism with stone trim, feature gutters, ostentatiously pitched roofs and strong vertical divisions to echo the rhythm of the street's older buildings. The 1990s gate at one end of Lasdun's block is a sort of Postmodernist Renaissance gatehouse, with simplified heraldic-looking carvings. The new building is not actually without its qualities as a piece of architecture (though when I was there I derived an adrenal satisfaction from loathing it), but it is certainly not what Lasdun wanted – his original overhanging concrete front was all sublimity and strength.

By the time I arrived there, the common rooms under the great stair down from the terrace had been cheered up with low budgets and the most dismal taste. The double-height graduate common room around which my college social life revolved had had its urbane shutter-marked concrete papered in woodchip wallpaper. A broad dado rail in dark, orangey wood veneer had been added, and above and below it the large expanse of wall was painted two shades of vivid, never-nice blue. The original furniture of chrome and black leather had gone or was going (I will one day stop regretting my failure to pinch one of the clapped-out Wassily chairs that had been relegated to the mezzanine and were on the cusp of being thrown out), to be replaced with successive batches of the banal institutional standard items of later decades. I had a role in choosing one set of new chairs, and a thoroughly unaesthetic process we made it.

If my initial reaction to New Court was disappointment, that was to change over the course of the following year of my living in it and three years using it as a social facility. Presided over by the offensive wall coverings of the graduate common room I played hundreds of hours of table football. I perched on the ugly sofas sipping mid-quality sherry from tiny goblets in an incongruous half-and-half world of village-hall aesthetics and collegiate traditionalism. I watched cricket on the mezzanine television, enjoying during breaks a tantalising glimpse of the Fellows' Garden trees through a long window. One hot summer night some of us went outside through the large sliding windows to enjoy the tense, thrilling moment between nearby lightning and the first giant drops of rain, a transitory mania making habitually sober types frolic on Lasdun's lawn like bookish Maenads. Snow brought out even the quiet students, and I watched with pleasure the frustration of those further down the block at the impunity with which their higher neighbours could paste them with snowballs from their own unreachable height.

In the basement I learned to print black-and-white analogue photos in Lasdun's darkroom. The only radio transmission which would make it past so many steel reinforcement rods was a local music station with the sorts of DJs who make you see that the wearisome national ones really are a cut above. Amidst the pleasingly metallic smell of developer, as the timer ticked away, I would dance round the darkroom to any rubbish playing, confident in the pitch black of my security from being seen, heard or interrupted.

In the summer I sunbathed my way through books on my terrace, and once at night I climbed quietly up the outsides of the rooms above me to the roof to look out over the lights of Cambridge. I wish I had tried it by day. Perhaps the gnawing embarrassment at the prospect of going past someone's window at the wrong moment deterred me more than the fear of being seen and punished. I think it was this sense of excessive anxiety about privacy which deadened the central grass of the block: the undergraduates of the early 2000s were too strongly aware of territory and private space to risk lounging on grass claimed architecturally by the room that overlooked it. Whilst many in the 1960s and '70s enjoyed breaking down bourgeois concepts of privacy, the daring new freedoms were never universally accepted. The thin blinds of the University of East Anglia were rumoured to have produced a lively traffic of peeping

Toms, in response to which students held vigilante patrols. By the 2000s this type of anxiety had become much heightened. I still remember the awkwardness of a group of besuited college estates people, who came out of the next-door room's window one day with their clipboards to find me sunbathing, sprawled on the roof in my underpants. We greeted each other with awkward politeness, and then felt uncomfortable until they could finish their business and go back in.

The claustrophobically narrow, low corridors, artificially lit and ventilated, and the steep internal staircases, whilst in themselves not places one would choose to linger, made the pleasure of emerging into the higher, brighter rooms more striking through contrast – a classical architectural technique about which Lasdun spoke explicitly elsewhere.[52]

Back in my room, small but well planned, I would look up at the hessian side walls and the exposed concrete beam above my bed and smile to myself with straightforward aesthetic pleasure, and with the less healthy kick of knowing that I was right, unlike the daily detractors who seemed genuinely shocked at what they saw as my attention-seeking eccentricity in expressing pleasure in this supremely unloved architecture. As one Fellow of the college put it, when I told him I liked the building, 'There are enough loonies amongst us conceivably for somebody to think it's a smashing fine do – that's up to you.' He reported that other Fellows called New Court 'the *Belgrano*', as it looked like a battleship and they felt it would be better off sunk.

In my room I had a particular fondness for a solitary stalactite which had formed where a slow drip of rainwater was seeping through a joint, carrying down the lime from the cement and re-forming it as in a cave, with a matching small crusty circle on the carpet below – all that develops if a stalagmite is hoovered weekly. I was slightly saddened one day to notice my stalactite lying broken on the carpet. I think it had grown long enough to be hit by the door.

I had two reservations about my room. Firstly – and intrinsically to the design – the rooms were deep but narrow, which is neither the most homely nor the most flexible proportion; with each room having a south-facing terrace they had to be tightly squeezed in side to side, the more so after the design was compacted to accommodate the planned road-widening. Secondly, the sound insulation was pretty poor. A report by the architects into changes they would wish to make in Stage 2 (it looked at the time like getting built) commented on the need to 'improve the methods of forming the joints between block work partitions and concrete mullions and beams to reduce possible sound penetration between rooms'.[53] In my room I could hear the words of a loud conversation next door. In that respect I was happy to be in a college whose students overworked and under-partied; the worst noises that made it through from either of my very nice neighbours were some splendidly earnest first-year student conversations about politics and philosophy, ending early enough to let me sleep.

The radiator was – as often in buildings designed in those days of cheap and cheapening energy and no awareness of the environmental dangers of wasting it – placed along the bottom of the single-glazed, metal-framed window to cut out draughts. Almost touching the radiator, and probably functioning to some degree as a storage heater, was a substantial precast concrete bench. This monolithic window seat was not grit-blasted like the rest of the precast, so its surface was as smooth as it was hard – comfortable and cleanable.

The concrete parts of the interior had worn as little as you would expect, and the hessian pinboard which covered the main stretches of wall was in strikingly good condition after thirty years, a testament to the excellence of the idea. A painted wall would have needed redecoration every couple of years to look so good under the onslaught of pins and Blu-Tack.

I was sad at the end of the year when I had to move out of the room. I still now pine to be back in surroundings where there is the calming solidity of concrete to touch, a balcony, and a daily dose of the hard-edged sublimity of the 1960s. For now, though, Balfron Tower, Trellick Tower and the Barbican remain as hopelessly beyond my reach as they were when I was a student.

viii

At New Court, Lasdun paid a considerable price for the magnificent sublimity of his King Street facade.

Only in the backs and underbellies of buildings can an architect really take awe-inspiring dominance to its terrifying, beautiful height, and only in the later 1960s did an increasing body of Brutalist architects get up the nerve to do so. Lasdun's lost facade to King Street seemed to revel in honesty about materials, structure and social function, taking this delight to the borders of rudeness. The reception of New Court by the press shows that their previous hesitancy about such muscular statements had been sensible: what causes thrilled awe in admirers can cause furious hostility in others.

Reputation and good publicity were important to Lasdun, and he could be ruthless in opposing coverage he felt to be unfair or damaging. As a leading architect he tended to have substantial control over what architectural publications said about his work, normally getting pre-publication previews of reviews. In the case of New Court he responded with obvious anger in a private memorandum to one draft article he disliked: the author 'is prepared to falsify history but should not be allowed to by debasing D[enys] L[asdun and] P[artners]'.[54] He also took offence at a proposed article in which a young architect speculated about the creative process behind New Court's design: 'DL made it clear that we were not a nursery school for budding writers and were not prepared to have seven years' work irrationally destroyed.'[55] Lasdun rang an editor of the *Architectural Review*, the journal where the offending article was to be published, warning that 'his [Lasdun's] wish to censor "fact" in [the] article would apply equally to praise and criticism, i.e. if he [the author] liked something for the wrong reason, based on incorrect facts, it would be censored'.[56]

Yet after so much effort to control how his building was presented to the world, when the long-discussed article came out, in a form at last approved by Lasdun, it was prefaced by an editorial entitled 'Anarchy' (of which Lasdun had only been told a few hours before). The editorial attacked the 'academic rape' to which King Street had been subjected, opening with, 'King Street, Cambridge, was – and half of it still remains – a paradigm of English urban society. Human in scale, modest in expression, a representation in Cambridge brick and stucco of that ideal of a diversity-in-unity to which we all subscribe.'[57] It then went on to contrast that with the 'Brobdingnag' of the three new developments for Christ's, Jesus and Sidney Sussex. The editor suggested in a private letter to Lasdun,

> We have taken great care to make it clear that the ultimate villain of the piece is a combination of the devil incarnate, the planning officer, and his chief aide, Ivor Smith [the architect of Jesus College's building opposite Lasdun's], whose long, low, flatulent block utterly destroys any semblance of curvature which you, with your building have intended, and will, with the second and third stages, undoubtedly create.[58]

Yet the editorial was the introduction to the article on Lasdun's project, not Smith's, and there can be no doubting that it implicated Lasdun in the crime which it argued had been committed against King Street.

Lasdun's misfortune here was that the pleasant if unremarkable street which he had partially replaced was, at the time when his scheme was first proposed, not likely to be a cause of controversy, nor long to survive the rising land pressure of central Cambridge. Architectural conservationism had been gradually on the rise from the later 1950s, with the foundation of both the Victorian Society and the Civic Trust in 1957. In the later 1960s the legislative protection for older buildings got stronger and stronger, with a series of measures strengthening listing, bringing in Conservation Areas and 'group value' to allow accumulations of decent buildings to be treated as collectively worth saving, and making it compulsory to consult amenity societies like the Victorian Society about the demolition of buildings within their historical remits.[59] Right at the tail end of the decade a huge swell of conservationist opinion burst on the UK, with simultaneous manifestations nationwide. Suddenly the kinds of agreeable but unremarkable streets and buildings which had always tended to be pulled down as part of the normal order of things came to be widely appreciated and efficaciously fought for. Through its prominence in an influential city and through the coverage in the *Architectural Review*, Lasdun's New Court found itself becoming a major early talking point in the battle to conserve the ordinary street. The sublimity and height of Lasdun's street elevation made it a photogenic enemy for those who preferred cottages to megastructures.

Perhaps Cambridge was particularly susceptible to this kind of conservationism because of its status as a conspicuously old university town: people so often have sentimental memories of their student days and the streets in which they lived, like those recorded with no trace of self-conscious irony by an Italian who wrote to *The Times* as early as 1968 to protest against the fact that Lasdun's scheme would mean removing an existing railing.[60]

Whatever the mix of reasons, Lasdun found himself at the centre of controversy over New Court in 1971. Whilst his public face remained as professional and authoritative as ever, in private Lasdun appears to have been shocked and hurt by the reversal in his critical fortunes represented by the coverage of his latest building. His correspondence suggests that he contacted the friends and supporters with whom he most liked to discuss architecture, perhaps in the hope of receiving their advice and reassurance.[61] He also drafted a memorandum, as far as one can tell purely for his own benefit, entitled 'What is a street?' In it he tried to apply a

Modernist approach of working-out-from-first-principles to the question of what streets are, and who is responsible for their character. At a time when architectural debates were becoming increasingly sophisticated and insightful about the difficult and subtle characteristics which make for a successful streetscape, Lasdun's memo seems clunkingly old-fashioned and awkward. It opens with a reductivist definition of a street as 'negative space created by the public walking level (levels) and the "physical obstructions", in and along it, (as building elevations, trees, etc.)'. It ends several inconclusive pages later in a melancholy and defensive tone: 'When the site [of a building] is in a street which some people claim "It should be preserved" without sufficient knowledge about the responsibilities of the various parties, no architect can meet the challenge which is not his.'[62]

Reading Lasdun's memo, his tone suddenly unconfident and puzzled, I feel a sympathy which goes beyond simple historical interest. To my great sadness I never met Lasdun, but nevertheless over the years I feel as if I have got to know him, and when I encounter his moments of struggle and adversity, like the media hostility to New Court, I feel a sympathy which departs from a historian's detachment. It is a closeness that has been fomented in part by talking to his family and his former colleagues, but more substantially, I think, through reading his remarkable office memoranda.[63] Lasdun used to keep exhaustive records of any interactions which might eventually prove relevant to the finished building. These escape the customary banality of committee minutes, with their 'it-was-resolved-that ...' blandness ironing out every wrinkle of individuality and contention. Instead the memoranda record Lasdun's excitement, his frustration, his anger, or his relief, as the immense projects of national importance which occupied his 1960s and '70s went through exhilarating moments of creative satisfaction, or terrifying lurches towards cancellation or damaging modification. The memoranda often convey the feelings of the moment, and are full of charming human details: Lasdun recorded of a crucial after-dinner meeting in 1960 where he was trying to get the challengingly Modernist Royal College of Physicians design through an ambivalent client committee, 'I doodled a sketch of the west elevation which at any rate impressed the President very much, but this may have been the brandy.'[64] He told an architect who was writing about the Christ's project that his article was 'hogwash',[65] and frequently triple-underlined in his broad 6B pencil ideas or phrases that he thought might hold a key to his design.

I feel I have shared some of the highs and lows of this committed, creative, serious, obsessive, irascible, resolute, insecure man, with his consuming dedication to the art of architecture, and his corresponding vulnerability to criticism. The day-to-day life of his projects comes through so vividly that there are moments in his archive where I could shout at him in frustration as he stubbornly defends a design too intransigently and damages his relations with an important client in the process. At other moments I have wanted to comfort him as the paper trail follows the turn of fashion against his architectural style, and his all-conquering confidence slumps into self-doubt, anxiety and puzzled bitterness.

Lasdun is an architect who inspires my tremendous admiration. Admiration of his professionalism (every project is run with absolute precision and thoroughness); admiration of his deep conviction in the worth of architecture as an art and its power to improve people's lives; and admiration of his endless willingness to persuade, charm, cajole, negotiate, dodge, fight, and fight again for the unprovable but strongly felt conviction that he knew what each building needed artistically. His commitment to his idea of good design was so strong that he sacrificed the possibility of considerably greater wealth for it, routinely refusing work in order not to dilute his central role in the design process, and sometimes dropping jobs at advanced stages because planners or clients would not let him build something he felt would be good enough. Susan Lasdun, the architect's wife, recalls an occasion when he commissioned a management consultancy to come and investigate ways of making the practice more economically efficient, but dismissed them as soon as their early recommendations suggested cutting the amount of design work that went into each project.[66]

If I am sad at the 1990s loss of the controversial north side of Lasdun's New Court, my feeling about recent developments on its south side is closer to rage. The lovely planting which characterised the south face of the building had been the subject originally of careful consultation and thought. A Fellow of the college wrote to the architects in November 1971 when the building was ready to be landscaped, 'I remember your general intentions very clearly, but was not happy with the suggested shrubs in the plan which the Superintendent of the Botanic Garden drew up – the effect would have been too prettified, and not bold enough for the scale of the building.'[67] The planting when I was there was excellent: informal, bold and cascading, with leaves rich in textures and tones that went beautifully with each other and with the concrete. Yet in the past decade the college has not only torn out all the planting, with the legitimate concern that it was making it hard to resolve leaks into some of the rooms below, but it has also brought in new landscaping as radically hostile to the building as it is possible readily to imagine.[68]

The terrace is now paved in concrete slabs whose gimmicky patterning of light and dark does nothing to mitigate the extent to which they kill the intended contrast between the hardness of the building and the soft grass of the terrace. The new paving is without sitting places, so the social potential of the lost grass is gone. On it stand potted shrubs of startling absurdity – Versailles-style topiary of the sort favoured by pretentious hotels. The condemnation 'too prettified, and not bold enough for the scale of the building' does not begin to express how wrong this planting is for Lasdun's architecture.

An even more recent loss is the lawn at ground level in front of the building, punctuated only by three carefully placed birch trees, whose beautiful grass lapped at the base of the building. This has been removed and replaced with a 'Darwin Garden' (Darwin went to Christ's College) of many fiddly little details, which fights furiously against the monumental clarity and scale of the building behind, greatly to the loss of both garden and building. The life-sized, realist sculpture of Darwin which perches with self-conscious Madame Tussauds casualness on a bench in the middle reflects the absolute opposition of taste between the avant-garde Modernist style of the college's architectural patronage in the early 1960s and its extraordinary artistic conservatism now. It is almost too obvious to be worth saying, but Cambridge benefits from its reputation and image as a very old university, and college members seem often to like buildings to *look* old, or at least deferential to the old. The apparent lack of aesthetic sophistication to which this contributes is surprising amongst a body of people so proudly sophisticated in intellectual fields.

The point seems to be lost on architectural traditionalists that New Court's radicalism of engineering and image was not at all disruptive to the traditions of college life. For Christ's College in the 1960s, as for the Corporation of the City of London when they built the Barbican, concrete Modernism offered all sorts of advantages: new ways of increasing the amount they could pack on to restricted sites; exciting aesthetics showing a forward-thinking sophistication; experimentalism which promised better-functioning buildings. But at the same time good architects working in a Modernist idiom responded, as architects always have, to the needs of the client. New Court exemplified the strength and independent-mindedness of Lasdun's architecture, but also the care with which he ensured that his designs corresponded to the real needs and nature of the client and users. The building enshrined collegiate privilege, hierarchy and territoriality, and maintained traditional social patterns. It is extraordinary how far the unconventional image of 1960s university buildings fooled the critics, in the long period of Modernism's unpopularity, convincing them that the phase represented a

The Darwin Garden

genuine and somehow externally imposed disruption of a collegiate tradition which inevitably involved stone, pitched roofs and pointed arches or Classical columns. Somewhere in the anti-Modernist backlash, Cambridge badly lost its architectural nerve. The change is all the more striking because from the end of the 1950s until the 1970s, the city had seen some of Britain's most acclaimed and interesting architecture, yet as recently as 2012, an exhibition and book could justly claim that this was a forgotten or disliked period in the history of the university and the city.[69] With luck the tide will turn before too much more damage is done to the great works of Cambridge Modernism.

Chapter Five

The Establishment's Radical
Professor Sir Leslie Martin, PhD

(barnabascalder.org/rc5/)

i

In 1959, two talented and spiky young architects got what turned out to be their big break. It came near the start of a nationwide building boom in the university sector: new universities were founded, old ones were greatly expanded with a new quality and quantity of facilities for teaching, research and student life. University College Leicester was upgraded in 1957 to full university status, and began a large building programme to accommodate new and expanded departments. Their facilities were determined in negotiations between powerful heads of department and the University Grants Committee, an opaque branch of the Treasury which determined the budgets for new building work according to tight formulae, but with enough discretion to be able to support innovative teaching or research facilities, special equipment and so on.[1]

Based in a manufacturing city, the newly upgraded institution was to have a top-class Department of Engineering, and the young, innovative head of it, Edward Parkes, worked well with the young, innovative architects, James Gowan and James Stirling, to think through the needs of its building.

With the possible exception of the architects themselves, no one involved in the process is likely to have foreseen at their appointment in summer 1959 that the result would be one of the world's great buildings, and would send waves of excitement round the globe. They produced a sneering, hip-thrusting Elvis of a structure, which for countless young architects seemed to show up the samey superficiality of the crooners it was to upstage. The new Engineering Building, built in 1961–64, embodies in its exciting, vigorous, unconventional architecture the best aspects of the optimistic post-war expansion of British universities.

Sunlit against a blue sky, its red-brick and red-tile cladding is almost painfully vivid. My first visit to it, however, was in ugly, fading light. The shockingly red brick and tile looked slightly liverish and off-putting, the building's windows were filthy, and it seemed squashed into a neglected corner of the campus. Having come to Leicester especially to see it, and knowing it well from beautiful photographs and above all the architects' own precise, toy-like drawings, I found at last seeing the real building partly elating, partly uncomfortable. With architecture of this level of fame and influence visiting can feel like a desecration of the pure architectural idea received from books. You knew it would be so, but it still comes as a shock to discover that real, flesh-and-blood pigeons nest and shit on them, that they have the same accretions of later signage and clutter as any other building, and that they sit with little fuss amidst other more ordinary neighbours. Passers-by do not look up at them, and users show the usual range of daily emotions, not the transcendent aesthetic excitement you are there to feel. This is perhaps more so with post-war great buildings than those of earlier periods. If you go round a medieval cathedral or ancient temple everyone else *is* there to admire it, even if many pay their tribute to its architecture only by making it the latest backdrop for their selfie-face. With post-war buildings, if they cease to serve a

function they get demolished rapidly. Most people in them are there to work, to study, or to live, and, as the camera-wielding gawper, one is the eccentric outsider and not the self-appointed elite of the tourist throng.

I knew how the building was set out: most of the irregular site is taken up by a large, rectangular, industrial shed for the substantial teaching workshops which were to make hands-on experiments with the latest engineering equipment the core of undergraduate teaching. Because of the land these workshops take up (most of the shed is road-level and single-storey, to ease future changes of heavy machinery, only rising to three at the rear edge), the remaining facilities were short of ground space. Thus lecture theatres, administrative offices and research laboratories are stacked densely in a small area of the site overlooking a large park. Experiments relying on an even water pressure necessitated a water tank raised to 100 feet.[2] Characteristically of post-war Modernists, the architects used this functional requirement to explain – and secure the necessary budget for – their arrangement of the whole administrative space as an improbably skinny tower, each level providing only a medium-sized meeting room or, if the floor is partitioned, a few small offices.

Under each of the two towers the lecture theatres cantilever out precariously, their shape making clear what they are – a wonderful way of turning 'honesty' into expressive art. The towers do not land squarely on the lecture theatres, which in turn do not land squarely on the ground, so the whole balancing act looks thrillingly dynamic, with the graceful strength and poise of a yogi.

Glazing is used to heighten the contrasts between the parts, and to hint at their functions. It does more than that, though, learning tricks of architectural effect, as well as borrowing the bright red brick, from the magnificent Johnson Wax headquarters building by Frank Lloyd Wright in Wisconsin. At Leicester as in Wisconsin, glazing is used to muddle and disorient the viewer in a manner

more Baroque than Modernist. The small panes of glass in the office tower leave one initially confused as to scale. How many panes per storey? How many storeys? How big is this building and how far away?

The clarity of the glazing in the laboratories – one ribbon-window running right round each floor – helps one to understand the scale but has its own disconcerting quality. The windows seem too small a proportion of the storey height, the weighty bands of brick dominating, and the glass apparently folding out under their mass, projecting in a triangular profile from the face of the building. With an unsettling appearance of instability – buttercream windows squashing out between overheavy layers of red-brick Victoria sponge. The lumpen massiveness of this block then lands on perilously few, thin, tall concrete columns, further heightening the viewer's awareness of the impressiveness, appropriately enough given the purpose of the building, of contemporary engineering.

The thrilling, hard-to-make expressiveness of the glazing, however, suggests that this was not a question of saving a few tens of cubic feet, but an outburst of creative excitement from a pair of young architects at a sweet spot in their careers: experienced enough to have shed the gaucheness of the new graduate, but with little enough work on the drawing board to give a good job like this an unparalleled level of personal focus.

In its original pristine form, Leicester Engineering Building was a spectacular international triumph of architectural success. It was visited by architects from all over the world until the head of department, though pleased with his building, joked that he ought to charge Stirling and Gowan for the electricity cost of turning on the lights for endless visiting groups to photograph it after dark.[3] It was copied and played upon by thousands of architects internationally from the mid-1960s through to the 1980s, raising the popularity of shocking red brick and tile, making some of its glazing and material choices into widespread clichés, helping to form the vocabulary of High Tech architecture, and establishing the worldwide reputation of its architects – primarily of the noisier of the two, James Stirling, after he and Gowan dissolved their partnership at the end of the Leicester job.

But where is Leslie Martin, the focus of this chapter, in all of this? We are already a few pages in and have yet to mention his name. This is a fair reflection of Leslie Martin's career: he was a quiet, courteous man, fifty in 1959, whose principal means of exerting influence was being disarmingly helpful on committees. Stirling and Gowan's futuristically industrial University of Leicester Engineering Building seems poles apart from the peaceful converted mill in the Cambridgeshire countryside where Leslie Martin lived and worked, spending his moments of relaxation pruning his orchard of rare apple varieties.[4] Yet without him the Leicester Engineering Building would almost certainly not have been the masterpiece it is.

Leslie Martin was something close to the curator of the post-war architectural scene in Britain, unobtrusively promoting the careers of talented architects on a scale unknown before or since. Many of the commissions his influence steered to these able designers have attracted huge international reputation, but he himself remains as elegantly behind-the-scenes as he was in his lifetime. Over the years I have been working on Brutalism, Martin has become a towering figure in my imagination, seeming to preside over the post-war architectural world in Britain with the implausible but plot-advancing powers of a Gandalf. But let us leave the man here, as he would have wished, and return to the strong-minded young architects he supported.

ii

When they were appointed for the Leicester Engineering Building, Stirling and Gowan were by no means the obvious men for the job. They were too new, too young, too unproven for a conspicuous and complicated building, and their partnership had never before worked on commissions at that scale or that level of technical difficulty. Martin, a careful judge of young architects, assessed that they were good enough from the evidence of their short careers to date. There was not yet much for him to go on.

Both Gowan and Stirling were born in the West of Scotland. Gowan was the son of a butcher and grew up in Paisley and Partick, moving to live with his grandparents when his parents split up.[5] Stirling's parents, a ship's engineer and a schoolteacher, moved from Glasgow to Liverpool whilst he was still a child, leaving him with a life-time fascination with and loyalty to both these big, beautiful, tough industrial cities. Gowan, pointed towards architecture by a careers advisor who was impressed by his artistic abilities, studied the subject at Glasgow School of Art in 1940–42. The school was at a peculiarly low wartime ebb, with Gowan recalling that the same man taught all the history and design classes, seemingly with no greater ambition than to turn out proficient draughtsmen as 'docile labour' for Glasgow's architecture firms.[6] Gowan nevertheless learned from the vestigial remains of its earlier Beaux-Arts curriculum the possibility of thinking about buildings in abstract compositional terms.[7] He then interrupted his studies to join the RAF as a radar technician.[8]

Stirling struggled a little in conventional education, thanks to his probable dyslexia. Only in obsessive, competitive birdwatching and egg-collecting was some of his later drive and ability shown before his war service.[9] In the Second World War he was a paratrooper, one of only two survivors when his platoon was fired on by an armoured car. In another incident he was invalided out after being shot clearing an occupied house in Normandy. He was decorated for his courage.[10] On his return to civilian life he enrolled at Liverpool School of Architecture with an ex-serviceman's grant, and with the bolshie confidence and purposeful focus which characterised quite a lot of returning servicemen going through universities, there established himself as a serious young architect. After commanding men under very dangerous conditions in the war, Stirling was one of a generation of students whom it was clearly exhilarating but intimidating to teach.[11] He was hugely influenced by a young historian at the school, Colin Rowe, whose sense of Modernism's links to history was unusual for the period and helped free Stirling to explore wider historical precedents like the industrial and dock architecture of nineteenth-century Liverpool. Stirling grasped his studies by the throat, and before he left Liverpool for London it was already clear that he intended to be a major figure in the architectural world.

When Gowan was demobilised in 1945 he resumed his studies at Kingston School of Architecture, an institution as unlike the wartime Glasgow School of Art as any he could have found in Britain. Kingston gave no history teaching, and employed very young Modernist architects to teach a design course based with fervent loyalty on the writing and design-work of the founder of the Bauhaus, Walter Gropius.[12] Gowan found the devotion which many there showed to Gropius, and a rival faction showed to Le Corbusier, 'reprehensible' – he felt that they used their chosen hero as a way of avoiding having to think out design solutions of their own.[13] Gowan was never to accept such pre-made solutions.

Stirling and Gowan both gravitated towards the excitement and opportunities of post-war rebuilding in London. Gowan found employment as an architectural assistant to subsidise his training at Kingston, working for, amongst others, Powell & Moya, a young practice which had won perhaps the two most enviable competitions of the immediate post-war years: the huge Churchill Gardens housing estate in Pimlico (the two partners were respectively twenty-three and twenty-four when they won it), which was to be a showpiece of Modernist reconstruction, and the Skylon, the prominent 'vertical feature' of the 1951 Festival of Britain. Gowan worked on drawings for both projects.[14]

After moving as assistants from office to office, not quite finding the architectural opportunities they sought, Stirling and Gowan both drifted into a practice which never gets the attention it deserves for its high-quality, exciting, early Brutalist schools and university buildings: Lyons Israel & Ellis. There the two men met. Whilst there Stirling got a commission from a friend's father for a development of flats squashed on to a tight site in Ham, in the south-western suburbs of London, and he and Gowan went into partnership to fulfil the commission (1955–58).[15] Langham House Close, as the project was called, was tough but not thuggish: exposed brick and concrete, learning lessons from Le Corbusier's Maisons Jaoul without copying them, and bringing a clarity and strength that seemed to many young architects a thrilling escape from the vernacular pitched roofs and cheapskate prettification of the older generation of Modernists. The building was to be hailed by Reyner Banham as one of the first swallows of the Brutalist summer.[16]

By the time Leslie Martin put them forward for the Leicester job, this medium-small development was still much their biggest completed commission, and although their reputation amongst young architects was high it was not necessarily of the type to attract powerful clients. The alarming tag 'Brutalism' was off-putting; James Stirling, the conspicuous frontman of the pair, was increasingly famous as a roustabout partygoer in the racy, hard-drinking London jazz and arts scene of the 1950s; and the pair had never had the chance to show that they could design a big building with a big budget and complex engineering, and coordinate themselves and any assistants to produce it within a budget and a timescale.[17] Without Leslie Martin's authority they would surely have been confined for years more to private houses and other small commissions for the enlightened rich seeking to show their avant-garde credentials.

Even as they started work on the Leicester commission they were still a practice so small that they had no assistants at all, just James Stirling and James Gowan, sitting before the tall windows of Stirling's flat in York Terrace, Regent's Park (at the time a far less pricey and prestigious address than now). With the Leicester fees, they started to bring in Michael Wilford and other assistants to help with the detailing, which made their illicit use of the flat as a cheap office increasingly conspicuous. They briefed assistants on the story to give if challenged on what they were doing in the block.[18] At night, Stirling slept on a divan in the corner.[19]

Details of the Leicester Engineering Building were worked and reworked between Stirling and Gowan in an atmosphere in which tensions increasingly descended into acrimony. Stirling was away teaching and giving lectures much of the time, the noisy public face of a partnership far more equal than it appeared from his prominence, whilst Gowan kept the office going.[20] Even as the practice moved towards break-up, however, the good of the building remained the most important thing and collaboration continued, with ideas tested in the clashes between the two principals. Wilford sat at a drawing board with one of the partners on each side of him, learning rapidly from both, and keeping his head down as they argued.[21] Together they developed an outline shape for the building, then nuanced and developed it with more attention than most partnerships were willing to devote to a single building.

As the designers drew and drew, changing and refining the scheme again and again, their repeated reworkings composed and exaggerated necessary elements into architectural art. They detailed the building with an equal level of fanatical thought and effort, taking inexpensive, tough materials and turning them by meticulous and innovative design work into high art. Where the building lapses into less well-disguised artistic intent is in the front towards the park: a windowless triangular block containing lavatories juts out beneath the tower, a ramp leading up to its roof which offers a terrace on which a liner-like ventilation pipe heightens the resemblance to a ship's prow, recalling Stirling's youthful fascination with the Liverpool docks.[22] From a practical point of view this extra entrance via the first floor had little to offer, and on each of my visits, like so many such first-floor entrances of the 1960s, it has been locked. The first-floor entrance and the Corbusian ramp which leads to it are testament to the preoccupation of the Brutalist period with raised pedestrian access, but here there is no attempt to integrate it with any wider system of pedestrian circulation, and indeed since it is built where the edge of the campus meets a pedestrian path and a large park, there would never have been the vehicle traffic to require special separation of pedestrians. Instead this convoluted upper entrance sequence must be seen as primarily aesthetic – a beautiful but perverse sculptural element almost always bypassed in favour of the ground-level doors.

Behind the clear, strong tower is a jagged sea of glass: the roof-lights of the workshops. The roof is something like a classic factory shed, with translucent saw-tooth ridges to provide diffused light.[23] It uses patent glazing – a proprietary system produced by a subcontractor designed for roofing large industrial buildings cheaply, with simple extruded aluminium strips holding the glass in place and somewhat basic waterproofing supplied by greased asbestos cable being squashed between the aluminium and the glass.[24] Yet the glazing, running broadly east–west, is at forty-five degrees to the rectangle of the workshop walls, and the roof meets the orthogonal end walls with a geometrically logical solution which was hugely ingenious in its apparent simplicity, and very difficult to construct using the patent glazing system. From ground level the first row of these crystalline glass boxes is echoed above by the more distant repetition of the pattern along the top of the higher section of workshop at the back. From up in the tower the roofscape of the workshops is magnificent, almost hypnotic in the strength of its diagonal stripes – a Bridget Riley painting you can study in.

In the tower, the architects gave particularly rich thought to the series of landings linking the staircases and giving access to the tall laboratory block and the even taller office block. There is something unnerving in the use of tiles to cover not only the floors but the ceilings and most of the walls; the visual conventions of up and down are partially missing. The glaring red on all sides, the merciless hardness of tile, concrete, and steel railings, unrelieved by visibly flimsy polystyrene ceiling tiles or anodyne plasterwork, and the complexity of the geometry of these small-scale spaces, make for a great deal of aesthetic impact in a relatively modest volume. As at John Soane's house in Lincoln's Inn Fields, there seems to be a gloriously excessive amount of architecture for the scale of the building.

Perhaps my favourite moments internally are the stairwells themselves. The contrast with the all-embracing redness and glaring windows of the hallways heightens the subtle tonal qualities of the concrete stair and walls. The cool grey comes as a welcome visual rest before the sensory assault of the next storey. The concrete is fairly ordinary, genuine in situ as it appeared the moment the formwork was struck, rather than being expensively textured as at the Barbican. Its candour about the process of its creation is a lesson to engineering students, as is the magnificent display of water pipes running up to the roof tank via an open shaft alongside the taller of the two staircases, large-scale, industrial and beautiful.

Compared with the delicate-looking office tower, the architects gave the workshop interiors much more aesthetic and physical robustness: they are large covered spaces into which any amount and type of machinery could be brought on roof-mounted crane tracks, and which could be subdivided or left open as changing uses dictated. The ground level is indeed uncommonly free. The only fixed points are a central corridor, and the concrete columns which support the roof. The architects have nevertheless managed to carry their thrilling architecture throughout the workshop block in the form of the roof, its spectacular presence running diagonally across every part, seeming vast and prominent, only a few metres above the viewer's head.

Unusually for a period where black-and-white architectural photography and greyish buildings were the norm, Stirling and Gowan used colour intensely throughout the Leicester Engineering

Building: the predominant red is offset by the milky white of the shed roof lights, and by the pink of the handrails – an almost luminous effect under artificial light, clashing subtly with the vivid brick and tile. The architects' careful choice of colours extended even to the tower glazing, which used Dutch glass rather than the normal English-made glass from Pilkington or Crittal.[25] They felt that the English glass had a faint green tint which they wished to avoid. The tower was later reglazed, with chunkier glazing bars which have fairly substantially reduced the beauty and subtlety of the building, though presumably they improved its weatherproofing. As one architect has commented, the new network of heavy-handed glazing bars 'hangs like a string vest on a Modigliani'.[26]

The faceting of each of the volumes of the tower, cutting off forty-five-degree corners, was to become a major cliché of 1960s architecture. Here it was generated initially by the boundary of the plot – the laboratory tower was chamfered in order to fit on to the site. But here and elsewhere this faceting lends compositional richness to buildings whose decorative restraint could easily have become drab. As the light changes and the sun moves round, the angled corners catch different levels of light from the orthogonal walls, not only helping the viewer to read the building as three-dimensional, but also creating a composition of lights, midtones and darks reminiscent of a cubist painting. At Leicester, Stirling and Gowan resisted the temptation to cut all of the corners at the same point: the laboratories have the broadest corner strip, the office tower's corner chamfers are substantially narrower, and the lift and stair towers are under half that width again (each a multiple of the width of one tile, so that tiles did not need to be cut). The result is once more to confuse and excite with the different apparent scales, and again to produce a richness of composition comparable with the best architecture of any period.

The office tower shows off clever concrete engineering: its paired corner columns behind glass land on a splayed and inward-sloping element which brings the whole weight of tower and water tank on to four impressively slender corner columns which then run to earth through the lecture theatre and foyer below. It has always reminded me of the space rocket in which Tintin visited the moon, and the architects were indeed of the generation fascinated as young adults by the emerging technology of the Space Race.

At Leicester, Stirling and Gowan were indeed lucky in their chief client: Edward Parkes, the first Professor of Engineering there, who was founding his department. From contemporary documents as well as interviews which he gave later, it is clear that he was a sophisticated and intellectually engaged architectural patron, who played up to the flattering idealisation of engineers as noble savages which went back to the roots of Modernism. From at least Le Corbusier's *Towards an Architecture*, the first polemical blast of which is entitled 'The Aesthetic of the Engineer', the engineer's honest, naive functionalism has been held up as producing ideal design solutions to the problems they address, as opposed to the style-obsessed architects who contort their buildings into shapes that are already obsolete even before the first brick has been laid. Parkes deliberately provided a light brief, just setting out functional requirements, in order to leave the architects free to create. Yet Crinson has shown that Parkes was concerned with the image that the building would project, writing to the architects about their proposal for paired boiler chimneys:

> I do not like the two free chimneys. They seem to me out of harmony with the rest of the design. Perhaps to you they symbolise engineering, but free-standing chimneys are not a common feature of modern engineering works, and I particularly wish to avoid giving the rest of the university the idea that the 'dark satanic mills' have come amongst them.[27]

Sure enough, they built a single chimney, and it looks much more high-tech than dark or satanic.

Parkes, Gowan and the excellent engineer on the job, Frank Newby, were all thirty-three when they started work. Stirling was thirty-five.[28] If Parkes was a self-aware perfect client, Newby was similarly the ideal engineer for the job. He and his wife were friends with Stirling and other exciting avant-garde architects of the 1950s, and he followed and joined in their theoretical and ideological discussions with intense interest. His collaboration on Leicester included working out a way to avoid the columns which Stirling had regarded as an unfortunate necessity under the hanging edge of the smaller lecture theatre.[29] In the end the weight of the tower above counterbalances the tilting weight of the theatre – Stirling was thrilled that the lecture theatre needed to be held up by substantial temporary supports until the weight of the growing tower above was great enough to hold it in place.

Given how little of the Leicester Engineering Building's concrete is visible (the clients specified that not too much concrete should be exposed),[30] there will be those who feel it has no place in this book. Is it even Brutalist? Stylistic terms tend to give rise to disputes, and architects themselves often repudiate them aggressively (Stirling did with 'Brutalism'). The discussion of such questions can descend into tedious geekery. It is worth noting, however, that Banham, having begun his book on Brutalism with the Smithsons' steel-and-glass school at Hunstanton, ended it with Stirling and Gowan at Leicester:

> In many ways, Stirling and Gowan's laboratory-block for Leicester University comes nearer to Brutalism in the emotional sense of a rough, tough building, and in the dramatic space-play of its sectional organisation it carries still something of the aggressive informality of the mood of the middle fifties.[31]

Perhaps it is enough to say that even if it is low in exposed concrete, the building has more of the hallmarks of Brutalism than of any other stylistic tendency of its moment: such exposed concrete as it has is truly 'as found' – not textured during or after casting, and showing the marks of the plugs which held the smooth formwork panels in place. The magnificent exposed water pipes are equally as found. The patent glazing system was a substitution to save money at the point that the building contract went out to tender. Originally they had hoped for larger panes of plate glass. In the way it was in fact built, however, the patent glazing argued for by Gowan became another material almost as found: a proprietary, standardised glazing system meant for factory roofs being magnificently distorted into something beautiful, unique, and not, as it turned out, entirely watertight. The building is a sibling of many other Brutalist greats in that every element can be explained in functional terms, with the expression of those elements (especially circulation, servicing and structure), heightened into visual art.

iii

The bringing-together of two first-rate young architects and one similarly outstanding engineer, all at the height of their youthful vigour and confidence, with an engaged, supportive client, was always likely to lead to an exciting building. Yet their coming-together was not a matter of simple luck here, but of artistically committed patronage.

Leslie Martin grew up in Lancashire, the son of an architect. He was an academically gifted youth, educated at the excellent Manchester Grammar School and then at Manchester University School of Architecture, where he was considered so outstanding that he was admitted directly into the third year of the course.[32] This precocity continued, with his rapid achievement of the atypical qualifications for a 1930s architect of MA and PhD, the latter a piece of architectural history research on the Spanish Renaissance architect who designed the Escorial.[33] At the absurdly young age of twenty-six, Martin was appointed head of Hull College of Art's tiny architecture school, which he must have shocked somewhat by bringing as guest speakers major international stars of Modernism such as Marcel Breuer and László Moholy-Nagy from the Bauhaus, Serge Chermayeff, Maxwell Fry and Jacob Bronowski, and the nationally important critics Morton Shand and Herbert Read.[34] This unbeatable team of international Modernist ringers must have seemed rather like the arrival of Fred Trueman in the *Dad's Army* cricket match. Martin's same gifts at networking and persuasiveness enabled him in 1937 to draw together a roll call of the leading figures in artistic and architectural Modernism to contribute to a new journal, *Circle*. The list of those involved in its nearly 300-page 'first' issue (there was never another) was outstanding: Le Corbusier, Constantin Brâncuși, El Lissitzky, Henry Moore, Piet Mondrian and Naum Gabo, with layout by Barbara Hepworth. *Circle* was co-edited by Martin's friend Ben Nicholson, from whom Martin had bought work starting in 1934, paying for his first Nicholson in instalments from his academic salary.[35] *Circle*'s one remarkable edition was made all the more legendary when the remaining unsold copies were destroyed in the wartime bombing of Faber & Faber's warehouse.[36]

Leslie Martin had a perfect Establishment manner, and was well spoken, never too pushy, never brash, always courteously rational. He remained consistently quiet-living. As a trained architect he was not conscripted, and spent the war working on designs for railway stations which could be prefabricated and built rapidly to meet urgent wartime and post-war needs. His own career continued to rise fast after the war, but not primarily through the route of designing prominent buildings. Leslie Martin's greatest talent and ambition was to organise and promote good architecture. He became a very energetic Deputy Architect for the London County Council (LCC) in 1948, and then in 1953–56 its Architect. In these roles Martin held huge personal power. With the massive effort of post-war reconstruction, and building new housing and schools for the Welfare State, the LCC was the largest architect's office in the world.³⁷ Martin here exhibited his lifelong tendency to devolve his power with intelligent thoughtfulness to those below and around him. The LCC Architect's Department had been divided into numerous smaller design teams since the war, and Martin, first as deputy and then as head, gave each of these teams a kind of benevolently supervised autonomy which brought new heights of creative and organising energy out of the many talented young architects under him.³⁸ The LCC was an exceptionally desirable organisation for which to work, and many of the major British architects of the post-war period gained formative experience there under Martin's generous tutelage.

This was not the limit of Martin's patronage, however. Even with hundreds of architects and support staff in his department, the LCC's in-house teams were not able to keep up with the quantity of work required by the extensive and populous County of London. Martin kept a list of private architectural practices to whom jobs could be given, often testing them with a comparatively small project before giving them larger ones if they did well. Along with Goldfinger, Chamberlin Powell & Bon, Lasdun and many others, Stirling and Gowan were probably added to this list by Martin. Young and inexperienced, Stirling and Gowan were given a first commission by the LCC in 1958, shortly after Martin's departure: a school dining and assembly hall on a small budget, safer for both sides than a big project. They completed the work in 1961, making a decent job of it within the limitations of such a modest commission.³⁹

In 1956 the pressure of Martin's massive workload at the LCC got on top of him and he had a nervous breakdown. The following year he retired to the comparative peace of academia, becoming the first Professor of Architecture at Cambridge. He was not a man to take things gently, though, and rapidly expanded his role into influencing architectural educational policy through the 1958 Oxford Conference. Characteristically, he took on the task of writing up the conference report, thus quietly enabling him to ensure that it presented a message which accorded with his own priorities. He systematically turned his own department into a model for university-based architectural research, answering (with his own and others' mathematical modelling of planning problems) the criticism that architecture was a technical and artistic discipline better taught in art schools or engineering colleges.[40]

Martin also joined every committee he could that was involved with appointing architects or planners. In spreading his architectural power through the Establishment, he had various very distinctive advantages. He was highly unusual in being an architect with a PhD, legitimating his expertise to his fellow academics. His knighthood (awarded in 1957) and Cambridge chair were stamps of authority to civil servants and the laity. To these badges Martin added a manner of calm certainty and rationality, and extensive experience from the LCC and elsewhere of committee work, making him an incomparably effective operator in the bureaucratic world of public patronage.

Using these superficially unglamorous weapons, Martin continued, after leaving the LCC, with his personal campaign of promoting good modern architecture. His particular focus was a university sector expanding as fast as it could build to accommodate the rapid growth in student numbers: from 9,300 university degrees being awarded annually just before the Second World War, to 17,300 in 1950, 22,400 in 1960, and 51,200 in 1970.[41] The expansion was under way before Martin went to Cambridge, but from his arrival there the architecture of universities nationally came rapidly to bear the same exciting stamp of artistically sophisticated modernism as the LCC had had under his guiding hand. Much of the detail of how Martin achieved his power is permanently lost – presumably quiet conversations face-to-face and by telephone were the ephemeral means by which he gained invitations on to committee after committee, and then came to dominate the architectural discussion on each. Shortly after his arrival in Cambridge, his influence started to be felt. For example, he ousted the not-quite-modern practice which was planning the town-centre science site, offering his own rough plan and then bringing in Lasdun to refine and execute it.[42]

Martin's most high-profile coup, though, was in the appointment of an architect for Churchill College, a new science and engineering-focused college founded in honour of the elderly war leader. Churchill himself made his architectural preferences clear – something grandly Classical, like County Hall in London. The budget, raised from Tory captains of industry, would have stretched to a fair amount of the Classical stonework Churchill wanted.[43] Somehow, however, Martin managed to take control of the appointment process, and invited twenty architectural practices to provide designs in a limited competition.[44] All twenty were uncompromisingly modern, and most of them were young and comparatively inexperienced for such a big and high-profile job. Names of competitors included Chamberlin Powell & Bon, the Smithsons, Lasdun, and Stirling and Gowan – a striking act of faith in a young practice which had only just got a small commission from the LCC at that date. The competition was won in the end by Sheppard Robson & Partners. They produced a pleasant and workable college, but managed slightly disappointingly to disguise its substantial budget in buildings which, whilst good, somehow fail either to be sensuously rough or glamorously luxurious.

Stirling and Gowan got a lot of architectural attention for their loopy but beautiful scheme for Churchill College – a single giant court which would have looked awkwardly incomplete until finished, and then have been hard to extend without spoiling it. This is precisely the wrong design solution for an institution like a college, which develops very slowly and incrementally over centuries. It was, however, a thrilling image, with intriguingly sculptural communal buildings sitting within the courtyard.

As his profile rose, Martin was consulted by many – or perhaps even most – clients wanting new university buildings in England.

At one end of his gamut of patronage was medium-scale, high-budget work: Cambridge colleges putting up new buildings. Stirling and Gowan got as far as the design stage of a new accommodation block at Selwyn College for which Martin put them forward in summer 1959.[45] They proposed a block which would have leaned inwards, curving along its length in a sinuous wave, its glazing providing a stuttering and fragmented reflection of the college's wonderful gardens.

At the other extreme of the scale, Martin was approached by universities to provide them with overall plans for several decades of their future estate planning and architecture, just as so many aristocrats of the late eighteenth century had sought the guidance of Capability Brown on the landscaping of their estates. Hull (where Martin had taught), the University of London, and the University of Leicester, all asked him to draw up schemes to resolve the messy leftovers they had been bequeathed by the incompletion of earlier classical plans, their estates strewn with buildings which ought to have been symmetrically paired had the enthusiasm and the budget survived for another decade or so. In each case Martin planned out the new parts of the campus in rough blocks, then distributed the resulting new building commissions to architects whose work he admired. These were often the same youngsters he had promoted at the LCC in their early post-student days, and whom he now helped to get larger projects as their practices and reputations grew.

It was as the master planner for Leicester University that Martin was able once again to succeed in giving work to Stirling and Gowan, successfully ending with a building after the two failed attempts in Cambridge.

Martin designed some of the university buildings himself; they couldn't be more different to the impolite Engineering Building. After one glorious but cloudy day wandering round Stirling and Gowan's masterpiece, taking photos, touching the brick, tile and concrete, getting shown by a kind member of staff on to the roof of a nearby tower to look down on it, and circling it again and again, my wife and I were looking for somewhere to stay in Leicester so that I could have another go at the photos next day in hope of winter sunlight to bring out the colours. We stumbled upon the website of College Court, a conference centre and hotel which I realised was a conversion of a 1960s hall of residence, College Hall, designed by Leslie Martin and Trevor Dannatt and built in 1958–60. We went straight along, and spent the evening enjoying the buildings. The room in which we stayed had been knocked together from a pair of student rooms, to fit in a shower and lavatory and make for a more lavish space than was originally offered to the all-female residents. The landscaping and some other modifications have about them the generic smoothness of corporate hospitality, yet the buildings have in general been treated with what is still for now an atypical level of respect.

An evening surrounded by Leslie Martin's architecture formed a strong contrast to the day in Stirling and Gowan's block from the

College Court

same years. Both are classics of brick Brutalism, each offsetting it with concrete, but where the Engineering building is a shocking red, Martin's is a courteous yellowish buff – a brick colour familiar in the Midlands and the east of England and not shrilly anti-traditional or industrial in the manner of so much Brutalist brick. The materials are only the start of the contrasts between these two projects, which are almost as different as buildings could be. Where engineering in Stirling and Gowan's building is flaunted proudly, at Martin's the structure is quiet and rectilinear, in service of simple shapes. Stirling and Gowan's building thrusts confidently and assertively into the air, its daring asymmetries lending it an appearance of the later stages of a game of Jenga, whereas Martin's lies low to the ground, standing more often than not on traditional load-bearing brick walls. Glass at the Engineering Building becomes crystals on the workshops, ribbing on the laboratories, and a net thrown over the offices; at College Hall glass forms windows – often nice big windows, taking in pleasant landscaping, but still windows in an intentionally unchallenging and conventional sense.

Where there are bursts of explicit artistry in College Hall they are handled once again with restraint and domesticity. A staircase here, a concrete column there, has a disproportionate massiveness that suggests some of the Brutalist love of ostentatious weight. We were there in a quiet period between conferences, and had the bar (the former junior common room) largely to ourselves, so were able to eat in a charming little social area screened off from most of the common room by a brick partition containing on each side a fireplace. The fireplace screen has openings, and projecting and recessed bricks, in a composition which, from the main room, resembles one of Ben Nicholson's abstract reliefs. With the kind indulgence of the barman, we spent a happy hour removing all of the furniture from in front of the screen, in order that I could photograph it free from clutter, then carefully replacing it all.

As the consultant planner for the University of Leicester, Martin produced core buildings for the University of comparable restraint

College Court fireplace

and similar brick to College Hall. Again they are organised with semi-formal rectilinearity, this time around a kind of central court and lecture theatre block, their planning soberly logical and their elevations unassuming to the borders of banality, saved only by the quiet precision of their detailing (for example, most of Martin's buildings are designed on modular grids whose dimensions conformed to the size of a standard brick, meaning that each wall or column is a precise number of bricks wide and they do not have to be cut to fit). His buildings are low-rise and elegantly undemonstrative.

Stirling and Gowan's architecture could scarcely be more different. Their building appears to embody a powerful and optimistic image of the place of engineering in modern Britain: assertive, anti-conventional, proud and industrial – a perky middle finger raised skywards to the rest of Martin's polite campus.[46] College Hall, sitting amidst suburban streets, carves out a little corner of Oxbridge: its ranges of accommodation are placed around courts, with communal facilities in the centre and a tiny patch of apparently wild nature to one side, an abstraction of a Cambridge college overlooking the Backs. The fireplaces in its common rooms evoke the social heart of Oxford and Cambridge student communal life, not needed for warmth in these centrally heated buildings. College Hall appears to lean on archetypes of a traditional, communitarian, rather upper-crust sort. It is a gentlemanly building, as against the brash industrial laddishness of the Engineering Building.

Little surprise, then, that a close associate reports that Martin found his first look at Stirling and Gowan's design 'disconcerting', and felt that it was 'not what he expected or wanted'.[47] In fact, Martin had originally suggested that the University of Leicester's new buildings should be very low, ducked below the brow of the hill, as his own buildings there are. He hoped not to mar the prominence on the city skyline of a fine Lutyens war memorial in the park next door.[48] Yet he did not attempt to oppose Stirling and Gowan building higher, brighter and more obtrusively in every respect than he might have wished, and despite his personal ambivalence about their style, he continued to back the young partnership; he put them forward as possible architects for the Cambridge History Faculty, which they again won, Stirling keeping the job when the two split. When the Cambridge historians had a wobble about their choice of such a flamboyant and controversial architect, Martin backed him, reassuring them that Leicester was recognised as outstanding in the architectural world, and that Stirling would learn from any mistakes he and Gowan had made on it.[49]

iv

Martin's persistence in steering interesting jobs towards the young practice does not seem to have been based on any personal partiality. They were not friends. Martin found Stirling's gaucheness and brashness uncomfortable and unattractive. Nor did he especially like Stirling's buildings in aesthetic terms, recognising their quality without warming to it.[50] The site he gave Stirling and Gowan in

Leicester embodies this ambivalence: at one level the position overlooking Victoria Park is one of the most prestigious and exciting in the campus, but at the same time it is round the corner from – and largely out of sight of – the centre of Martin's new campus, like some teenager's bedroom where Stirling and Gowan are free to make a youthful architectural row without disturbing the mature, collegial peace of Martin's courtyard.[51]

Perhaps the most spectacular example of Martin's consistency in backing a good architect whatever the difficulties encountered was not Stirling and Gowan but the Danish architect Jørn Utzon. In 1956 Martin was a leading figure in the four-man competition-judging panel which appointed the young Utzon as architect for the Sydney Opera House. The competition was judged anonymously, and when the winner was revealed to be rather inexperienced for such a big job, the option was available to the panel to impose on him a collaboration with a more experienced firm. It took Martin and his fellow panellists, in Utzon's recollection, 'five minutes and a drink before dinner to decide that I was OK and that I did not need to have any partners collaborating with me on the project'.[52] On this occasion the complexity of the project, its political sensitivity in Australia, and the overambitious engineering of its famous roof vaults led to a sixteen-year struggle to get the Opera House designed and built, with Utzon eventually being driven off the job amidst very public battles.[53] Even after this high-profile controversy, Leslie Martin continued to back his personal sense that Utzon was a good architect worth supporting, and he helped to get him the commission for the parliament building in Kuwait City. In the younger architect's grateful words: 'Just consider a man who selected someone for the Sydney Opera House, and that person was then kicked out – and then picking him again for Kuwait and supporting him. It sounds improbable – but that was the kind of person Leslie Martin was.'[54]

Nor did Martin leave the firms he patronised to fend for themselves once appointed. In project after project he stayed involved after the selection of the architect and backed the designer in all discussions with the client, pushing through strong-minded modern architecture whatever the institutional resistance. Utzon recalled this characteristic of his:

> In his role as a client advisor, he carefully selected architects and, having introduced the parties to each other, he supported the architect through the entire project [. . .] all my work in Kuwait was done with a client who never questioned anything concerning my ability. Such was the personal authority Leslie Martin gave people.[55]

Sometimes the energetic backing Martin offered his architects bordered on impropriety. Denys Lasdun implemented the largest component of Martin's own London University development plan, for instance, involving extensive demolition of Georgian Bloomsbury. In 1966 the controversial scheme came before the Royal Fine Arts Commission, a body which gave influential opinions on proposals for important or large-scale new buildings, and of which Martin was a member. Although he had drawn up the development plan, chosen and collaborated with the architect, and was still consultant to the client, he declared no conflict of interest when the scheme came before him as a member of the Commission, but rather led the pro-Lasdun faction, vociferously supporting the design in which he was so closely involved.[56] It is indeed wonderful architecture.

This ruthlessness in wielding his huge influence might seem at first like a victimless impropriety. Martin was impressively ungrasping about it, not only not chasing work himself, but also on occasion refusing consultancy fees for his advice.[57] Yet such was Martin's control of the substantial and architecturally prestigious boom in university work that it enabled him to damage careers by omission as well as to make them by patronage. Whether intentionally or not, Martin's repeated recommendation of the exciting youngsters of British Modernism did substantial damage to the careers of an older generation to whom he did not give work. Non-Modernist architects like McMorran & Whitby, the talented classicists who designed much of Nottingham University's beautiful green campus, got less and less work, but so too did an older generation of nearly Modernist practices like Easton & Robertson.

Perhaps the most surprising omissions from the list of Martin's favoured architects, however, were members of the pre-war contingent of convinced Modernists. Martin had himself been a member of MARS (an early example of the embarrassingly not-quite-right acronym: Modern Architectural ReSearch), an exclusive club of British-based Modernist architects founded in 1933. However, in the 1960s he appears not to have secured work for most of its members who were still practising. With the exception of Ernö Goldfinger's inclusion on the LCC's list of private architects, Martin appears to have cut out these older Modernists. The informality of Martin's influence means he left no record of why he did not offer substantial work to Maxwell Fry, Frederick Gibberd or Berthold Lubetkin, all important leaders of 1930s British Modernism. Perhaps in the former two cases it was because neither Fry nor Gibberd had the painstaking attention to detail nor the enlivening flair of most of the Martin-backed youngsters. Lubetkin, however, was an outstanding architect on any terms, and I find myself wondering whether Martin's failure to support his flagging late career may have been partly because Lubetkin's level of prestige, experience and confidence were such that he would not be susceptible to influence on the planning questions that were dear to Martin's heart.

Whatever the motivations behind it, the preferential treatment which Martin gave to exciting younger architects contributed substantially to a radical separation in British architecture between the 1930s and the 1950s–60s. Whilst a number of established pre-war figures hung on in important roles, Martin's promotion of the young is one of the major reasons why British Brutalism was such a diverse, exciting and energetic architectural moment.

V

If, through patronage, his stylistic influence was immense, Martin's endorsement of sweeping urban regeneration was to have an even more profound impact on Britain. In his Cambridge years, perhaps the contribution which absorbed most of Martin's vast energy was his attempt to bring serious theoretical analysis of planning and architectural problems into close association with architectural education and practice. He and his associates were early in bringing computers to bear on the problems of town planning, enabling them in the 1960s to run large-scale simulations of different possible urban configurations with multiple variables taken into account.[58]

The planning theory proclaimed by Martin and his associates was part of the substantial post-war overreaction to the increasing presence of the car in cities. This panic was understandable – car ownership had been growing very rapidly and showed no sign of slackening, and the effects of ill-controlled parking and ever-heavier traffic on existing cities were very alarming, and promised to get continually worse. They included increasing levels of road deaths, but also, it was widely thought, a less quantifiable corrosion of the social patterns of city life. The Beatles' lovely Rita and her parking meters, first introduced nearly a decade before the 1967 song, were not proving an adequate answer.

Martin and his collaborators at Cambridge observed that the larger the block size, and thus the further apart the roads, the larger was the area of carless, pleasant space within the block, where they hoped community feeling might flourish. Even more importantly, by disposing buildings round the perimeters of each block you could provide at least equal density to that available by building high, without recourse to the expense, prominence and unfamiliarity of tower blocks.[59] Yet this improved street layout could come only at a high price: getting rid of roads and changing building patterns requires an immense scale of demolition and reconstruction.[60] Now that the supremacy of the car in town centres is no longer taken for granted in the UK, these sorts of solutions seem heavy-handed and destructive in relation to the scale of the problem they addressed.

The same effortless authority which Martin exercised in patronage of younger architects also manifested itself in the faith the British government showed in his planning ideas. Nor was the aggressive radicalism of town planning at the time at all a monopoly of the Left, even if criticisms of post-war planning may have suggested so since the 1980s. It was Harold Macmillan, despite his later image as a grouse-moor fuddy-duddy, who employed Leslie Martin to report on how the buildings and streets of Whitehall should be developed to meet the needs of a civil service growing in numbers and responsibilities.[61]

Within an architecture and planning world where so many were looking out for possible chances of commissions at most opportunities, and with varying degrees of subtlety, Martin's urbane lack of neediness set him apart. Known for turning down work or passing it on to others, he was able to reshape the jobs he did accept, to suit his understanding of their needs. Thus he initially turned down the job of replanning Whitehall because the government was in too much of a hurry and because too narrow a scope was proposed for the plan. In order to persuade him to change his mind, the government broadened the terms of the commission.[62]

There could on occasion be an element of smoke and mirrors about Martin's calm expertise. A former assistant recalled of him:

> His report/meeting technique was that of making quite brief, but very meaningful, statements while having (usually) plenty of detailed back-up material to present if challenged on any point. I say 'usually' as on one rare occasion we attended a meeting with insufficient preparation. However he ensured

that he had to hand several (empty) files and rolls of paper to which he pointed (without displaying their lack of content) when a point was queried, saying grandly but, as always, pleasantly 'we of course looked in detail at all that . . .', then rapidly moving on.[63]

In London, Martin and the traffic specialist Professor Colin Buchanan held, separately or together, planning consultancies for areas which cumulatively made up the entire area south of Euston Road, and all of Whitehall. If their attempts to replan these had been carried through, many of the government buildings of Whitehall would have been demolished over a number of phases, and replaced with a series of perimeter-blocks on stepped sections round pedestrianised courts.[64] Oxford Street might have been turned, on Buchanan's suggestion, into a deck-access shopping concourse like Birmingham's 1960s Bullring, and Leslie Martin would have demolished much of Bloomsbury for a new British Library (which in the end was to be built in St Pancras) and new buildings for London University (many of which did come about amidst bitter controversy).

Whilst Martin did not intend to destroy everything in the areas he replanned ('we can modify the theoretical frame to respect historic areas'), it is hard to change the street grid without very substantial demolition work, and his Whitehall scheme, drawn up in some detail, kept the chosen 'historic' buildings as isolated art objects punctuating the proposed new development, rather like St Giles Cripplegate popping up unexpectedly in the heart of the Barbican.[65]

Martin, and most politicians of the early 1960s, thought the improvements they could make by reshaping existing cities would be worth the financial and historical cost. Perhaps he also shared the less heritage-minded attitudes of the time; the clarity with which the Victorian industrial city reflected massive disparities of power and wealth seems to have offended the egalitarianism of the 1960s far more than it now upsets most people.

Nevertheless, there is something rather frightening to modern eyes about the calm authority with which Martin proposed, and his clients endorsed, such extensive replacement of existing city fabric. It is the more surprising since many of the younger architects he admired were explicit in decrying the mass demolitions proposed by 1930s Modernists in their city planning ideas, most famously Le Corbusier's brilliantly self-publicising proposal to demolish most of Paris and start again with a giant park criss-crossed by vast roads and airport runways, and dominated by a remorseless grid of high-rises.[66] Whilst Martin still referred to Le Corbusier's 1930s planning as late as 1972, architects like the Smithsons and Denys Lasdun were publicly stating from the mid-1950s their ambition for their buildings to fit into and contribute to the existing urban fabric (an ambition explicitly attacked by Reyner Banham as a softening and a betrayal).[67]

If Martin's planning was damaging to old buildings, it called into being plenty of new ones, and he reshaped post-war Britain through his distribution of these commissions to architects who felt the full excitement of what concrete could do for city planning and architecture. Martin's calm authority gave the necessary weight to the youthful enthusiasm of his chosen architects, helping to bring about a climate in which big buildings could be built with thrilling architecture and the full support of the kinds of institutional clients who would generally avoid the risks attendant on innovation and artistry.

vi

The University of Leicester's Engineering Building is not especially large by the standards of the projects Martin handed out, but it rewarded his faith in the young architects as resoundingly as any project under his patronage. Its three-dimensionality and disconcerting sensuality has for me, inasmuch as any building can, something of the richness, illusion of motion, dynamic imbalance and aesthetic impact of Bernini's famously luscious, tactile sculpture the *Rape of Persephone*. The glass tower is hoisted easily into the air by the rugged, bulky lecture theatre just as Bernini's substantial Pluto lifts his weighty Persephone. Where Bernini's rough-carved hand of Pluto meets the smooth, plump flesh of his victim's thigh, puckering it under his force, Stirling and Gowan's tile and brick drop back to reveal the slender concrete legs holding up the tower, apparently pinching into its elevated base. Bernini's sculpture has no ideal angle of view, but changes constantly and enthrallingly as you move round it looking up, taking in new details and re-composing the whole; Stirling and Gowan's tower does the same, hardly recognisable from one angle to the next as solidity gives way to transparency; regular gridded glazing to cascading waterfalls of glass; heavy, dark brick to translucent window; tall tower to taller behind it.

If it sounds as though, by dragging in Tintin's space rocket and Bernini's sculpture, I am getting overexcited about this mid-sized, mid-budget building, I am not the only commentator to have given way to poetic or mystical responses to it. To Stirling's delight, children at a nearby school called it 'the fairy palace' because of its shimmering unreality at night under electric light.[68] At the other end of the spectrum a prominent US architect managed to confect from it a level of overanalysed sophistication which starts to depart into its own fairyland:

> The office tower can be conceived of as a solid chunk of glass – a conceptual solid. In this sense it is possible to see this tower as having existed in some pre-physical or conceptual state as a primitive crystalline solid; a glass cube which was eroded and chipped away to reveal its present configuration – which is merely some fragmentary or partial state in its evolution in time.[69]

Another architect was more straightforwardly

'knocked out by the extraordinary formal presence of the tower and lecture theatres and then, as twilight descended, by the quite otherworldly experience of the field of crystalline luminosity of the furrowed glass roof of the workshops, [. . .] a brilliantly contrived aggregation of objects brought together at the edge of a great glass table.'[70]

Norman Foster found that

it had a tension, an originality and a sculptural drama that was born out of everyday ingredients of function and materials. [. . .] One is aware of the visible cut and thrust of forces, an almost acrobatic display.[71]

The quality which won this ecstatic reception for what is in the end just a building of concrete, brick, tile and cheap patent glazing was achieved largely within the rules of Modernist restraint.

Glazing aside, the building is generally in decent nick, and the department has uncommonly civilised visiting rules for a 1960s building – most managements of post-war Modernist buildings in the UK have not yet realised that they need to accommodate architectural tourism. The workshops look terrific after fifty years of hard use, and changes in equipment and technology. The tower is doing pretty well, too, though the difficulty of getting window cleaners to the glass of the tower circulation areas is witnessed too clearly by extensive smears of green slime. University furniture has for the past few decades tended to be ugly, so the wonderful little meeting rooms of the tower are marred by dirty glass and clumsy-looking tables and chairs, but the intrinsic building is doing well, even with its heritage protection only making Grade II* – if ever there were a building whose international influence and carefully thought-out beauty deserved a Grade I, this is it. Whilst the underlying fabric of the building is essentially being well looked after, though, the pleasure of visiting it is undermined by the same kind of clutter which mars almost all post-war buildings in the UK. Unavoidable, and there for understandable reasons, are the shrieking colours of fire signage and safety equipment (though their garish red fits in better with Stirling and Gowan's colour palette than in most buildings). More solvable would be the zoos of ugly furniture, retro-fitted cable runs, penguin huddles of recycling bins in lumpen plastic, and – worst of the lot at Leicester Engineering – posters. Some well-meaning initiative to share research work with passers-by has led to the installation of poster panels not only on the concrete of the stairs (presumably seen by whoever did it as blank space available for decoration, or even – horror of horrors – as being 'in need of brightening up'), but much more bizarrely on some of the windows.

My intolerance of these expressions of human activity within good buildings is easily attacked: the building is there to serve an educational purpose, not to be a sculpture for the delectation of passing aesthetes. Of course I have sympathy for people's desire to make a place their own, and to customise everything from their choice of clothes to their wall decoration and their telephone ringtones. However, if you happen to find yourself, whether by choice or not, in the quiet movement of a great symphonic concert, you switch off your ringtone. If you happen to find yourself in one of the two dozen best buildings of the twentieth century, you send round an email rather than putting up a poster.

Through the changes of fifty years, what remains clear is the exceptional creative energy of Stirling and Gowan's masterpiece. And Martin's role in this is all the more impressive for its invisibility: once he had got the architects the job, and supported them in its execution, the fact that he did not attempt to impose on them his own architectural preferences gave Stirling and Gowan the freedom they needed to produce such a startlingly original and full-blooded building.

From the many projects in which Martin's quiet presence had a critical role, a composite picture emerges of a man utterly of his moment. With his inconspicuously elegant suits and artistically unruly hair, Professor Sir Leslie Martin, PhD, was the perfect committee architecture and planning advisor for the competitively progressive governments of the 1950s and '60s, and particularly for the fast-growing, ambitious university sector of those years. He was efficient, cooperative, impeccably well networked and calmly authoritative, justifying his advice with his immense architectural expertise and his scientific investigations of planning needs. Yet the agenda which drove him was that of the hard-edged radicals of 1930s European Modernism – friends from his *Circle* days. Where Le Corbusier had had himself filmed in an eccentric bow tie and thick-framed glasses, scoring a defiantly thick charcoal line through a map of central Paris, Leslie Martin sat courteously in meeting after meeting, taking burdensome work off others' hands and putting people in touch with relevant specialists. But fundamentally the scale of the two men's visions was much closer than their methods. Martin, sometimes as efficient committee technocrat, sometimes as thoughtful and generous teacher, and sometimes as avuncular supporter of promising young architects, was discreetly pursuing a consistent policy of radical and fast-moving modernisation of the built environment. His aims were, in that particularly 1930s Modernist way, an inextricable blend of the artistic and the socio-political, and in the detail of how he pursued them he was ruthless to the borders of fanaticism, but within the terms of the 1950s and '60s: radicalism by committee. Through hundreds of hours of meetings, Martin secured and exercised patronage and planning consultancy which were to shape the course of post-war British architecture.

Chapter Six

'Too Commercial – No Convictions'
Developers' Brutalism

(barnabascalder.org/rc6/)

i

'I have an awful feeling we're not going to get our fees on this job,' says a sharp-suited architect to a cravatted interior designer, in an unfinished nightclub on top of a multi-storey car park. Their client, a corrupt local businessman, has just been thrown over the edge of a concrete staircase by Michael Caine.

In a commanding position on a hilltop towering over Gateshead, the car park, Trinity Square, is vigorously angular and sculptural. The whole building was cleverly arranged as a continuous shallow ramp in a squared-off spiral, avoiding the wasted spaces of separate ramps up to flat floors. This allows Caine the pleasure of driving fast up the entire spiral, tyres squealing, concrete columns whirling past.

In its bulky hilltop prominence the car park formed a kind of one-building acropolis for Gateshead, flicking the obligatory V at Newcastle, visible just across the Tyne. Built from in situ reinforced concrete, the car park looked jointless, a vast public sculpture, sharp-shouldered and assertive with something of the bruiserish

The original facade concrete and tile of the Anderston Centre towers

Trinity Square, Gateshead. Photograph: Mark (Flickr: kpmarek)

seductiveness of Michael Caine himself. Capping all of this, however, lifting the car park into the pantheon of British Brutalist greats, was the rooftop nightclub which overhung the edge of the uppermost deck, in which the fictional architect lamented his lost fee. It was never in fact occupied, but it could potentially have been one of the most stylish and imaginative venues a 1970s lush could ever have driven home drunk from.

The cameo in Trinity Square is perhaps the most famous sequence of a memorable film, *Get Carter* (1971), which paints a revolting picture of self-serving corruption: property developers who are almost indistinguishable from the violent gangsters, illegal pornographers and other sundry lowlife who surround them; men who care only about money and power. With police sirens screaming, the mercenary architect thinks only of his fee. It is a portrait carrying the distinctive jaundice of the early 1970s, when the 1960s public and commercial building frenzy was still ongoing, but being seen with increasingly bitter alienation by many. The real-life Newcastle was shortly to add another detail to this sordid portrait when the town's mayor was caught accepting bribes from an architect; both men were sent to prison.[1] This sweaty pursuit of money could hardly be further from Leslie Martin's elegant refusal of fees for his advice on worthy public buildings for higher education. Martin's circle certainly felt a clear superiority to the 'commercial' architectural world of developers with their speculative office blocks and shopping centres.

Yet the feeling of difference tends to be one of emphasis: even in the 1950s and '60s, the height of the Welfare State, there were almost no architects in private practice who did not accept commercial work from time to time. From the standpoint of the most left-wing salaried architects, working directly for local or central government, all private practice was commercial, whether it made its profits from business or from the state. Perhaps because of the element of truth in that view, Leslie Martin's favoured circle of architects tended to be noisy in declaring the distinction between themselves and what they considered commercial architects, emphasising their own public sector work and downplaying the shops, offices and houses which had often helped launch their careers. Truly commercial architects, by contrast, were happy to be seen as businessmen whose practices specialised in such work.

From its completion in 1967 to its demolition in 2010, Trinity Square embodied for many all that they felt was wrong with post-war British architecture: an overbearing, unsightly, lumpen shrine to the mighty pound and the mighty car plunked unceremoniously in the middle of a city centre torn apart by commercial speculation and road-building fever. Where the goals of many 1960s buildings are easy to approve of – education, health and improved housing conditions – the speculative self-enrichment which lay behind many commercial schemes is less sympathetic, with architects like Richard Seifert who worked largely on such commissions easily sidelined as traitors to the Welfare State ideal. Yet speculative offices and shopping centres make up a large body of Brutalist architecture, and there were some very talented architects working in the sector. For all the criticisms levelled at it, those of us who loved Trinity Square found its abrupt bulk, dominating Gateshead like a crouching monster, exhilarating, even beautiful.

ii

The ubiquity of 1960s commercial architecture perhaps makes it easy to take for granted, yet one might have expected the post-war period, with its massive growth in state building activity, considerably increased planning controls, heavier taxes and a narrowing wealth gap, to present thin pickings to commercial property speculators.

Indeed, Lewis Silkin's 1947 Town and Country Planning Act represented the largest attempt to bring the country's building activity under state control, introducing the requirement for local government to give planning permission for new developments, and bringing in green belts around major cities. In order to smooth the path of infrastructure and the redevelopment of cities, the Act considerably strengthened powers of governmental compulsory purchase. Silkin even levied a 100 per cent tax on 'betterment' – the profits of property speculation – effectively nationalising the industry by making it unprofitable for the private sector.[2] Unsurprisingly in such circumstances, the immediate post-war years saw little in the way of commercial construction. Property owners hung on for more profitable times. In addition to the taxing-away of the profit motive, building materials were rationed, with priority being given to council housing, schools and emergency repair or reconstruction after bomb damage.

Yet by 1954, all this had changed. Churchill's Tory government cancelled Silkin's betterment tax in 1953, and the following year they removed restrictions on building materials. The combination of the two measures promoted a very rapid boom in new office and shop development, and handed huge profits overnight to some property developers. One of the leading developers of the 1960s, Harry Hyams, bought a site in London's Grafton Street for £59,000 just before the 1954 lifting of building restrictions, which raised its value immediately to £100,000. He spent £250,000 demolishing and rebuilding, resulting in an office block worth around £840,000. Since taxes on increased property value were only levied if you sold the building, this gave him a tax-free nominal profit of £531,000 on a speculation of £309,000.[3] Hyams and most of the other leading developers of the 1950s and '60s had almost no overheads, with perhaps a secretary or two and an accountant, working from their own luxurious houses (or in the case of Jack Cotton, from the suite in the Dorchester Hotel in which he lived).[4] One estimate suggests that with this sort of project Hyams was able to generate £25 million in personal profit by 1967, which would at that time have been enough to buy 3,750 of that year's luxury car, the Rolls-Royce Silver Shadow, or to build the campuses for nearly twenty new universities on the scale of York or the University of East Anglia.[5] No wonder that when an elderly Hyams suffered a burglary at his country estate in Wiltshire in 2006, he was said to have lost £30 million worth of art and antiques, with the thieves rumoured to have deliberately avoided hard-to-dispose-of paintings like a Rembrandt and a Rubens.[6]

From 1954 things became even worse for local-authority planners trying to keep the speculative frenzy in check: the Conservative government introduced a rule specifying that if planning permission was refused for a proposed development, the council could in some circumstances be responsible for compensating the developer for lost income from the rejected scheme, even including profit margins. It increased the caution that local authorities felt in challenging developers and their expensively ruthless legal representatives.[7] Nor were the developers obliged to take much risk for their impressive returns. Once their credit-worthiness was established by a few successful speculations, a bank or sometimes the building contractor would lend 100 per cent of the initial cost of acquiring the site and the costs of redeveloping it.[8] As soon as the block was let, insurance companies were eager to take on the debt. The collateral represented by the building made the long-term mortgage a safe investment, securing low-interest payments for the developer, who could service them from rents. The value of the mortgage was based not on the cost of the speculation but on the amount of rent it brought in, so the developer would be lent a sum much bigger than he had spent. It also meant that the first rents were the crucial determinant of the value of the mortgage, which had the strange side effect of meaning that sometimes it brought in more money not to let the building at all for months or years until rents rose: empty blocks did not incur rates, and if you could afford to service the short-term loan whilst you waited, blocks rented out for higher first rent made for much bigger total profits than blocks rented out hurriedly during slower moments in the property market.[9]

Unsurprisingly, a wider public became increasingly aware of the vast wealth which successful property developers could accrue, and Harold Wilson's Labour administration, elected by a slender margin in 1964, took action to try to calm the feverish fight to acquire developable sites in London. The Chancellor of the Exchequer, George Brown, brought in legislation within the first year of the administration to prevent the building of any new offices in London.[10] Hyams jokily named his final development before the ban came into effect 'Mohican House', as it would be his last for the time being.[11] Here, too, however, the quick footwork of the leading property developers saw them thriving in the changed environment. Firstly, they diverted their new London activities from offices to hotels, and started planning new developments outside the capital to prepare for the migration of business to other towns during the construction freeze. However, there was a second effect of Brown's attempt to halt profiteering from office developments: an increase in office rents. By the early 1960s many smaller speculators had started trying to follow the paths of the big tycoons, and by the mid-1960s there was the beginning of a glut, with prices dropping proportionately. Brown's clumsy intervention meant that developers like Hyams, who had blocks under way at the time of the ban, were able to let out office space at unprecedentedly high rents and borrow against them with correspondingly massive profits; his Drapers Gardens development was the most expensive office space ever when it was let and is thought to have made his company in the region of £7.3 million profit.[12]

If the leading developers were able to profit even from a ban on new London offices, they were equally effective in exploiting other planning regulations. From the war until 1963 a regulation known as the Third Schedule, brought in by Silkin to allow modest extensions to existing buildings, but badly drafted, allowed new developments to occupy the same cubic volume as any building they replaced on the site, plus 10 per cent. The rule made nonsense of local authorities' attempts to plan urban densities according to the burden extra workers placed on transport and other infrastructure. Instead, the Third Schedule handed huge floor areas to developers who had a large existing building on their site.[13] It also produced an incentive to demolish anything you could: at the very least you would be able to get a 10 per cent increase in volume, but in addition older office blocks had had their amount of useable space considerably curtailed by their dependence on natural light and air from tall windows. New 1960s offices had much lower floor-to-ceiling heights and deeper plans made possible by improved electric lighting and mechanical ventilation, and could often offer much more than 10 per cent increase in lettable space.

Not only were many developers and their architects able to ride roughshod over the restrictions attempted by the planning system, they were also efficient in co-opting new planning law where it might increase their profits. The powers of comprehensive development which Silkin's Act had given to local authorities were beyond the fantasies of earlier commercial property speculators: to buy up and demolish entire areas of cities, redeveloping them as substantial new city-centre complexes, would previously have involved agonisingly slow and difficult negotiations with tens or hundreds of property owners, and the risk that some of them might realise their power over the development and demand ransom-level payment for the final properties needed for the project to go ahead. Councils could now buy out large areas at a comparatively low price, though it still took time and effort.

These powers were intended for public infrastructural and re-planning projects, but developers were quick to recognise their massive commercial potential. They and local authorities thought up appetising deals whereby the council would use its new powers to buy and flatten a down-at-heel inner-city area, and the developer would then put a substantial new commercial development on it: typically shops and offices, but in some cases with housing too. The developers and local authority would then share the considerable profits they hoped would accrue, and the council would have an up-to-the-minute image for the city centre, replacing grubby-looking Victorian 'slums', enlarging roads and parking facilities for the automobile age, and appealing to the monument lust of local mayors like that of Preston who, opening a shopping centre, let slip his excitement at his modest shot at immortality: 'I do believe that in years to come posterity will pass this plaque and will remember who it was who was Mayor of Preston in 1966.'[14]

There are examples of these local-authority-backed speculative property developments in almost every British town and city, and behind each its individual story of mass-demolition, profit-maximising design, and then, as a rule, several decades of afterlife as failing shops or office space of diminishing value. Trinity Square was a wonderful piece of architecture, even in its neglected years before demolition, but many commercial schemes of the period defeat even my admiration for bulky concrete; there can be something particularly unattractive about their form of decay. The shopping centres of the 1960s, their units typically too small for today's chains, are often marbled with pound shops and closed roller-shutters, and many of the period's office buildings are scarcely more thriving. Such a block features in the title sequence of Ricky Gervais's *The Office*, firmly establishing the atmosphere of unglamorous, hopeless, frustrating, pointless drudgery that pervades the series.

iii

The most prominent of Britain's unashamedly commercial architects was Richard Seifert. Where most architects of the 1960s would have agreed that they had an important role to play, few of the leading names would have admitted to sharing his 'enormous sense of responsibility on an architect [. . .] to do the best for his clients and not just put up a building which didn't stand up financially to any proper exercise'.[15] An architect's first duty was, as Seifert saw it, to maximise profit for the client. And as Hugh Casson, earlier one of the leading architects of the Festival of Britain, put it, Seifert had 'an unswerving loyalty to his clients. Most architects feel that their loyalty lies also to society in general.'[16] When Seifert put himself forward for selection as a prospective architect for the National Theatre, the appointment committee of senior architectural figures dismissed him curtly: 'Too commercial. No convictions.'[17]

There may have been an element of anti-Semitism in some of the hostility towards him, with sneers at his change of name from Rubin to Richard.[18] Born in Zurich in 1910, Seifert emigrated with his family to London whilst still a child. He studied architecture at the Bartlett, and then went into practice from 1934, but it was with the commercial property boom of the 1950s that his career took off. By the 1960s he was running nine architectural offices employing a total staff of 300, with commissions for office blocks and shopping centres coming in left, right and centre.[19] Yet the frequently repeated observation that Seifert's towers had changed the London skyline more than anyone since Wren was invariably rueful in spirit.

Even after I had become a fervent admirer of the classic Brutalist projects (housing, public projects and university buildings), I retained for a long time – and still do to an extent – a wariness about developer architecture of the 1960s. This is thoroughly inconsistent of me, as I love much of the speculative architecture of earlier periods, which has only been cleansed by the passage of more time from all the same self-serving motivations which make me queasy about commercial Brutalism. Arriving at Glasgow Central Station for my job interview in 2007, I was immediately smitten with the faded mercantile flashiness of the city; its cliff-like sandstone office buildings from the nineteenth and early twentieth centuries walled me into impressive, busy corridor streets, and the long straight roads – on a rectangular grid more American than British – shoot apparently vertically up hills at their ends, or terminate in fine pompous churches and civic buildings. The commercial buildings of pre-Modernist Glasgow are as big as planning laws or the market would take at the moment of their creation, pushed right to the fronts of their building lines, and towering over the pavements, their facades a zoo of every passing fashion in architecture from the early nineteenth century through to the 1930s.

Living and working bang in the centre of the city I did not take long to decide that the way I wanted to teach architectural history in Glasgow was to use the vast wealth of interesting buildings there. After a year or so I was entrusted with my own special subject group of fourth-year students wanting to study Brutalism with me, and I cast around for projects to visit with them. Alongside some more obviously architecturally distinguished buildings, I took my little tour groups of clever, committed students to a large city-centre redevelopment of the 1960s that I had spotted on one of my exploring rambles.

The Anderston Centre in Glasgow is one of Richard Seifert's largest city-centre schemes, a complex of high-rise council flats above a podium intended for shops, all raised above street level on the roof of a substantial car park. It is incomplete, and what has been built

'TOO COMMERCIAL – NO CONVICTIONS'

The Anderston Centre, Glasgow

has the tawdry dishevelment which makes so many commercial schemes so hard to love: its shops have failed and been converted into cheap office space. Parts of it are empty and none of it feels valued.

I remember with affection my students' well-disposed bafflement as I led them round the un-navigable podium, each blind corner seeming to promise threats to one's personal safety, or to feel like an intrusion into someone else's unenviable territory. The experience was completed by roaring traffic on the nearby M8 and (my memory insists) ever-gloomy autumnal weather. We had repeatedly to turn back at intended walkway continuations fenced off in a range of later, cheaply jaunty fencing designs of the sort which especially disgust cool young architects. Even for the most diehard admirer of Brutalism, the Anderston Centre is painful, with half-hearted, almost budgetless interventions made piecemeal over the years in inadequate attempts to make it a pleasanter place.

Perhaps the most egregious is an effort to make special the podium-level entrance to one of the blocks of flats. It is a pair of

white-painted metal posts topped by a cut-out in the shape of a simplified Classical pediment – a touchingly naive gesture of Postmodern faith in the power of traditional architectural motifs to make people feel connected and at home. It is so forlorn and pathetic that I have come over numerous visits to feel something like a perverse affection for it, but I cannot find anything picturesque in the repeated assaults on concrete and brick by cream paint and ill-matched plastic fascias. The towers themselves have been overclad in new insulation – environmentally, improving heat-retention is absolutely the right thing to do, but as one Twitter detractor pointed out, this type of new surface has all the panache and monumentality of an old laptop.[20]

These tatty additions, along with a surrounding of dreary commercial high-rise from later decades, ensure that, though the Anderston Centre is large and tall, from almost every angle it fails to be sublime. For a lover of sinister cityscape it has its occasional moments – the sheer face towards the western car park is bleak enough to excite, and the paired ramp and stairs to Waterloo Street, heavily fenced in, have a toughness of material and scale which I enjoy, complete with stalactites formed by long-standing drips, and free of the twiddly additions which undermine much of the rest. At the extreme west of the podium a few facades have seen such neglect that they still have some of their old muscularity, and through filthy windows one can glimpse the comforting grey of a concrete waffle-grid roof slab. But in general the range of materials and shapes of the original design was somewhat excessive, its original jauntiness perhaps increasing the tawdriness of its failure and the less than half-hearted additions. Its evident lack of success comes in the singularly unpoetic form of accident solicitors, rather than the bleak sublimity of total failure and dereliction.

The Anderston Centre is disconnected from the streets around it by the largely impenetrable sides of its raised podium, and since the walkways and travelator which were intended to connect it into a wider pedestrian network were either never built or have been demolished, every point of access feels like a back route, and probably an unauthorised one. Unsurprisingly, the shops which filled its podium level have long since gone, and the conversion of their premises into office space has turned the pedestrian streets between them effectively into extended light-wells, incongruously accessible to the public but with few reasons for anyone to be there. In the days before prostitution went online, this unfrequented deck was a celebrated red-light area, but now it even lacks illicit uses as far as I have ever seen. Office workers cross it to get to and from work, but outside these brief busy periods, people are scarce. Even the high flats do not seem to generate much footfall.

On the podium is a staircase whose jazzily showy engineering and strong shape are characteristic of Seifert's commercial schemes – popularising and jollying-up Brutalism the way Art Deco had borrowed and decorated motifs from 1920s Modernism. On one visit I found beneath the bottom flight a melancholy little huddle of bowls containing water and what looked like cat food. It is hard to

imagine much living on the bare, paved deck, but areas whose conventional use has failed often come to house eccentric activities like those of this benevolent rat-feeder with his or her incongruous heart-shaped bowls printed with flower patterns.

How did such a financially and architecturally baleful scheme get built in the centre of one of Britain's great cities? On the council end, Glasgow's local government had a fanatical zeal to improve a city notorious for having the worst overcrowding in Britain in its central slums, with associated social and health problems. The common association between social ills and the architecture in which they occur led to a consuming haste to demolish squalid nineteenth-century housing and put up modern, Modernist replacements which would end the overcrowding and dirt. Most of this was targeted specifically at housing, and Glasgow probably built more high-rise social housing per head in the post-war decades than any other European city, either side of the Iron Curtain.[21]

Particularly in the city centre and inner suburbs, there was also an ambition to improve office, shop and industrial premises and, with the characteristic Modernist preference for clarity of function, to separate each from the others and avoid the jumble of functions present in the Victorian city.

Large areas of Glasgow were declared as 'Comprehensive Development Areas' (CDAs) by the council, and confirmed by central government, indicating that they needed as a matter of priority to be demolished wholesale and replaced. The huge Anderston Cross CDA, of which the Anderston Centre was to be part, stretched from the south-western corner of the city centre across much of the West End.[22] The original street after which it was named was one of a number of points where arterial suburban streets converged at the boundaries of the city centre. Like Trongate, a similar confluence which largely survives at the eastern edge of the centre, Anderston Cross's nineteenth- and early twentieth-century commercial and transport importance was reflected in grandiose stone buildings. Photos show them as having the charismatic bad taste and brio of Victorian and Edwardian commercial architecture which Glasgow does better than anywhere else I have seen.[23] A major bus and tram terminus, with a railway station too, Anderston Cross was poor and rough in the way which is historically common around transport hubs. To its west the industrial and commercial infrastructure which supported the river Clyde's massive shipbuilding activity stretched for over half a mile. It was the sort of dense, polluted, mixed-use area which 1950s planners saw as a problem requiring urgent and radical solution.

At the westernmost end of Anderston Cross CDA an industrial estate was given approval in 1965 and built over the following years for companies including the Dunlop Rubber Co. Ltd.[24] This concentration of industry on one part of the site segregated the noise, traffic and pollution of factories and lorries from a large development of social housing which was the next area of the CDA coming in towards the city centre.[25] The innermost part of the CDA, on the fringe of the city centre, is the Anderston Centre. However, you would never guess from a visit that this was part of the same development as the rest of the CDA; they are separated from each other by the huge breadth of the M8 and its attendant slip roads at a variety of levels. The unachieved original intention to connect the parts of the CDA by a pedestrian walkway over the motorway was for decades memorialised by a celebrated 'bridge to nowhere': the central section had been built at the same time as the motorway in order to avoid having to close the road for building works at a later date, but the link to the Anderston Centre was never made because the second phase of the Centre, with the walkways to which the bridge would have connected, was never built.[26]

The part of the Anderston Cross CDA on the city-centre side of the M8 was to combine compatible uses in a way regarded as desirable for a commercial district, with a bus station, a raised podium of shops over extensive parking (connecting at its margins with a new large hotel and possibly a casino), eventually a swimming pool, and potentially other facilities which came and went from the plans over more than a decade of negotiations and changing property market, as developer enthusiasm waxed and waned.[27] Above the shops were to be commercially let offices, and towering over the whole, one- and two-bedroom flats aimed at young people who would enjoy its central location.[28]

The council's plan was to use its considerable powers of compulsory purchase, demolition, and road replanning, to delineate and clear a viable site. Private developers would then use their expertise in the property market and their sharpness about the construction industry to design and build the new development, paying a good rent to the council, and sharing the profits with them. In the late 1950s, when the idea was floated, this seemed like a thoroughly mutually satisfactory arrangement which would allow the council to put the profit back into some of its many expensively large regeneration projects elsewhere in the city. The developers were clearly bullish too, and the original deal provisionally agreed in 1963–64 was that the council would get back every year a rent amounting to 8.5 per cent of the original cost of buying and clearing the site, plus 50 per cent of the remaining profit after the developers had taken a rent calculated as 10 per cent of their construction cost.

The intention was to develop the entire site in one phase, to secure the critical mass of shops, offices and transport required to attract tenants and shoppers in viable numbers. An interesting sidelight is cast on the use of pedestrian segregation here: the argument was put to the council that the land for the development needed to be made available all at once and soon, 'to enable the Centre to be developed comprehensively in accordance with the most modern principles of vehicle and pedestrian segregation'.[29] In other words the walkways, as well as being fashionable in terms of planning theory and architectural expression, could be used as a lever to put pressure on local and central government to push through Compulsory Purchase Orders to clear the whole site for rapid development rather than developing piecemeal as successive parts of the site became available. The sociological drive of the 1950s avant-garde to prevent cities becoming segmented by their roads had become a tool to secure more favourable terms of development for private speculators.

If this was indeed the developers' tactic – holding local government to ransom with the threat of an incomplete walkway system – the Anderston Centre seems to have resulted in the town planning equivalent of a murdered hostage: only one stage of the Centre was built, replete with incomplete walkways and poor connections to the wider city.

The development must have seemed full of promise in June 1959 when the council determined the boundaries of the large CDA, and still thoroughly viable in the early 1960s as they pushed the scheme through three public inquiries and successively won each of the six Compulsory Purchase Orders which covered the area. Even in those peak years of mass demolition, however, it took time and controversy to clear such big areas of city with so many

property rights to untangle, and for so many competing and contradictory interests to be negotiated or steamrollered. It was 1965 before the necessary planning processes had been gone through for the development as a whole, and detailed planning, design and financial discussions, as well as demolitions, dragged on for the following five years, with Stage 1 only going on site in 1970, twelve years after the CDA had been declared.[30]

By 1967, when the scheme was starting to look closer to becoming reality, the original pair of developers – chosen by the council in 1963–64 from a shortlist of those keen to get involved – suddenly pulled out.[31] The speculative commercial development bubble of the earlier 1960s had burst. As a chartered surveyor advised the council:

> From 1965 to the present day, this competition has slowed up considerably, money being very difficult to obtain and at higher interest rates with institutions requiring a greater share of the equity than hitherto. At the present moment, a 10% return to a developer with 60% of the equity is the sort of return that almost every company expects to obtain, and we cannot foresee any reduction in these terms in the immediate future, if at all. [. . .] There are now a number of examples of shopping centres which have not been successful for one reason or another, e.g. Doncaster, Piccadilly Manchester, Bangor, Derby, Burton-on-Trent, etc.[32]

After two successive pairings of developers had fallen through, the council was left in a bad position to negotiate. Yet cancelling the development would have been problematic too: the railway station had been closed since 1959, and the blight of deserted buildings, short-term tenants who could not afford better, and minimal maintenance – regular afflictions of areas proposed for demolition – had been accumulating for almost a decade. A letter from the transparently exasperated Depute City Chamberlain in June

1967 recommends accepting reduced terms from the latest developer pairing, Taylor Woodrow and Standard Life:

> I feel bound to say that [. . .] I have been disturbed by the attitude of Taylor Woodrow [. . .] and I have given serious thought as to whether I should recommend the Corporation to seek other developers.
>
> However, there is no guarantee that in the circumstances an alternative developer acceptable to Standard Life could be found and that subsequent negotiations would not be protracted, and in view of the urgent necessity to get things moving in Anderston I agree that the proposals tentatively agreed last Tuesday with Standard Life and Taylor Woodrow should be submitted to the Corporation for approval.[33]

The council official clearly felt that the council had been systematically chiselled by the developers:

> Numerous meetings were held between the developers and Corporation officials between March 1964 and March 1966 at which, on almost every occasion, some effort was made to wring some concession from the Corporation and to whittle away the original agreement.[34]

The developers had even pulled back from the original aim of developing the whole area at once, perhaps wanting to put a toe into the water first, or to minimise their exposure to a now-risky project:

> At the meeting held on 6th May 1967 Mr North insisted on the inclusion in the Heads of Agreement of an option clause which alters fundamentally the original conception of development of the area as an integral whole.[35]

Any spirit of cooperation towards a common goal seems by 1967 to have worn pretty thin, and the council, with the reluctant backing of its officials who clearly felt they had little choice, went ahead with an agreement which limited their land rent to far below the original percentage of purchase and clearance costs, and cut their share of remaining equity from a half to a third, in return for building Stage 1 only of the full scheme, with no guarantee covering further stages or the neighbouring hotel which had been proposed.[36]

If, at the Anderston Centre and other projects, developers could be ruthless in their pursuit of profit, Seifert turned his considerable intelligence and professionalism to the same end. 'There are something like 350 Acts of Parliament governing building operations. I find it difficult to understand how an architect can possibly advise his client to their advantage if he does not know the law.'[37] He found it important 'to meet the planners and make them realise that you knew more about it than they do, or as much, and therefore I used to get the best advantage out of my planning applications.' What he meant by 'best advantage' was specifically 'best plot ratios' – the largest amount of lettable office or shop space.[38]

It was a combination of hard work and pushy pluck which famously secured huge increases in developable space at Seifert's Centre Point and Natwest Tower, both in London. For Natwest Seifert got around height restrictions in the vicinity of St Paul's Cathedral by producing a deliberately ugly scheme which conformed to the planning restrictions, and an elegant one which broke them, in order that popular opinion pushed through his oversized scheme.[39] For Centre Point Seifert and the developer, Hyams, struck a deal with the London County Council where the LCC acquired the land needed to replan the important traffic junction beneath in return for Hyams and Seifert being allowed to build exceptionally high.[40] So intelligent and thorough was Seifert's pursuit of planning loopholes that he became a byword for them; the LCC repeatedly had to change its bylaws to close gaps he had exploited, and planners came to dub the new regulations 'Seifert clauses'.[41]

This profit-driven architecture was parodied by John Betjeman, who made 'Colonel Seifert' an early target of the architectural column he inaugurated in *Private Eye*, 'Nooks and Corners of the New Barbarism':

> Any suggestion of human scale has been skilfully avoided. [. . .] The high-rise 16 storey block is cleverly unrelated to its low-rise neighbour, thus making the composition financially viable. [. . .] Colonel Seifert & Partners, the designers of this ambitious project, are to be congratulated on steering it through the gruelling process of committee stages.[42]

Seifert also became a prominent target for 1960s and '70s conservationists – the Anderston Centre was typical of many of his schemes in its indiscriminate swallowing up of the buildings and streets which predated it, irrespective of their qualities.

Seifert was not of course responsible for the management of his buildings once completed, but his reputation certainly suffered from Hyams's handling of perhaps the most elegant building to come from Seifert's office. Centre Point, towering thirty-four storeys over Tottenham Court Road, was designed primarily by Seifert's gifted partner George Marsh, and has always had its admirers for its graciously curved slenderness.[43] However, Hyams indulged in the profit-boosting trick of keeping the building empty until prices rose. The controversially high structure failed to bring new jobs, and instead stood for many as a monument to the inhuman power of money – the 'tomb of the unknown developer'.[44] It was an obvious high-profile target for the homelessness campaigners who in 1974 infiltrated the security company looking after it in order to lead a protest occupation.[45]

Unsurprising, then, that Seifert's was the largest of the ten or so commercial architectural practices which took on between them the considerable majority of the major speculative commercial developments of London, and many nationwide, in the 1960s boom.[46] Seifert's partnership rose from a small practice with around twelve employees in 1955 to a massive organisation with a turnover of £30 million in 1964–65, and £300,000 estimated profit.[47]

Seifert was indeed a slick businessman. He is rumoured to have been invited to take shares in Harry Hyams's development company Bolton – a privilege granted only to those Hyams valued, as it gave the recipient a stake in his immense profits.[48] At one time Seifert had nine offices open across the UK, with projects coming in at up to one per day, mostly for the UK but with commissions around the world. Seifert lived in a large house in Mill Hill, drove a Rolls-Royce, and had a weekly box at the opera.[49] Whereas James Stirling was fairly typical of internationally leading architects of his period in being reasonably well off but not super rich, dying in 1992 with a fortune of around £1 million (probably mostly bound up in property, a furniture collection and artworks), Seifert's commercially successful career left him far richer.[50] It seems characteristic of his pleasure in playing with the financial and legal structures at his disposal, however, that at probate after his death in 2001, his estate was valued at less than £50,000 – presumably his house and the rest of his fortune must have been transferred to his heirs via instruments free of inheritance tax.[51] Even his death was run on sound commercial lines.

iv

Beyond his financial legacy, Seifert's critics could easily paint a picture of him as having left behind thousands of buildings put up primarily to generate vast tax-free profits for people who were already fabulously wealthy. In the process, he left the comparatively poor residents of the Anderston Centre's towers living in dystopian isolation above a deck which would provide a good setting for one of J. G. Ballard's tales of urban dislocation and moral and social collapse. Seifert, his opponents might argue, lumbered numerous cities with little pseudo-gardens and pigeon plazas that no one will ever use, towers which rise above their neighbourhoods as bullish tributes to the power of property speculators, and office spaces devoid of any interiors which might lift the spirit.

How great a contrast to the buildings of the Welfare State, whose architects foreswore Seifert's massive profits to use their skills for the benefit of those less well off than themselves. Yet from the standpoint of the local-authority Communists, almost all architects in private practice were essentially commercial, running their own businesses and accepting private sector commissions, as well as making profits from their work for the Welfare State. From this standpoint Seifert was on the same side of the fence as Chamberlin Powell & Bon, the difference being merely that a larger proportion of CPB's profits came from public clients than did Seifert's.

When the 1970s brought a collapse in the UK building industry, the architects who had sniffed at Seifert for taking developer money almost all joined the 'commercial' architects in seeking work from the suddenly rich oil states of the Middle East. Nevertheless, at a time when there was plenty of public-sector work around in the UK, Seifert and other leading commercial practitioners chose to make more money by prioritising speculative office design, whilst others focused on Welfare State work, often with a real sense that they were doing the right thing. But morality was not the only motivation for concentrating on these public-sector buildings: the major architectural magazines gave far greater attention to public commissions than to speculative projects, and awards, titles, influence and prestige tended to go to the architects of prominent government-funded buildings like the Royal Festival Hall, the National Theatre, new university buildings and so on, not to designers of office blocks, however competent and prolific. In other words, the career path for an artistically ambitious British architect of the 1950s and '60s was to get public projects – housing, schools, university buildings or arts projects – and to do interesting, innovative, photogenic things with them. Architects in that period had to choose between the highest prestige and the highest profits in a way that had not been necessary in most earlier periods, nor again since the rise of the great architectural practices of the following generation, Foster Associates and the Richard Rogers Partnership, which have managed to pursue careers of both commercial and critical success.

There may have been, in this 1960s ostracising of 'commercial' architects and their clients, an element of social or cultural prejudice. Thatcherites *avant la lettre,* they did not all talk or present themselves like the public schoolboys who presided over most of British politics and culture in the post-war years. Behind the criticisms levelled at the developers and their architects may linger a whiff of class resentment at this new power elite of self-made interlopers – the mocking 'Colonel' used by Betjeman when writing of Seifert is a jibe at the architect for being so uncouth as to use his wartime rank in civilian life.

Whatever the prejudices lined up against them, it would certainly not be fair to suggest that Seifert and his fellow commercially oriented architects were uniformly uninterested in the appearance and architectural qualities of their buildings.

Seifert's firm had flashes of real quality, yet for the enthusiast of rough concrete there is something overslick about most of his elevations – he leaned more towards the architectural suavity of the German-American Marcel Breuer and the great US office designers Skidmore Owings & Merrill than towards the roughness of Le Corbusier or Paul Rudolph. Worst are the decorative flourishes with which he softens his pedestrian levels, most often in the form of crazy angular excrescences superimposed over the real structural shapes of his supporting columns.

For lovers of expressive concrete Seifert is at best second in the pantheon of commercial architects. Within the Owen Luder Partnership, another practice which did a lot of work for developers, the design architect Rodney Gordon produced in the 1960s three schemes which were not just the best examples of speculative work, but took Piranesian excess as far as any British Brutalist.

The first, Eros House in Catford, has been the victim of one of the ugliest, most destructive re-claddings I have ever seen, with its bull-nosed elegance utterly destroyed by the piggy little eyes of its new windows, peering through cheap-fridge-door-style cladding. Relative to Gordon's other two belters this is conservation. Both the Tricorn Centre in Portsmouth, which to my shame and great sadness I never saw in person, and Trinity Square in Gateshead have been demolished.[52] As usual with commercial architecture they proved vulnerable both to changes in shop trends, like the pressure for much larger shop units than they were designed to accommodate, and to small-town local politicians' zealous love of being seen to do something. In a distant echo of the 1960s Mayor of Preston, the Corporate Affairs Manager for the developers destroying Trinity Square celebrated the destruction: 'Beginning the demolition of the car park is a momentous day for Gateshead.'[53] Either or both of these two could have become major monuments for their cities if intelligent reuse had enabled them to continue to work, but they were demolished just before the public recognition of their quality could rise to a level where they would be kept.[54]

The Tricorn was probably the best of the three great Rodney Gordon schemes, epic in its complex external expression of varied functions – shopping, offices, residential and parking – and joyfully sculptural in its overarticulation of these necessary elements.[55] If the indifference of developers to the urban impact of their schemes was generally damaging, it had at least one excellent side effect in the case of Gordon and other good architects: the developers exercised very little control over the appearance of their buildings. As an estate agent for Charles Clore, one of the most successful developers, reported, 'He [Clore] leaves it to me to find the architect. I usually have a model made. He loves a model, you see. When he sees it, he usually says "I like that". I've almost never known him to say he didn't like one.'⁵⁶ The compromise of working for a commercial practice was one Gordon was happy to make: 'If it meant selling my grandmother or working for Owen Luder, provided I was free to implement my ideas, I would do it ... And without a second thought I did.'⁵⁷

Rodney Gordon was perhaps the most visually imaginative and energetically creative commercial architect of the 1960s in Britain. He and Seifert had, however, no monopoly on producing decent commercial schemes. Fitzroy Robinson, in London and nationally, had various lovely moments including the wonderful office block (its future currently uncertain) squashed on to a narrow site between the road and rail approaches to the Blackfriars Bridges, lowering and seductively sinister, like the malevolent spaceships come to destroy the planet on which film designers often lavish their best efforts.⁵⁸ This and dozens of other lesser-known commercial schemes nationwide, however good they are or once were, are especially vulnerable to degradation through cheapskate attempts to renew their image, or to radical alteration or demolition spurred on by the same speculative acquisitiveness which brought them into being in the first place.⁵⁹

Whilst some fashionable architects seemed to dress their buildings in exposed concrete as the latest trendy style, Rodney Gordon's Brutalism comes straight from his guts – an atavistic grunt frozen in concrete in all its intrusive, uncouth virility. The quality of design artistry comes from talented and committed individuals and teams wherever they happen to crop up. This, though obvious, is rarely stated and contrary certainly to the pattern of official recognition of buildings, where the tendency is for ministers to agree to list buildings of public or institutional importance, or those which cost more to build, more readily than buildings whose architecture is better in those unquantifiable ways that made the Tricorn Centre so remarkable.

The situation was more complex than is often allowed. Rodney Gordon, the real-life architect of *Get Carter*'s Trinity Square car

The Tricorn Centre
Photograph: James Mann (Flickr: sunspan_1)

park, was neither as posh as his film counterpart, nor as exclusively money-minded; and the suave, upper-crust architects who gained many of the plum public commissions could be at least as ruthless in their pursuit of prestige, power and work for their practices as Seifert was in his pursuit of developer profits.

V

The picture of commercial Brutalism is generally cheerless, and having a last walk around the Anderston Centre before leaving Glasgow, I was struck by the sad waste of so much hope and effort. The building seemed like a monumental warning against badly implemented halfway houses: the market was distorted by regulation into supporting ill-thought-through schemes, whilst the public sector's involvement saw it bearing much of the cost of a development which brought little advantage to the city to recompense it for mass-demolition.

It is rather difficult to admire the involvement of speculators in this sort of development. There is an opportunistic, uncommitted quality which, whilst economically rational, is deeply unattractive, especially when contrasted with the contemporary national effort of the Welfare State to provide housing and education. The council, meanwhile, could be charged with some combination of naivety and greed. They began compulsory purchase and demolition without having secured a contract with developers, so the developers were not obliged to meet the council's initial expectations – indeed, it would have been well-nigh impossible to enforce any contract, given the tendency of developers to form disposable separate companies for each major project, meaning that any one which went wrong could be dropped without miring the others in debt.[60] As soon as they had started the process of acquiring and clearing the land, the council's initial negotiating position was weakened: they needed developers, and the developers could therefore name their terms. The half-cock Anderston Centre was the result.

Yet even amidst the sad wreckage of the Anderston Centre – a never-fledged corpse, now decaying – there are moments of real architectural quality. The highlight is the former bus station, where the elegance of Seifert's partnership's handling of precast concrete systems comes out at its simple best. To accommodate double-deckers in the bays below, the offices stand on attenuated legs, and are arranged into blocks of different sizes around the quadrangle of the bus station. The precast system is suavely varied so that different buildings have differently spaced windows in a manner reminiscent of the Smithsons' Economist Building. It is a facade of some refinement and considerable elegance. It has weathered well, and even shorn of its buses after a later public-transport rearrangement it remains a gratifying reminder that almost any situation which gives rise to lots of buildings will inevitably give rise to some very good ones. The Anderston Centre may be a monument to the adversarial legislative bodging of Conservative and Labour administrations in the post-war years, and to the sharp-elbowed

The Anderston Centre Bus Station. Photograph: Peter Atkinson (Flickr: SpaceLightOrder)

money-chasing of developers exploiting both sides, but even there, and even after the awful patching-up of the Centre over subsequent decades, there is some architecture which any city should be pleased to have. And as always, time brings changes in taste and perception. The feeling was widespread in the 1950s that the soot-blackened Victorian offices of Glasgow – functionally outdated by then and partially empty – were ugly and ill-maintained, were punctuated only by insufficient and impractical public spaces, and called to mind a period of feverish commercial speculation whose record would be better eliminated from the streets.

In 2014 an avant-garde orchestra, the Scottish Ensemble, co-operated with artist Toby Paterson to produce 'City Spaces & Strings', a combination of visual art and music performed in an abandoned office space in the Anderston Centre.[61] There is something surprising about radical art choosing such a commercial setting. It suggests that, for a generation born after the controversy of the Anderston Centre's creation, the toxic stench of destructive profiteering has been dispelled, leaving only the object itself, poetic in its half-abandonment, and almost tragic in its evocation of a period when even big business seemed to believe in the viability of radical new directions for city design and architecture.

Chapter Seven

Good Ordinary Brutalism
The University of Strathclyde Architecture
Building and the Newbery Tower

(barnabascalder.org/rc7/)

i

I recently returned to the University of Strathclyde School of Architecture Building where I worked for five exciting years. The building is at the top of a short but very steep hill. A walk I had done daily now had the prickle of nostalgia after three years elsewhere. The rush up the hill in the mornings to get to my lectures in time kept me fit, or at least fit enough to have regained my breath by the time my slides had loaded on the lecture-theatre computer. This time I was in no hurry, however, and was able to take in the Architecture Building properly, as I had done on my first arrival there for interview eight years previously, loitering with the uneasy self-consciousness of someone killing time dressed for a job interview.

The Strathclyde Architecture Building stretches along the crest of the hill, a long, narrow building that looks from the air a little like a Yale key. Most of its length is concealed by other buildings as you approach. All you see is the end of its bulky podium, windowless and geological. On top of it, delicate by contrast, the last few bays of staff offices. All walls are in blue-black engineering brick, and

above the podium concrete beams are exposed, and the offices and studios are lit by a neat system of metal-framed Crittall windows and copperised green felt cladding panels. A jutting roofline of white skylights projects into the sky. The sloping site means that the building towers over you as you approach.

The path to the entrance takes you along the edge of the building on a series of wide, shallow steps. They are awkwardly spaced, somewhere between a single large stride and two small paces, and I never in five years worked out whether I was better taking them at a comical stretch or trotting up them as if doing dressage. I tended to compromise on a bit of both, jog-hobbling up and down them with the irregular gait of a three-legged donkey. As you raise your eyes again at the top you are confronted by another substantial cliff of dark, slightly shiny brick, this time forming a retaining wall to hold up the higher ground at the top of the hill. To escape this canyon there is a narrow staircase to your right, again following the outer wall of the building. Its high walls are of the same dark brick, crushing you in and disorientating you as you rise. There is no horizon, no colour, no view to either side – it is an intense, claustrophobic experience. As one reaches the top the full length of the building becomes apparent, the orderly repetition of its projecting window bays, and the long shaded walkway running beneath the overhanging walls above providing an exaggerated perspective, whilst a rather charming garden of singingly green grass in front gives welcome relief from the sublimity of the approach, all the brighter and more welcome for the contrast with the sober architecture.

On my most recent visit all of this was exactly as usual, but when I got into the building I was filled with sadness: I had almost never entered the school before without a friendly greeting from some student or colleague, and only in the depths of summer had I seen it without that beguiling bustle which attends architecture schools: busy students working long hours in companionable anxiety about deadlines; staff bustling from room to room with important-looking papers and the body language of having too much on;

groups of smokers loitering sociably outside the entrance; models, drawings, posters and the artful clutter of clever, gifted young people scattered everywhere. Even in the lavatories a student had noticed the similarity of the cubicle lock to a duck's beak, and drawn the rest of the duck's face around it in a rather charming little cartoon.

Now, however, the building seemed empty. In the whole course of my visit I did not see one person in it. The last architecture students had stencilled various titles on the walls to accompany an exhibition of their work, and that was the only remaining sign of all that creativity and energy in the echoing studio spaces, now shorn even of furniture.

I did not have the heart to go and see what had become of the beautifully top-lit library with its useful collection of periodicals, where I had waited years before to give my pre-job-interview presentation to the staff. The little seminar room where I had given it, and first set eyes on the diverse bunch of architects and academics who were

Disused design studios in the Strathclyde Architecture Building

to be my colleagues, was empty and dark. When challenged on the lack of decoration in his buildings, Denys Lasdun used to say that the people were the decoration.[1] As someone who has always liked Lasdun's walls and terraces in all their austere concrete splendour, I have never felt the need of decoration. However, back in my old department, my footsteps echoing off the brick of the internal walls, I sorely missed the people.

Even when bustling and cheerful, the Strathclyde Architecture Building was only my second-favourite Brutalist building in Glasgow. Right from my arrival in Glasgow in 2008 I immediately admired the Newbery Tower, a rugged, stocky little block at the Glasgow School of Art. I had never before heard of it or its architects, but it gave me pleasure, every time business or sociability took me past, to glimpse its picturesque roofline popping up peek-a-boo on the approach, and then to come face-to-face with its soaring yet weighty concrete and its crisply tough glazing system.

When I first knew them, both the Strathclyde Architecture Building and the Newbery Tower were busy, useful buildings full of happy students, many of whom admired their strong Modernist architecture. Neither now serves its original purpose, thanks to the swings of fashion and managerial decision-making.[2] They are just two stories amongst thousands of similar ones. Both buildings were purpose-built studios created by local practices of the sort who do not tend to figure much in histories of movements: they did not write much about their work, they did not tend to be (or claim to be) first to do anything in particular, and they were not widely published and copied. Stepping away from connoisseurship and grand historical narratives, however, it seemed to me that these two very good and quietly successful buildings had something important to say.

ii

The Strathclyde Architecture Building was designed and built between 1964 and 1967 as part of a considerable expansion in the newly chartered University of Strathclyde. Previously the institution had been an engineering and technical college founded in the early days of the Industrial Revolution by a former professor of oriental languages at Glasgow University, who saw the burgeoning Industrial Revolution all around him and abandoned his erudite niche in favour of applied science. At his death, he left his fortune to establish what he called, in polemical contrast to Glasgow University, 'a place of useful learning'.[3] In the 1960s it became one of Scotland's answers to the seven English New Universities, building upon its technical and technological strength, but becoming a proper university with humanities and social sciences, and considerably expanding its campus with mass demolition of tenements and commercial buildings to create a large area of new buildings right in the city centre.[4]

The Architecture Building was designed by Frank Fielden, the head of the school at the time.[5] I always enjoyed the legibility of the building, which seemed set out to teach architecture students about how to plan a building: the entrance hall welcomes you with a large abstract concrete mural, regrettably painted white at some point, but still handsome.[6] To each side of the mural are doors into the department's intimate lecture theatre, wood-lined and humane. Around three sides of the lecture theatre is a gallery space for visiting exhibitions. This is also used for student pin-ups, the intimidating moment where nervous, exhausted architecture students who have been up all night display their work on the walls for panels of staff and visitors to come round and peer at, interrogating the students on their design decisions. There tends to be a strong smell of glue from the frantic last-minute completion of models which are still drying as they are examined.

The rest of the ground floor was originally given over to the laboratories for Building Science and Structures. The architecture seems to suggest that these offices and labs are of less importance than those on the upper levels: they are overhung by the cantilevered first floor, and served by a narrow, low-ceilinged corridor. The open stair hall rising clear to the rooflights two floors above invites you instead to rise through the building, and on each of the other two floors the staircase opened out into the design studios, at least until fire regulations demanded the walling-in of the stairwell. Even so, the studios dominate the two main floors in a way which clearly sets out the department's agenda: design is the centre of the architecture degree, and other activities all feed into producing good designers. The studios take up the whole of one side of the building as a sort of very wide corridor. On the middle floor they are lit by large windows which, because they face north, never bring in the glare of sunlight but consistently provide an even light which is good for drawing. On the floor above, the windows are only slits, making for more wall on which to pin up drawings. The natural light comes instead from abundant large skylights, again angled north to keep out direct sun. The 1960s was consistently preoccupied with how buildings exploited natural light for rooms that would be occupied for long periods, and here it is done with practicality and elegance.

The south side of the building was given over to offices, and these were protected from glare or overheating by avoiding large areas of south-facing glass. The walls were boxed out so that windows faced east or west rather than to the sunny south. The one exception was the head of department's office (originally the staff common room), which had a full south-facing window with impressive views out over the city above roof height. My slit of window had a fine diagonal view out over the roofline of central Glasgow and to distant hills beyond. My desk was one of the 1960s originals, made specially for the department out of ash-wood, and sized to fit into the window niches of the offices. This left room for a table round which I could squeeze eight students for seminars, and some bookshelves screwed into the exposed brick walls. On other walls pinboard enabled me to decorate as I saw fit. Details like the door handle were of a quietly nice quality, shaped to the hand. I loved the simple aesthetics of the room, and its informality of scale and expression. I felt very much at home there.

Along the centre of the building, sandwiched between the offices and studios which all needed natural light, were lavatories, the lift, and a couple of teaching rooms. Always my least favourite bit of the school, these windowless teaching rooms were part of the move in the mid-twentieth century to deeper-plan buildings where parts could be entirely surrounded by other rooms, lit and ventilated by the cheap electricity of the 1960s, especially where, as here, users would not be in them for sustained periods. It very substantially increases the amount of useful space you can fit on to many sites, but for me the slight stuffiness, the incessant hum of air plant, and the whistle and peripheral-vision flicker of fluorescent tubes, mean that rooms without windows are rarely agreeable. When I was scheduled to teach in them I tended instead to wander round with the students to find a quiet corner of the bright, airy design studios.

The building was not perfect. Much of the structural work occurred over a cold winter when, to stop the concrete being weakened by freezing, it was wadded with straw to retain its natural heat from the setting process, but control on the building site was far from perfect. One of the architects recalls that some of the builders were found to be sleeping in the straw instead to save themselves the cost of lodgings. At another point a consignment of stolen whisky was found hidden in that same busy straw. No wonder that the quality of the surface finish of the concrete was disappointing, and it had to be covered in a layer of render on completion.[7]

Apart from the concrete problems, the building made a good case for the merits of 1960s finishes. By the time I left it had taken forty-five years of rough wear: architecture students use spray glue and spray paint everywhere, they drop scalpels and Stanley knives, spill ink, hammer and saw things inexpertly, scrape tables and chairs across floors, carry large pieces of wood carelessly round corners, improvise ways of hanging things from ceilings, and Blu-Tack, glue, tape, pin and nail all manner of things to all parts of every surface. The exposed brick and concrete, built-in pinboard, wood-block floors and rubber tiling of the entrance hall had taken all this with grace. There were plenty of marks of use, but on rough, tough materials these seemed like a well-earned patina rather than tawdry decay. Even the curse of new cable runs, tacked into ceilings and walls and wreathed in generations of electrical and electronic additions, seemed almost at home amidst the unpretentious robustness of the department. Forceful but not intimidating, sophisticated but rugged, didactic but practical, the Strathclyde Architecture Building had everything going for it as an architecture school.

iii

If the concrete work at Strathclyde was problematic, that at the Newbery Tower was sensationally good. Built a few years later, the Newbery Tower takes a rather different approach to a similar brief, stacking the studios vertically rather than spreading them along a larger site as at Strathclyde. Part of a development plan for the expansion of the Glasgow School of Art, the tower was designed by the successor firm to that for which the great star of Glasgow's architectural history, Charles Rennie Mackintosh, had worked at the time that he designed the original Glasgow School of Art building, a thrillingly idiosyncratic piece of architecture blending ideas from the Arts and Crafts, Art Nouveau and Scots Baronial movements, and attracting later somewhat propagandistic claims that it was one of the founding buildings of Modernism.[8]

The practice, known as Honeyman & Keppie when Mackintosh worked for it, had by the 1960s become Keppie Henderson & Partners. Throughout the 1960s and '70s it produced a succession of decent, well-made Brutalist buildings in and around Glasgow, none of which attracted more than passing interest from the national architectural press, but which together make up a locally important body of work of impressive variety and quality, attractively integrating in their design vocabulary influences from the British and international leaders of the Brutalist movement.[9]

Keppie Henderson's master plan for the expansion of the Glasgow School of Art was characteristically Brutalist in its bold simplicity, consisting of three new blocks ranged on two sides of the original building, composed together like a Russian Constructivist sculpture of the 1910s – simple cuboids juxtaposed with each other.[10] The Newbery Tower was to be the vertical counterpoint of the horizontal Mackintosh building and the two new horizontal buildings of the master plan.

As in so many 1960s schemes, the provision of efficient external circulation was allied to an eagerness to make room for democratic outdoor space, whether this is in the rather tokenistic form of the commercial developments of the previous chapter – drawn in salesman's technicolour by hired perspectivists and crowded with happy, glamorous strolling couples – or in the more convincing form of the South Bank's river-front walkway. In central Glasgow in particular, this little square offset the unrelieved density of an urban grid produced during a previous century of immense land-values, where throughout the substantial city centre tall buildings land directly on the pavement, with few squares providing relief. The architects sat the Newbery Tower back from the street on a low podium. This would also have linked it to the neighbouring 1970s block across a small square, had the planned demolition gone ahead of a pleasant but unexceptional early twentieth-century blonde sandstone building. Nevertheless, by stepping back from the building line the tower's height was made less dominating, and more space was created across which to view Mackintosh's remarkable entrance facade.

The Newbery Tower managed an uncommonly satisfactory balance for such a tall structure. From the streets around, it appeared only intermittently, almost always peering unintimidatingly over the shoulder of some neighbouring building. From further afield – from the M8 motorway or from one of Glasgow's other hills – it stood proud above the roofline of its neighbours, marking the location of one of the city's major educational and cultural foci with the same appropriately fearless pride as the University of Glasgow is marked by its John Oldrid Scott Gothic tower of the 1880s.

Modernist towers seem often to be mistaken by the public for an intrinsically cheap option. In fact, the additional constructional and structural difficulty of building high meant that it was always a more expensive choice. The decision of the Glasgow School of Art to build high was the luxury option, worth it both for the extra space it opened up and for the architectural elegance and civic prominence it provided.

In practical terms, the height of the Newbery Tower made viable the architects' proposals for a small square as the School of Art's outdoor space, whilst still producing plenty of new, purpose-built accommodation for art and design studios. The programme was simple: above a raised entrance storey came seven open-plan floors of studio space with double east–west aspects, supported by circulation and service cores to north and south. This is reminiscent in concept and expression (though not materiality) of the great American Brutalist Louis Kahn's hugely influential Richards Laboratories at the University of Pennsylvania, where he separated off staircases, lifts, pipes, cables and ducts into almost free-standing towers surrounding the laboratory rooms themselves, which were therefore freed of clutter but well serviced.[11] This idea of dividing up a building's programme into 'served' and 'servant' spaces spread rapidly round the world through extensive international journal coverage, and provided a major point of reference for late Modernist and High Tech architecture.

The Newbery Tower's simple composition was originally to be executed in specially made, extra-long bricks of the sort used in the neighbouring first phase (1963) of the Keppie Henderson redevelopment of the art school.[12] By 1969, however, when the building went on-site, the influence of one of the major monuments of Brutalism had struck: Paul Rudolph's Yale University Art and Architecture Building. Rudolph was the Dean of the Yale school,

and therefore both architect and client, giving him an enviable level of freedom to explore his latest ideas on architectural expression. He required the contractors to cast the concrete into vertically corrugated formwork and then smash each rib individually with repeated blows of a hammer, exposing the aggregate.[13] This extraordinarily strongly modelled texture, often nicknamed 'corduroy concrete', shows the shape of the building even in neutral lighting, and honestly reveals the constituents of the concrete as cement, sand and coarse aggregate, the last of which in particular can often disappear beneath the former two whose finer grain makes them settle to the surface of the formwork. There may be echoes, too, of Auguste Perret's desire to bring out the stone aggregate within concrete to make a claim for concrete as the modern inheritor of the prestige of stone. At a more prosaic level, Rudolph hoped that the channels would contain and conceal rainwater staining.

The Newbery Tower used these prominent vertical ribs, broken with a hammer. It cross-bred the new Rudolph trend with ideas from Le Corbusier, alternating Rudolph ribs with wooden boardmarked concrete like that at the *Unité d'habitation*. In the irregular rhythm of widths of plank between projecting ribs, the Newbery Tower also echoed another characteristic stylistic trait of Brutalism, perhaps originating with Le Corbusier's collaborator, the designer and early electronic musician Iannis Xenakis. Xenakis came up with *ondulatoires* – windows divided vertically by mullions spaced irregularly according to patterns determined by the wavelengths of musical notes.[14]

The thought, care and expense put into this one-off, craft-intensive concrete treatment suggests the importance of materiality to the architects. The technique produced two characteristic Brutalist effects. Firstly, it expressed and memorialised the means of production in the surface appearance of the building, uniting aesthetic, construction, structure and space in a single material expression. Secondly, the deep ribs of the surface produced an exceptionally pronounced verticality, prominent in all lighting conditions

and from near or far. This concrete treatment was originally carried into the interiors around the core elements, but as so often (including on much of the exposed brickwork inside Strathclyde's architecture department) this continuity was later blurred by painting the internal concrete white, perhaps to make the rooms within lighter, or less excusably to smarten it up.

Internally, the stairwells had arched cuts through their central concrete spine, recalling in elegant tribute the similar cuts through the stair spines of Mackintosh's building.

The cores rose above the main roofline of the building, each of the seven separately articulated elements rising to a different height, probably under the influence of an unbuilt Lasdun scheme for controversially prominent science towers in central Cambridge.[15] Though the effect was later muddied by scrappy added roof elements, this turned these eminently practical shafts for stairs, lifts, services and structure into a picturesque roofline reminiscent of the towers of San Gimignano (a precedent for the beauty of unadorned high buildings often cited by Modernists), or the varied skyline of a Gothic cathedral.

Between the Newbery Tower's rough-ribbed, in situ cores the architects hung decks of open-plan studio space, and their material treatment expresses this functional and structural distinction with the usual Brutalist clarity. Windows running the entire width of the floor slab, including rounding the corners to the cores, indicate that the cladding contains or conceals no structure. Simple black window frames and, originally, exposed concrete floor-deck edges, were alternated with bands of lightly verdigrised copper.[16] The concrete deck edges were later clad in black glass, presumably concealing added insulation. It was an atypically sensitive intervention.

Despite the clarity with which these materials manifest their nature as cladding, the elements are neither light and shiny like those of the earliest glass curtain-walled office buildings of fifteen or so

years earlier, nor slick like Norman Foster's remarkable frameless glazing at the Willis Faber and Dumas insurance building five years later, where the near-black glass is held in place with almost no external indications as to how. Instead, at the Newbery Tower, the glazing takes its expressive cue from the staircases: there is a proportionate chunkiness to it which gives the building as a whole a literal, physical robustness echoed, to a sympathetic eye, by a poetic robustness of expression.

At a single look, then, anyone who knows a little about mid-twentieth-century construction can examine a picture of the Newbery Tower and tell how it was built, what it was built of, and can read the structure and programme in the external shapes and material treatments. It is in its own way as unobtrusively didactic as the Strathclyde Architecture Building.

iv

When I arrived in Glasgow in 2008 both the Newbery Tower and the Strathclyde Architecture Building were doing fine, still with most of their original architecture intact, and as far as I could see still serving well their original purposes. During my five years in the city both were to come under threat, and now one is gone and the other seriously compromised. They make dispiritingly clear case studies of the ways in which good ordinary buildings, especially Brutalist ones, can suffer sudden attrition.

At much the same time, Strathclyde and the Glasgow School of Art came out with plans for changes to their estates. My recollection is that the first indication I had that the Strathclyde Architecture Building might be in trouble was a proposed estate plan showing departments moved and 'consolidated' into existing and new buildings: the new plan no longer had an Architecture Building on it. I initially assumed that this was a mistake, but in fact it emerged that the intention was to move us into an existing engineering building, and, it appeared, demolish the Architecture Building.[17] University financing was putting considerable pressure on universities to compress their teaching into fewer or smaller buildings and sell off the remainder of the estate, and we were informed by the management that Strathclyde had investigated and found that it had 40 per cent too large an estate.[18]

The Glasgow School of Art, meanwhile, wanted to 'redevelop our campus to provide a high quality learning, teaching and research environment and accommodate growth'.[19] It had concluded that its buildings were 'very poor'. They proposed to redevelop the site opposite their original Mackintosh building, then occupied by the Newbery Tower, its near contemporary the lower-rise Foulis Building, and the little yellow-stone student bar building that had survived the demolition plans of the 1960s. It was the obvious spot to bring together the two main buildings as the shared core of the institution, and had the additional advantage that you are less likely to get snarled up in planning disputes and preservation campaigns when pulling down post-war buildings than ones from any earlier period, whatever the merits or demerits of the buildings slated for demolition.

With student numbers rising, the school undoubtedly needed a bigger lecture theatre than any it already had, and some teaching spaces for larger classes. These could have been provided, as one of the competitors in the architectural competition for a new building proposed, by keeping the Newbery Tower at the core and building new facilities around it. The school, however, argued that its campus 'fails to provide a learning, teaching or research environment which is in any way adequate to meet the ambitions of the school in terms of its quality, its flexibility, its cost-effectiveness, or the image it projects to future students'.[20] The 'cost-effectiveness' case is undermined on the following page, which indicates that 'the redevelopment of the estate also has major financial implications', requiring the institution 'to generate significant additional income over the planning period'.[21] Perhaps a key motivation was 'the image it projects to future students': an impressive new building would make an architectural splash, and furnish a stunning image for the prospectus.

The attitudes of the managements of both institutions suggest that architectural merits of the sort discussed in this book are not very often recognised by those with the power of decision over estates. The notable exception is in the case of celebrated older buildings, which have made it over into the category of 'heritage' with sufficient prominence to make people venerate them. Thus the Glasgow School of Art is well aware of the importance of its Mackintosh building. The GSA logo is Art Nouveau in the manner of Mackintosh, the architecture school there is called the Mackintosh School of Architecture, and a proportion of the building is given over to a gift shop, heritage tours and a Mackintosh museum. Quite rightly, when an appalling fire there in 2014 burned out the finest part of Mackintosh's building, the library, staff and students were deeply upset. Yet even the Mackintosh building, an established masterpiece now, had its period out of fashion. Mackintosh's style was loathed and mocked in the early decades of the twentieth century by the architecture staff and students working in his building, as excessively personal and undisciplined. His designs 'appeared to be derived from drug-induced hallucinations'.[22] If they had had the funds it might perhaps have been demolished. Yet each generation fails to learn the lesson that all architecture, and perhaps especially the strongest-flavoured and best, has an unfashionable moment for several decades after its completion.

I was at a drinks event in the GSA when I first heard the news that the Newbery Tower was to be demolished, and when I expressed my dismay my interlocutor from the GSA management seemed baffled and amused at my defence of the building. I think it was taken for an attention-seeking rhetorical stance. This dismissal of the Newbery Tower had the weight of general opinion on its side at that time. The *Guardian* published an article on the proposed replacement for the Newbery and its neighbours, making no mention or illustration of the buildings to be demolished. Of seventeen people who commented on the online version of the story, six spontaneously abused the existing buildings.[23] They found their hostility to the Newbery and its neighbours so self-explanatory that they needed say nothing more than that they are 'horrendous' and that any replacement 'could hardly be worse'. A good architectural guide, written in 1989 when Brutalism was at its lowest ebb, went straight for the concrete: 'Coarse concrete crowds in on Mackintosh's masterpiece with bruising Brutalist indifference.'[24]

The Newbery Tower, then, was an obvious target for a management wanting to make space for a new building in a densely built-up area. Few would be upset by the demolition, and those few would not carry public opinion with them. The new building would have immediate fans simply for replacing its unfashionable predecessor.

I do not recall the discussion of the Strathclyde Architecture Building taking in any account of its architectural quality initially. I had the impression that the department was seen as underperforming financially relative to some others in the Faculty of Engineering, whose balance sheets were swelled by contracts from industries including arms and oil.

As for the claim that the building was too large for the department, it would have surprised its architects: when it was built the total number of students at the school was considerably smaller than the number at the time I was there.[25] Each student had originally had a personal, allocated drawing table, whereas in my time the larger number of students meant that they had to 'hot-desk', finding available space – though some of the best students in one particularly good first-year cohort took things into their own hands and set up their own corner of the studio as suited them, reserving their drawing space largely by the impressive expedient of working there for very long hours every day.

Both Strathclyde Architecture Building and the Newbery Tower were seen by some as outdated, yet it is hard to see why. I knew the Strathclyde building far better, and can personally vouch for its effectiveness not only practically, but in terms of developing a 'studio culture', where students work together and spur each other on to better and better work. As for the Newbery Tower, many of its students loved it, and despite claims that it was functionally obsolete, it was in fact more adaptable to new functions than almost any older building. With the vertical structure and services confined to the staircase cores, there were no columns or structural walls dividing up the floors, so they could be used as single large rooms, or be divided into as many or as few rooms as were wanted, for the cost of erecting or removing a partition.

In fact, even in less flexible buildings, architectural adaptability is decreasingly important in many cases, as the infrastructure of learning, work and leisure becomes ever more portable. Many people can now do their job from a laptop anywhere with a Wi-Fi connection and a plug socket, as the coffee-shop boom of recent years shows. Late-twentieth-century concerns of office layout, lighting and cable runs begin to appear increasingly archaic. When a building is liked it is easier than at any previous point in human history for people to adapt to it, rather than having to adapt the building to the activities it houses. The Glasgow School of Art itself shows this clearly in its continuing use of the Mackintosh building. Its rooms are ossified almost entirely by both structural and heritage restrictions, yet the departments and offices housed there generally appear to be sufficiently proud of their prestigious and attractive surroundings to accommodate themselves like a hermit crab to the shell of a building designed inflexibly around a Victorian and Edwardian curriculum of fine and applied arts, originally intended for much lower student numbers and barely recognisable conditions of education – what use now its 'Elementary Ornament Room'? The school considered abandoning the building in the post-war period, but must be constantly grateful that it held its nerve.[26]

If I have little sympathy for functional arguments against the Newbery Tower and Strathclyde Architecture Building, their environmental performance – especially their poor thermal insulation – is a much knottier and more intractable problem. The awareness that 37 per cent of all the UK's CO_2 emissions come from the running of buildings, in particular heating them, is driving the architecture world to give serious thought to reducing the energy consumption of existing as well as new buildings.[27] This is a tricky business in Brutalist architecture. The desire to produce legible buildings, using reinforced concrete simultaneously as structure and surface, often inside and out, means that many Brutalist buildings are composed partly or largely of solid concrete walls, and that floor decks are often exposed to the outside of the building. Steel reinforcement carries heat too easily out of the building, resulting in poor insulation and sometimes problematic condensation inside, if the temperature difference inside to outside is substantial. Adding new insulation is desirable but often difficult: added externally it alters the proportions and covers up the exposed concrete which is central to the building's aesthetic. Added internally it reduces the sizes of rooms which are often already planned tightly on hard-squeezed budgets. Floor-to-ceiling heights can be particularly problematic here, with 1960s dimensions on occasion being close to feasible minimums.

Brutalist windows are often poor at insulating, too, frequently having metal frames which conduct heat very fast, and almost always being single-glazed. These can be satisfactorily replaced with double glazing if care is taken in commissioning high-quality replacements of similar frame thickness, appropriate finishes, and similar proportions to the original glazing. Many Georgian listed buildings in Edinburgh's New Town have had their windows recently double-glazed with this sort of care, and the results, whilst detectably different in the way in which they carry reflections, substantially improve the insulation and leave the building looking broadly the same. This kind of care for post-war Modernist buildings is, however, very rare indeed. Much more often the managements of Brutalist buildings (often publicly funded bodies under pressure to accept the lowest tender) select the cheapest option, which generally means an offensively inappropriate and obviously cheap replacement glazing – often glaringly white uPVC with proportions loosely aimed at the 'period' house market – and the hideous clumsiness of thicker frames round the opening lights than round the fixed ones. Ruining the windows is perhaps the most efficient way of removing all architectural quality from a facade of any period or style, and still leaves them with less good insulation than a new building put up to today's regulations.

Yet the idea of replacing energy-inefficient buildings with energy-efficient ones is not the panacea some suggest. It costs a great deal of fuel to demolish an existing building, dispose of its materials, manufacture and transport materials for a new building, and then to build it. One can add to this the wastage of the already-used resources that built the building in the first place – 'embodied energy'. The energy taken to demolish an inefficient building and replace it with an efficient one is so great that it will typically take in the region of sixty years for the new building to pay off the rebuilding energy cost through its annual power savings.[28] Given that the typical life aspired to for many contemporary building components is only fifty years, it casts serious doubt over whether demolition and replacement can in most circumstances be supported by any environmental claims at all.[29]

So doing some basic maintenance and otherwise keeping the Newbery Tower running as before was a sustainable option. Had the Newbery Tower been sensitively environmentally upgraded instead of being demolished, it might have come out of the comparison even better. It is potentially quite expensive upgrading a Modernist building in such a way as to respect its aesthetic; it is, however, very substantially cheaper than demolishing and rebuilding.

I have a further beef with current discussions of environmental performance in buildings: they seem to be based on an ambition to produce T-shirt-warm interiors with the precious warm air jealously retained in tightly sealed buildings. The assumptions of the 1960s and before were much less cosseted, and gave higher value to fresh air. In new schools in the 1940s, for instance, the ambition for the heating system was that if it was 0 degrees Celsius outdoors it ought to be 15.6 degrees in the classroom, and 7.2 degrees in the corridors.[30] People wore more layers, and were, at worst, sometimes a bit chilly.

I decided when living in Glasgow to put my money where my mouth was in my opposition to badly replaced windows and ugly retro-fitted insulation. My flat had lots of very large, single-glazed sash windows, so I decided to try not heating it for a winter. I undoubtedly stole heat from my neighbours – even when there was ice inside the windows it never dropped below 11 degrees Celsius in the bedroom and 8 degrees in the kitchen/living room – but it was liveable-with for someone in reasonable health. In cold weather I had occasionally to wear a hat, and thin gloves to keep my fingers mobile whilst typing, and I generally wore two jumpers in the flat. But with two duvets on the bed (a lovely way to go to sleep, warm amidst the cold) I was comfortable, and suffered no colds. The unwelcome dash to the shower in the morning was a small price to pay for the eco-smugness to which I felt the gimmick entitled me. This is probably further than most want to go, but even turning down your thermostat by one degree is claimed to save around 340 kilogrammes of CO_2 per year, and if you tolerate a bit of cold, the period of winter when heating is needed becomes considerably shorter.[31]

My radical conclusion on insulation, therefore, is that we ought to learn to personalise it: if more individuals are prepared to wear a jumper, we will no longer need to demolish – or rip the windows out of – every pre-1990 building. With the heating lower, managements will have an even harder time trying to excuse as 'sustainable' the demolition of good buildings during the inevitable period of unpopularity which follows any architectural style twenty to sixty years after its flowering. It is wasteful, stupid and vandalistic. The

Newbery Tower should still be there, sensitively double-glazed, heated to 16 degrees Celsius when necessary, and full of happy students snug in their jumpers, with up-to-the-minute equipment or extra staff paid for with the money saved by not rebuilding.

Whatever the strength of the case in favour of keeping the two buildings functioning as before, and upgrading them sensitively, it was outweighed for the managements of the universities by numerous other considerations. At the Glasgow School of Art discussion of the merits of the existing buildings was drowned out by a clamour of other opinions and special-interest pleadings which threatened to overwhelm not only any discussion of the merits of the Newbery Tower, but even the excitement at the major new building.

A few commentators quirked eyebrows at the fact that the invited competition to design the building was won by a major international competitor, Stephen Holl Architects, rather than by a local practice (many of whose architects, after all, were educated at the Glasgow School of Art).[32] Some admirers of the original GSA building felt that the design proposed by Holl was too tall, too light and too prominent a neighbour for Mackintosh's masterpiece.[33] I personally admire Holl as an architect, and did not have objections to the replacement as a design, merely to the loss of the Newbery Tower.

Local residents, too, took an interest in the development. I went along with two friends to one of the public consultation evenings, where the head of the Glasgow School of Art and one of the architects from JM Architects, the local practice working with Holl on the new building, took the audience through the proposals, and then using great smoothness and elegance dealt with a series of increasingly bizarre questions and comments: a neighbour was understandably anxious about parking and traffic during construction; the mother of a pupil at the next-door school announced that the building work could not go ahead if the noise would disrupt her child's study for exams; one audience member proposed that the School of Art ought to organise a pagan ceremony to thank the hill on which it sat for protecting us all. At that consultation none of the audience even mentioned Holl's design, let alone the question of whether the existing architecture ought to be preserved. With too little serious discussion of architecture in the media, and next to none in schools, this surreal harvest of personal anxieties is more typical than one would wish of the results of public consultation.

Amidst such clamour, voices arguing for conservation of the Newbery Tower became just another group to be handled with courteous tact, then ignored; we were scarcely to be taken more seriously than the pagan worship lobby. And this is what listing is for: to protect buildings with legal force until their managements can learn to appreciate them and work with them rather than against them.

Newbery Tower was put forward for listing by a member of the public, though the elegant style of writing of the letter (anonymised by Historic Scotland before release under Ross Brown's Freedom of Information request) makes it clear that it was at least an exceptionally well-informed member of the public, and more likely a professional historian or architect: 'one of the last remaining high quality examples of Caledonian brutalism at its most exciting', a 'vertically stacked factory of creativity'.[34] Historic Scotland came to the conclusion that the building was not an early enough example of its style to be considered important, and therefore could be allowed to go unlisted.

Strathclyde's Architecture Building was also considered by Historic Scotland as part of a listing review of the university as a whole, and was listed at Grade B for its architectural quality, and for its status as the first purpose-built architecture school in the UK in the post-war period.[35] There was much celebration from those of us who loved the building, and from those who opposed the department being moved out of it: listed, it could not be demolished, nor did it seem likely to me that the university would get listed building consent to build walls into the open studios which make up so much of its interior, and divide them into teaching or research spaces to suit other departments. Without obvious alternative users who might want to buy it from the university, architecture was surely more than ever the natural department to be housed there. If the 40 per cent reduction in estate was needed, it might also make sense to bring Product Design or some other design-based course into the building.

V

It came as a real surprise to me to learn that plans remained in place for us to move out of the building. The mystery deepened when the proposed replacement architecture department was revealed. Its main window would give only on to a steeply rising metal roof, in striking contrast to the fine views from the purpose-built building, and it would presumably depend on extensive artificial light and ventilation, unlike the well-lit, airy studios of its predecessor.

Student representatives made a wonderfully cogent case against the move at meetings with management. The students secured national publicity in the architectural press, held special events to celebrate the building's architecture, and have now founded a preservation society to ensure that the quality of the building is upheld in practice, rather than being chipped away at by little changes despite the listing.[36]

The camaraderie produced by this battle was magnificent, and the student campaign was conducted not only with integrity, energy and commitment, but also with charming sharp humour. But though La Fontaine's lamb can out-argue the wolf, he still gets eaten. The department moved. One of the key reasons I left Strathclyde, where I had so loved teaching, was that I could not bear to be displaced from the lovely, bright, open, well-designed building we had had into the call-centre atmosphere of the new rooms, squashed into a building exceptionally lacking in architectural distinction.

As I see it, the material result of all this unpleasantness is that the architecture department is stuck in an ugly and disagreeable new setting, whilst its own fine building provides, as far as I can gather, a sort of ill-fitting transit camp for other departments being shuffled around like chess pawns in the prolonged reorganisation of the university. On my latest visit it seemed half-empty and drained of human activity. Yet the Newbery Tower story ends even more bleakly.

Once listing was refused it was doomed, but between the certainty of its destruction and the closing-off of the site for demolition preparations there was a period of months in which the building was used exactly as usual, and looked its normal self, yet was condemned. It felt slightly unreal that such a manifestly resilient building should be on the point of disappearing for ever, and I am not sure I really believed it until the demolition work began.[37]

Glasgow School of Art alumni arranged a goodbye party for the Newbery Tower, at which hundreds of past and present students came for one last visit, graffiti-ing the doomed walls with pens provided by the organisers for that purpose, and breaking out of a fire escape to flock on to the roof of the next-door building, with an excellent view of the Newbery Tower, until a harassed janitor herded us all back down.

Picking up on the controversies, students from both of Glasgow's architecture schools co-organised a debate on whether the GSA should have kept the Newbery Tower or gone ahead with Holl's new building. One of the architects for the replacement building spoke for it, and I spoke for the Newbery. The contentious atmosphere was heightened by the floodlit demolition of the building proceeding just outside, so the audience had all just seen it at its most dramatic and with its pathos considerably heightened. My memory insists, though I cannot be sure, that we could hear the drills smashing through the concrete as we spoke.

After the debate was over, I climbed round the security fence surrounding the now-deserted demolition site, and used my bicycle light to pick my way through the rubble, the rough concrete chunks pushing up uncomfortably through the soles of my shoes, to the northern stair tower, still largely intact at the time despite the demolition of the decks. My main goal, apart from one last visit to the building, was to retrieve a piece of concrete which bore the distinctive and carefully crafted in situ texture on it. I searched and searched through the rubble, finding no fragment that would do. My assumption is that the density of reinforcement bars in the concrete led it to shatter into fragments on demolition, aggravated by the fact that the pieces had quite a way to fall from the demolition level to the rubble heap below. A keen hillwalker at the time, I scrambled my way up the staircase, its stairs having vanished beneath a steep, even, scree-slope of fragmented concrete, broken glass and dust, dotted with larger chunks of (maddeningly untextured) rubble, planks, sections of metal framing or service duct, and so on. On each floor one could pause and peer down over the missing deck into the void below, indirectly but atmospherically lit by the surrounding street lights.

In general I find construction and demolition fascinating. It is always informative and often hauntingly beautiful to see the serendipitous cross-sections produced by anything but an explosive demolition. Yet in this case my sadness at what I saw as the wanton destruction of the building made me take detours in order not to see the shrinking ruin, and I found afterwards that I had taken no photos of it during demolition, despite its being extremely photogenic, very informative, and a useful example of a contentious planning decision. I suspect my sense of guilt at not having fought harder for the building was a large part of this evasiveness.

The two examples contained in this chapter have only been chosen because I happened to live and work in or near them at the time they came under threat. The Casework Committee of the Twentieth Century Society considers what buildings erected since 1914 it ought to put forward for listing, and what proposed changes ought to be permitted in listed structures of that period. It can be heartbreaking. So many of these good but less well-known pieces of architecture all over the country are being hacked around or demolished when they could easily be sensitively adapted and reused. The scale of wasteful demolition and arbitrary vandalism is mind-boggling, and the continuing failure of so many people to recognise that 1960s Brutalism is a style with as high a proportion of good buildings as any other means that it is the easiest period of any to mistreat. Projects like scotbrut.co.uk, a research website compiled by Ross Brown, are uncovering the sheer quantity of good, ordinary Brutalism which remains uncatalogued, unanalysed and undiscussed, but even since he launched the project in 2012 many of the buildings covered by it have been painted, overclad, hacked around or even demolished.

The bar for listing is considerably higher for post-1945 buildings than for older structures. The considerable majority of extant buildings in Britain was constructed in the twentieth century, and yet in England the proportion of all listed buildings built since 1945 is 0.2 per cent.[38] Unless one truly believes that since the end of the Second World War the massive quantity of building for all purposes by all manner of architects on all levels of budget is in some way systemically inferior to all earlier phases, it is clear that a great many buildings are unprotected which would be good enough to be listed if they were from any other period.

Much the best way of saving buildings is to ensure that the users and managers are clear on the qualities of the architecture around them, and work with it rather than against it. The case of the Strathclyde Architecture Building, however, shows that energetic, convinced campaigning can do a lot to save a specific building even in the teeth of hostility from management. Listing cannot prevent wasteful mismanagement, but it can keep a building there

to await more enlightened days, just as Liverpool's now fantastically popular and successful Albert Dock was preserved from demolition (for a Seifert office scheme) despite being empty and derelict at the time.[39]

Meanwhile, back in Glasgow there is an almost Arthurian spirit amongst those who led the campaign against the move out of the Strathclyde Architecture Building: one day, somehow, the department will return in triumph from its ignominious exile, to enjoy once again proper studio space and a handsome building.

The Newbery Tower during demolition. Photograph: Alan J. Stuart (Flickr: Werewegian)

Chapter Eight

A Concrete Violin
The National Theatre

(barnabascalder.org/rc8/)

i

Crossing Waterloo Bridge from north to south on a sunny evening is one of the best ways to see London.* Docklands glints in the distance between the uprights of Tower Bridge. The City's zoo of commercial high-rises surrounds the dome of St Paul's, Wren's most assured and convincing architectural moment. In the other direction the London Eye revolves slowly above the heavily civic Edwardian solidity of County Hall, and the turreted silhouette of the Houses of Parliament is picked up and exaggerated by the magnificently pompous Loire-Chateau roofline of the Whitehall Court flats. I fell in love with this walk back in 2002, when I was doing my MA, and since then have taken any excuse I could find to divert over the bridge. The city around changes over the years, but the big red buses continue to trundle past, the water still flows underneath, and the panorama of fine buildings shifts as one moves, an architecture geek's pleasurable game of *Where's Wally?*.

* A view that is currently under threat from the unappetising Garden Bridge proposal.

During the course of my year at the Courtauld, one building came to stand out from this handsome crowd. By turns sullen, harsh, glittering, crystalline, buzzing with audience or austerely empty, rain-mottled or shining near-white in the sun, the National Theatre slowly began to preoccupy me. As an undergraduate history student I had done a special subject on English Baroque architecture, and was bewitched by the austere magnificence of Nicholas Hawksmoor's churches. Their slightly abstract classicism is handled with a chunky strength that I find utterly overwhelming, but at the same time there is a meticulousness and care to the composition of those massive stone shapes. I found myself feeling a very similar attraction to this new discovery, the National Theatre.

As autumn stripped the leaves from the trees along its river front, and brought the darker evenings, the National's flood-lit pyramidal mass was reflected in the river's ripples. The sense of expectation and ritual pleasure of theatregoers in its foyers was visible in their posture and movement even from the distance of the bridge. In spring the return of leaves came not as a sign of hope and re-generation but as the unwelcome cloaking of a loved sight, as well as the forerunner of coursework deadlines and a reminder of the imminent end of a course I was loving.

Growing up in London, I had known the National Theatre building all my life, and my discovery of its architecture during my MA year was all the more exciting for its feeling of dawning understanding. I had been to productions at the National since I was little. I recall running my puzzled child's fingers over its mysteriously fossilised wood-textured surfaces, wondering what it was made of and how. I have never forgotten an amazing production of *Wind in the Willows* in its Olivier Theatre, which I saw when I was about ten, with Toad Hall or Mole's house rising and twisting miraculously out of the stage. Wear what 3D glasses you like, cinema has nothing to touch a really good production at the National Theatre.

A CONCRETE VIOLIN

It had always seemed to me as much a timeless part of London as the Houses of Parliament, and its building as solid, as inevitable, and as fixed as any mountain. When I started to research it for my PhD I was to find that nothing I had thought about it was true. Both the institution and its home came into being only by the skin of their teeth. The building itself, so clearly complete, turns out to be a reworking of the uncancelled half of a larger project, and its appearance of four-square solidity is an architectural illusion: the robust-looking concrete forms a structure which vaults great spaces with the most ambitious ingenuity. The concrete itself, so easily mistaken for a cheap option, is in fact exquisitely crafted. The uncompromising distinctiveness of its theatres arose from the most indecisive briefing, and the whole project emerged from the most improbable consensus between political opposites.

When I embarked on my research on the National Theatre it seemed to me a magnificent, mysterious building, releasing only slowly the secrets of its complicated layout. Even after three years of full-time research, and more work on it since, it retains this sense of mystery for me. I do not feel the cosy sense of quotidian

familiarity that I have had with Strathclyde's Architecture Building or the informal, slightly punky cool of the Leicester Engineering Building. Around the National Theatre I stand a little straighter and I speak a little less loudly.

ii

The long and messy story which eventually led to the National Theatre building began over a century before the appointment of its architect, Denys Lasdun. Its earliest origins can be taken back to a publication of the late 1840s by an Enlightenment publisher, Effingham Wilson, who called for a theatre to bring about a higher standard of plays and productions than was marketable within the commercial theatre. This theatre, as Wilson envisaged it, would be funded by public subscription led by an aristocratic and industrial elite, an idea that lingered for nearly a century, with on-and-off fund-raising efforts attracting sporadic donations. Only by 1938 was a site negotiated and enough money raised for a foundation ceremony to be enacted by George Bernard Shaw. The building, opposite the Victoria and Albert Museum on a modest-sized corner site, was to be designed by the greatest of Britain's twentieth-century non-Modernist architects, Edwin Lutyens.[1] It became one of so many projects suspended for the Second World War.

Things did not come to a complete standstill, however. The National Theatre idea began to find favour with a new supporter, the consistently Labour-led London County Council (LCC), Britain's biggest and arguably its most progressive council. Faced with the unprecedented scale of destruction of London buildings in the Blitz, the LCC took the step, at once propagandistic and practical, of using the wartime pause in building activity as an opportunity to rethink the planning of a city struggling under the weight of increasing traffic, and full of housing which, even before the war, was in bad condition and overcrowded. Their *County of London Plan*, published in 1943, gave general principles for post-war planning and reconstruction, but also explored a number of important or exemplary areas in more detail, to illustrate the sort of opportunities redevelopment would bring about. One of the areas on which they focused was the South Bank of the Thames, a particularly tough area of industrial decay right in the heart of London, and the location of the LCC's own headquarters at County Hall.[2] Hoping to extend the cultural and economic life of central London over the Thames, the LCC seized upon the National Theatre as a potential addition to their South Bank plans, and offered to swap the Kensington site for a larger one in their new cultural complex. When the South Bank was used as the centrepiece of the 1951 Festival of Britain, the LCC contributed the Royal Festival Hall to it as the one permanent building, and the Queen laid a foundation stone next to it, on the site now occupied by the Southbank Centre, to mark the eventual hopes for a National Theatre.

Right from its post-war inception, the National Theatre was brought into being by a surprising coalition: a left-wing LCC wanting to democratise an elite art form cooperating with members of the old Right wishing to maintain theatre's artistic standards at public expense.[3] This LCC support was a policy of Isaac 'Ike' Hayward, Leader of the Council from 1947 right through to its dissolution in 1965. Son of a mining engineer in South Wales, Hayward left school at twelve, worked in the mines for three years, and then became an engineer. Drawn into social concerns via the Temperance Movement, he rose through the trade unions, becoming General Secretary of the Transport and General Workers Union, and thence moved into the LCC as a tough Labour whip.[4] A conspicuously cultivated autodidact, Hayward gave his committed backing to the LCC's financial and political support for the arts, including most prominently the South Bank developments, the gallery of which bears his name. To Hayward and other left-wing supporters of the arts it was self-evident that along with health services and education, the working classes should be given access to the best of the arts; arts organisations needed to be subsidised to bring ticket prices within reach of everyone. The Attlee government thought similarly, and in 1948 brought forward a bill to offer £1 million towards the building cost of the National Theatre.

The bill had wide support on both sides of the house, but the man who had done most to push it through was Oliver Lyttelton, chairman of the latest iteration of the century-old pressure group which had been pushing for a National Theatre. An aristocratic old Etonian, a Guardsman in the First World War and Armaments Minister in the Second, Lyttelton was almost a precise antithesis of Hayward. Lyttelton's speech in favour of the 1948 bill was as conservative as you might expect. His answer to the self-posed question 'Why found a National Theatre?' began with plodding humour – 'A question which perhaps only the Secretary of the Philistine Society [. . .] could appropriately ask' – and was unapologetically elitist:

> What is the need [. . .] for the National Gallery, for St Paul's Cathedral, "Lycidas" or the "Eroica" Symphony of Beethoven [. . .] In fact, we only begin to enter the realms of art when we begin to leave the realms of necessity.[5]

His next argument is nationalistic – France and other European countries have state-sponsored theatres (although so soon after the war the notable publicly funded theatre traditions of Germany and Austria are conspicuously absent from those he lists). The third of his arguments appeals essentially, and with striking historical inaccuracy, to social snobbery:

> A national theatre in Great Britain would help to keep undefiled the purity of the English language, the accents in which it is uttered, the grammar and the syntax in which it is cast, by setting a standard springing from the glorious English of Shakespeare of which we are the proud but I must say somewhat negligent heirs.[6]

Perhaps the most surprising reason of all is, as he puts it, 'filial piety'. His parents had supported the project and so he wants to push it through out of loyalty. He even deals explicitly with the extent to which the pattern of aristocratic patronage has now changed to one of influence on public spending rather than personal donations to good causes. In other words, the old Right was using the mechanisms of the Welfare State to pursue its long-standing elitism and to confer prestige on the aristocracy.[7]

Lyttelton's 1949 National Theatre Bill stated that the National Theatre project would not start within the lifetime of that Parliament – post-war reconstruction was in full swing, and it would have seemed an unjustifiable luxury to begin a theatre whilst many were without a permanent home. In fact it was to be 1962 before the National Theatre Company was founded and work got under way on commissioning a building.

By that time the two contrasting camps, united only by their shared belief in the existing virtues of theatre, had been joined by a third group of supporters: the avant-garde London theatre world. London in the 1950s had seen a particularly noisy and exciting explosion of new theatrical ideas, in particular the playwrights known as the 'Angry Young Men' who rejected the witty upper-class tennis parties of Coward and Rattigan in favour of the rough-edged rebelliousness of a post-war generation of working-class young people in tough industrial slums. The theatre critic who had set the seal of his influential approval on this new type of theatre, Kenneth Tynan, held a mock funeral service, in full-fig mourning, by the abandoned foundation stone which had been laid for the National Theatre back in 1951. Tynan and others in his circle were not believers in 'high art' – the influential director Joan Littlewood mocked the position of men like Hayward as 'piping Beethoven down the pits' – but they were certainly believers in the power of the right sort of new theatre to bring about individual self-discovery and political change.[8]

iii

By the start of the 1960s the National Theatre Bill was feeling increasingly remote, yet there was still no sign of an actual National Theatre Company, let alone a new building for it. The central figure in turning the dormant promise of government support into a reality was Sir Laurence Olivier. The most prominent British theatre actor of his generation, and one of the most admired, Olivier had the superstar status to maximise positive publicity for any project to which he lent his support.

His wide popular appeal was surprisingly accompanied by a certain credibility with the tough new avant-garde of 1950s London theatre. Unlike most of the suave matinee idols of the 1930s, whose critical reputation dipped in the post-war years, Olivier negotiated with striking success the change of mood which swept in with the Angry Young Men. He did this through a personal relaunch in which he abandoned his untouchably glamorous image from the years of his marriage with Vivien Leigh and sought to associate himself with the younger, grittier, kitchen-sink playwrights. Olivier asked the most prominent of them, John Osborne, to write a play around him (*The Entertainer*, 1957). He left the fadingly glamorous Vivien Leigh for his co-star in *The Entertainer*, an actress from the cool Royal Court Company. Even the names speak of the change of tone, from the Hollywood shine of Vivien Leigh to the earthiness of Joan Plowright. He sold his stately home, Notley Abbey, and appointed Kenneth Tynan as his dramaturg at the National Theatre, after Tynan had savaged Olivier's opening production as director of the new Chichester Festival Theatre.[9]

As hoped for since the 1940s, the National Theatre project, revived by Olivier's support and with the continued back-room lobbying of Oliver Lyttelton, was at last given government approval in 1962. It was to involve commissioning a new building with two auditoria, one large, the other a small experimental theatre for new productions.

The cost was expected to come in at around £2.3 million. Part-funded by the LCC, it was to stand on the Council's showpiece South Bank, joining the Royal Festival Hall and an art cinema as the nuclei of an arts centre. Whilst the Conservative government which founded the National Theatre could present the announcement as support for the arts, they actually embodied in the foundation an attempt to cut the number of separately funded performing-arts organisations in London: they proposed that the new theatre would house a National Theatre Company which would swallow up the Old Vic Company, and the recently founded Royal Shakespeare Company. The merged organisation would share its auditoria, too, with the Sadler's Wells Opera.[10] The creation of a new National Theatre and Opera House could, in other words, be supported by those who thought it was a good addition to London's arts facilities and also by those diametrically opposed to them who felt that less money should be spent on the arts, so all these mergers were a positive step. The National Theatre's apparent acceptance of these terms kept the project alive at the cost of deferring the row over how much should actually be built and what companies should occupy it. Once the basic idea of building a National Theatre and Opera House was established, the merger with the RSC was swiftly dropped by the companies themselves, and over a period of time increasingly full-featured facilities for opera and theatre made their way into the brief.[11]

From the moment Olivier and Lyttelton got the National Theatre moving again it was clear that they needed to get construction work on the new building started before 1965, when the LCC would cease to exist – it was impossible to be sure that the support for arts projects which Isaac Hayward's LCC had offered would survive the reorganisation, so a reasonably efficient process was required to choose and brief the architect, select contractors and begin to dig the foundations. As James Callaghan (until recently Chancellor of the Exchequer) told Lasdun later in the context of National Theatre funding, 'the scheme must be committed, even by stretching all approved facts to their limits. The money will be forthcoming once it is started.'[12] Whereas a project denied funding in the first place is only controversial with those who really care about it, a stalled building site is an untenable daily embarrassment.

The committee set up to commission a building, the South Bank Theatre and Opera House Board, ignored the government's proposal of two auditoria shared between opera and theatre. Instead they asked directors from the opera and the theatre each to draw up a separate outline brief for the ideal auditorium. The opera house representatives did so quickly and efficiently.[13] Olivier did not. The same anxious sensitivity which made him such a resonant and astute actor made him cripplingly afraid to take high-profile public decisions on his own authority. Accordingly, to produce his short briefing document, he brought together a 'Building Committee' which reads like a list of those whose criticisms he feared rather than those who would be the most cooperative and useful members. It included the cream of London's directors: Peter Brook and Peter Hall of the RSC; George Devine of the Royal Court; Michael Elliott, freelance at the time but previously at the Old Vic; and joining them in the early months of the committee's life, John Dexter and Bill Gaskill of the new National Theatre Company.

With characteristic élan they started by deciding that it would be wrong to perform the task they had been brought together to accomplish, of drawing up a brief for an architectural competition. Fearing that an architect appointed in this way would arrive with a preconceived design which would end up being built without enough input from the theatre specialists, Peter Brook proposed that 'what we want is not a competition but an audition. We want a smell of his talents.'[14]

The RIBA asserted the right to regulate all architectural competitions in the country, so their panel chose the shortlist for these 'auditions' from the long list of architects who had applied.[15] They also invited a few big names (including Denys Lasdun) who had not applied of their own accord, perhaps because they were too busy, perhaps because they thought it beneath their level of prestige to enter open competitions, which tend to be seen as opportunities for big breaks for lower-profile architects.[16] The wonderful annotations of the provisional shortlist for interview are a pleasure for a 1960s architecture nerd: if Seifert was 'too commercial, no convictions', Peter Smithson, next in the alphabetical list, was 'too many convictions – not a collaborator'.[17] Goldfinger was 'difficult to work with', whereas Lasdun, on several iterations of the list, was always just marked 'v. good'.[18]

The written submissions of the twenty shortlisted firms display a wide variety of tactics in trying to bring in such an exciting commission: only two architects stressed that they already had experience of designing theatres; others actively boasted that they had not. Stirling and Gowan promised that the only thing they would bring over from previous jobs was the 'intensity of aptness' that they gave to each building they designed. Bill Howell of Howell Killick Partridge & Amis was even more assertive, beginning his letter: 'We have never built a theatre, but considering the record of those who have, we do not think this is necessarily a fatal drawback.'[19]

If Lasdun's previous good reputation took him into the interview phase already in a strong position, his deep conviction both in the value of excellent Modern architecture and in his ability to provide it, carried the day. Whilst Stirling and Gowan's interview performance earned the annotation 'impressed some, but why?', the sheet summarising the discussions after the interview opens 'unanimously Lasdun'.[20] So great was the level of conviction of the panel that Lasdun was the right architect for the National Theatre that they finished the discussion twenty minutes early, skipping a planned third interview stage, where the remaining candidates would be asked to submit rough outline schemes for the National Theatre and Opera House. So confident was the committee's unanimity on Lasdun's excellence that they appointed him straight away.

Reporting back to the South Bank Theatre Board, its secretary Richard Lynex recalled a 'gruelling three days' of interviews, with a tricky interview panel:

> It would hardly be an exaggeration to say that no two of them think the same about anything. But after the twenty interviews every one of them, without exception, had independently come to the conclusion that Lasdun was outstandingly the best of those interviewed. It was an incredible result, and I can only regard it as a direct intervention of Providence.
>
> [They wished to abandon the final stage of the appointment process because . . .] if a second name were put forward and were to be selected by the Board they would be getting someone markedly inferior.[21]

This appointment process, based on previous work and attitude, certainly suited the architect they selected, Denys Lasdun, who had a lifelong mistrust of competitions for the same reason Peter Brook disliked them – they can cut off the client from the designer and result in designs based on cliché or guesswork. Each building, Lasdun felt, required research into its specific users. This would enable the architects to produce a design which would meet their needs at more than a basic practical level.[22] Lasdun did just what the Building Committee had hoped: he waited to talk to the users before starting to design based on their specific needs. Once the auditoria had begun to take shape, and the outline needs of workshops and dressing rooms were becoming visible, Lasdun's team would carry out a series of hypothetical 'movement studies' to determine which of the elements needed to be close together.[23] Even at that stage the purpose would be practical rather than aesthetic. As Lasdun put it in one of the meetings with the Building Committee, 'We cannot get to the poetic till we have bled dry the functional.'[24] Lasdun went along to the Building Committee with every reason to expect that it would be his ideal collaborator in coming to a very good theatre design.

However, having done a good job shaping the selection process, Olivier's briefing group did not then disband. Instead, not trusting the official client's expertise in theatre, it constituted itself as an unofficial rival to the South Bank Theatre Board as the representatives of the clients. The South Bank Theatre Board reluctantly accepted the demand of the Building Committee that it should have direct access to the architect. The South Bank Theatre Board would remain the official client, signing off decisions, but it appears to have felt that it could not afford the bad publicity of taking on this powerful group of theatre figures with their great ability to attract media coverage.[25] The exasperated tone of the secretary of the South Bank Board even before Lasdun's appointment indicates the spirit of testy resignation with which the Board accommodated the self-appointed Building Committee: 'As we shall have to try to carry these chaps with us, I don't think that this further indulgence is anything more than tiresome, although there is little sense behind it.'[26] It is annotated, presumably by the chairman, Lord Cottesloe, 'Quite right. C.'

The Building Committee was right in thinking that its assembled theatrical expertise was an asset of almost incomparable potential, but the South Bank Theatre Board was right that a group composed of such high-profile figures would be a loose cannon. The central problem of the Building Committee was its appallingly weak and unprofessional chairing. As month after month of meetings went by, Olivier and his co-chair Norman Marshall failed with absolute consistency to keep any shape to the discussion, and it rambled from topic to topic with neither resolutions nor votes. An exasperated Lasdun felt that 'I have been given some interesting personal vignettes, some of them cancelling out, some not', but that the brief was not ending up any clearer.[27] Even things as basic as how many theatres they would build within the complex remained for a long time contentious and unresolved.

The transcript of the Building Committee's first meeting, on 3 January 1963, most of a year before the appointment of Lasdun, augurs ill; Olivier sums up their role with a characteristically resonant phrase which may or may not mean very much: 'We are to study the practical aesthetics of the question.'[28] He then leads the way, but is rapidly the victim of multiple interruptions, one of them by his co-chairman, Norman Marshall:

> L. OLIVIER: To start off the discussion I would like you to put forward your thoughts on what a National Theatre building should be, and I will begin with a short record of my experience gained at Chichester.
> G. DEVINE: Do we assume that there will be two stages; and if so, when?
> N. MARSHALL: Have we any guarantee that we will get the second theatre? This affects the entire problem.
> K. RAE [the secretary, and here as elsewhere a voice of well-informed moderation]: Two theatres, eventually, are an integral part of the National Theatre plan.
> N. MARSHALL: Are we to design an all purpose theatre for ten years or so?[29]

This point unresolved, Devine adds the general principle that 'we must make clear our assumptions when we submit our findings'. Hall at once returns to the question of the number of theatres, and in characteristically categorical fashion makes two loosely related statements:

> The Old Vic [the nearby theatre in which the NT Company was initially housed whilst awaiting the new building] is not suited to be the proscenium theatre of the National Theatre. The only way to get a second theatre is to be absolutely uncompromising about the first.

Marshall attempts to bring the former point to a resolution, but Olivier instead chooses to disagree about the whole notion of having two large theatres:

> Let us have one flexible theatre and use any extra space on the site for rehearsal rooms, a small experimental theatre, etc. With two theatres we will get confusion. Let us have one perfect theatre, its capacity not exceeding eleven hundred.

At this point, he resumes his speech on his experience at Chichester, having declared his preference, but neither giving the committee the chance to express their feelings on that preference, nor putting his proposal to a vote. By the time the architect was appointed there was still no brief, and no signs of one emerging.

The written records of this and other introductory meetings were given to Lasdun on his appointment as the nearest thing they yet had to a preliminary briefing. The architect was nonetheless sanguine about his ability to deal with 'the usual inter-Committee difficulties'. He felt he had seen everything that dysfunctional committees could throw at an architect, as 'we were used to working for Universities'.[30] He set out to lead the Building Committee towards making some decisions and clarifying their collective position, bringing drawings and models to meetings in order to focus the discussion, and repeatedly trying to work them round to talking about specifics.

iv

At the time when the National Theatre was commissioned, theatre architecture was in flux. Victorian and Edwardian theatres had had proscenium stages, where scenery could be lavishly and thrillingly illusionistic. When the curtain dropped between scenes, the audience had no idea whether its next rise would reveal a drawing room, a street or a forest, lowered quickly whilst the orchestra drowned out the mechanical rumbling of the fly tower. Theatregoers stared from the gilding and plush of the auditorium into the exciting world of the stage, the two divided by a kind of picture frame: the proscenium arch.

The rapid spread of cinema in the twentieth century posed a challenge to theatre's position as the home of flamboyant spectacle: even the grandest theatrical production could not keep pace with the technical capabilities and budgetary extravagance of Hollywood. And just as photography contributed to a reduced appetite for realism in painting, cinema undermined the desire to compete over stage effects. What theatre had to offer now was not illusion but the reality of sharing a space with real actors who were performing specifically for that audience and with the thrilling immediacy of the stage: there could be no retakes, and each performance would establish a particular dynamic between audience and actors. The proscenium stage suddenly seemed to throw up unwelcome barriers to the actor–audience relationship which was now the central attraction of theatre: the action was taking place in another room, glimpsed through a hole in the wall, and there was a divisively confrontational quality to the way that actors stared out at the bank of audience, who stared back, often further separated by the gulf of the orchestra pit.

In the post-war years there had been an international enthusiasm for rediscovering older patterns of theatre which were believed to unify actor and audience: the Shakespearean courtyard stage or the ancient Greek theatre, in both of which the audience had been curved round the actors on three sides, sharing the same space and swapping, it was felt, scenic illusion for intimacy and communion with the action in the shared room. Flat scenery would not work on such a stage – the open stage; and although three-dimensional scenery of any size or complexity would not be easy to get on and off, for the right play and the right director something new and thrilling could be achieved.[31]

The aim of the prolonged Building Committee discussions was to work out what type of auditorium the National Theatre ought to have as its main stage. If it opted for the safety of the proscenium it would be embarrassingly old-fashioned. If it took a gamble on the open stage it might be unable convincingly to produce much of

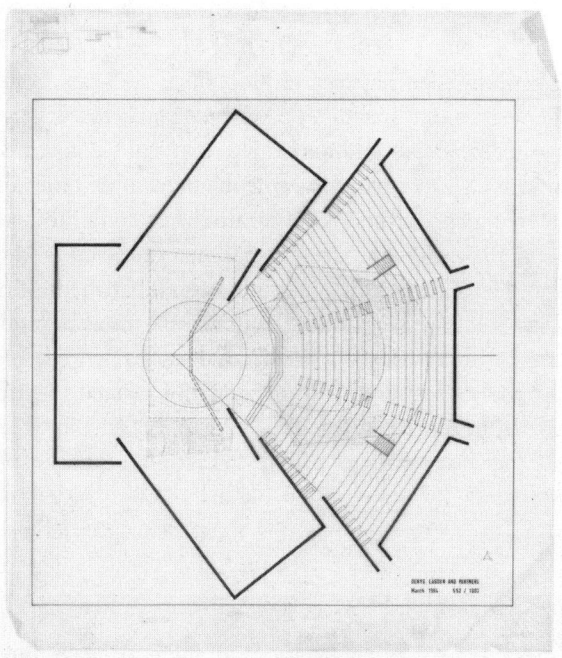

Scheme A for the open theatre

the great repertoire of plays written for proscenium theatres – almost everything between *The Tempest* and Brecht. Their search was for 'an open stage with full scenic capability'.[32] It was an ambitious goal.

The process began with Lasdun producing a comparatively conventional proposal to promote discussion: 'Scheme A'.[33] It was essentially a stripped-down proscenium theatre, without the actual proscenium arch that normally divides auditorium from stage. Its shape was derived primarily from sight-lines, and made for a slightly ungainly set of walls.

Based on the Committee's reaction to this design, within four months of his appointment Lasdun and his team had produced

Scheme B, a highly unconventional auditorium proposal which responded to the Committee's sense that the architect's first proposal still divided auditorium from stage. As Lasdun put it, 'if you really care about the unity of audience and actor, this means a room'.[34] Scheme B certainly provided a room – a single square space one quarter of which was given to a right-angled stage, surrounded on two sides in the other three quarters of the room by banks of seating. A balcony running round both auditorium and stage would have further heightened the architectural unity of the room. This initially met with considerable enthusiasm, though all including Lasdun wished to refine and develop it further. Brook thought 'the conception was generally excellent', though he worried that the right-angled stage would be challenging.[35] The great stage designer Jocelyn Herbert wrote to Lasdun the day after seeing the design:

Scheme B for the open theatre

I feel I must write and say how exciting and stimulating I thought your conception and model of the N. T. I am sure there are and will be problems, but finally they don't matter because they will all be based on thinking about the old theatre and not about your challenging new norm. I really do congratulate you on the first really creative new theatre design that I have seen.[36]

Things appeared to be on track, and knowing that there would need later to be much refinement of the stage design, Lasdun set to work producing an outline design for the entire National Theatre and Opera House complex in time to get it signed off in 1965 by the LCC.[37] The fundamental elements of auditoria, workshops, dressing rooms, offices and foyers were becoming clearer, so the first stages of aesthetic composition could begin, initially through placing blocks representing parts of the building in different dispositions on a model showing the context of the site proposed at that time, bounded by Hungerford Bridge and County Hall, the Thames and Howard Robertson's lumpen Shell Centre.[38] This exercise enabled Lasdun and his team to try out quickly a wide range of different relationships between the component parts of the complex, thinking about the functioning of the whole, but also seeking an overall massing which would have a good relationship to its surroundings, and produce exciting external spaces. From there they refined the design to a sort of wide valley of terraces, rising from a low central square shared between opera and theatre, up into the foyers of each building; these stacked terraces would be topped on each side by the large, simple cuboids of the fly towers.

In an architectural practice which he kept intentionally small – rarely over twenty architects, so that he could ensure personal supervision and keep the final veto on everything which emerged from the office – Lasdun had the unusual resource of a full-time in-house model-maker. This enabled him to design in three dimensions throughout, rather than in two-dimensional representations of 3D, which for all their strengths can end up colouring the design process. Lasdun recalled, 'My right-hand man has often been Philip Wood, the model-maker, and I don't use a scale, a ruler, I have, whatever model we're doing, a human being whose eyes are 5 foot 6 ½ from the ground, just a silhouette, and then move it around, and I look through that eye of the human being, and I find that gives me a very good guide.'[39] Lasdun felt his architecture 'doesn't lend itself easily to drawings. I have to have models, I even have to have models that you can take into the park and see the sun shining in one side through a window in order to try and establish what the light is.'[40] The National Theatre design process involved hundreds of models at widely varied scales from overall massing to 1:1 details.[41]

v

Yet whilst Lasdun was dropping everything to devote his full attention to getting the outline design finished in time, the Building Committee proved bizarrely uncomprehending of the urgent fact that the LCC was about to be disbanded, and with it might go the National Theatre building if the Council's funding for Lasdun's design had not been agreed by then. Both Olivier and Marshall were members of the South Bank Theatre Board and well aware of the rush, yet nowhere is there any record of their explaining to the Building Committee what Lasdun was up to and that there was a hurry.

To make things worse, the Building Committee also included members whose best interests were not necessarily served by a successful National Theatre: directors from the National's leading rivals, the RSC and the Royal Court. If Olivier had hoped to have the powerful figures of Peter Brook and Peter Hall inside the tent pissing out, it rapidly appeared that they might instead be inside the tent pissing everywhere. In February 1965, just as the National Theatre geared up to apply for funding for its magnificent facilities,

A heap of models used by the architects in the design process of the National Theatre

a troubling article appeared in the *Sunday Times*.[42] The article briefly set out auditorium design developments in Britain since the war, with sketch plans and outline details. It traced the ever bolder experimentation, with new ground being broken by the current design of the National's main stage, which, like the others, was illustrated by a sketch – the first time the design was ever shown publicly. The article went on to declare that, for all the innovation of the National Theatre, 'it is Peter Hall [in the RSC's proposed Barbican Theatre], however, who returns to the actor and *his* demands'. Peter Hall is mentioned repeatedly in the brief article, and he is quoted verbatim on the Barbican Theatre. The budgets of the various illustrated theatres are all given. Most are costed to the nearest £10,000 or £100,000, the National Theatre is given as roughly £2 million, and the Barbican, with suspicious precision, as £1,307,500. A memorandum in Lasdun's files accuses Hall of the leak, and reports Olivier as confirming that it was indeed Hall.[43]

Lasdun was utterly furious at the leak, which became one of the major reasons for his alienation from the rogue Building Committee. He petitioned to have Hall thrown off, and withdrew all the copies of designs for Scheme B that he had earlier given them. Lasdun clearly feared further leaks – he had been sufficiently concerned with managing the press campaign for the National Theatre that at one point he had had paper put up over a basement window to prevent press photographers snapping models through it.[44] But this was much worse than just an unauthorised preview of his design: as the National Theatre approached the delicate task of lobbying for funding, its opponents could claim that its building would be too expensive and already old-fashioned compared with Hall's proposed Barbican Theatre for the RSC.

Whilst Lasdun was busy lending his charismatic voice to the many months of attempts to get funding despite this damaging leak, the situation became even worse behind his back. In April 1966 the Building Committee decided that his withdrawal of the plans was a move to build Scheme B as it stood rather than continuing to develop it with them. Michael Elliott said that 'if Lasdun hesitates and doesn't produce something new, his reputation is at stake. If we are united, we can conquer him.' Peter Brook added, 'The point of a theatre is not how geometric the building is. Attack Lasdun – we've been the victims of a sort of confidence trick.' The transcript draws a veil over the remainder of the meeting, recording only that 'there followed more discussion on the best way of dealing with the architect'.[45] Given the vehemence of the attacks in the transcript, the mind boggles as to what they felt the need to censor.

It was a bizarrely long twenty-five days after this meeting that a shifty Olivier came to see Lasdun, for what the architect reported as 'a gentle icebreaking preparation for the fact that Scheme "B" now appears to have been unanimously rejected by the Buildings [sic] Committee who are speaking with one voice'.[46]

In the meantime, whilst the Building Committee and Lasdun struggled to try to come to an open stage design which would meet all the company's needs, the South Bank Theatre Board had decided that they would not be happy to risk a National Theatre which did not include a true proscenium theatre, and insisted on having one.[47] Proscenium theatres were thought to be well understood, and the Lyttelton was the subject of so little interest in Building Committee meetings that one of its members later referred to it as the 'any other business theatre'.[48] Lasdun did not attempt to bring them to pay more attention to it, presumably fearing another prolonged and row-blighted set of discussions without clear conclusions.

The contrast between the theatre's discussions and those of the opera could hardly be more pronounced. The Opera House briefing process was civilised and efficient, backed up by conversations between Lasdun and opera specialists including Benjamin Britten, who felt that 'people need a fairytale setting at the [opera] theatre and then to be told the truth. He did not think it beyond us to produce our own kind of fairytale. The theatres in Germany were, to him, like the buildings from which people had just come – offices.'[49] Informed by these discussions, Lasdun produced a highly attractive scheme for the main opera auditorium, which would probably have been a very effective opera house and would certainly have been a handsome and theatrical piece of architecture. It adopted a classic horseshoe shape, its sides composed entirely of staggered boxes which embraced the stalls and gave a muscular decorative pattern to the gracefully curving walls.[50]

Once the outline design took shape, a daunting task lay ahead in getting the greatly increased funds needed for the wonderful proposed facilities. By not contesting the original terms of reference (two shared auditoria for a budget of £2.3 million), the South Bank Theatre Board had ducked the question of how big and expensive the National Theatre and Opera House would end up. This had allowed the project to get under way, but at the cost of deferring until later the row about price and scale. In their confidential meetings and in the privacy of the architect's office, Lasdun and his clients had worked together on an ideal scheme which now consisted of two opera auditoria, one of them large, the other small and experimental; two large drama theatres, one of them open stage, the other proscenium; and a smaller experimental drama theatre. These five auditoria would be supported by extensive dressing rooms, foyers, production facilities and offices to allow the very best productions at all scales.

The massively increased scale and budget could no longer be disguised: £14.5 million.[51] In the prolonged back-room political bartering and lobbying, Lasdun's magnificent model travelled round Parliament and was shown to the press and public to rally support, and Lasdun himself had numerous meetings, lunches, informal chats and so on with anyone who might be able to lend useful backing, public or private.

Despite all the efforts of Lasdun and the other energetic advocates of the scheme, in March 1966 the Treasury decided against the

The model of the unbuilt 1965 scheme for the National Theatre (right) and Opera House (left)

Opera House. They offered instead only half of the cost of the theatre alone, to a maximum of £3.75 million. The GLC (Greater London Council), which was turning out despite the earlier uncertainty to be as robust a supporter of the arts as its predecessor the LCC, contemplated shouldering nearly £11 million, the rest of the entire cost; however, when the government warned that it would permit no increase in the Arts Council's support for the running costs of the opera company in its present home at Sadler's Wells, the threat of a substantial ongoing subsidy commitment scared the GLC out of its prospective generosity.[52] Though officially the Opera House was only postponed, no one thought it would actually happen now.

Without the Opera House, the battle was to get the surviving National Theatre scheme under way. As Callaghan advised Lasdun, any overspend could then be begged for as it arose. To get the go-ahead, Lasdun had somehow to squeeze the project until contractors would agree to build it within the £7.5 million budget cap. He and his team made every possible saving on the scheme – from building the restaurant and experimental theatre as unequipped empty shells right down to leaving the water pipes unlagged.[53] At this point the chair of the South Bank Theatre Board, Lord Cottesloe, showed that his loyalty was exclusively to the theatre, and that he would be willing to sacrifice the architect's reputation to that cause. He attempted to bounce Lasdun into allowing a budget limit for the entire building and equipping project to be written into the architects' contract.[54] This would have been unusual, and in the case of construction works on this scale utterly outrageous, the more so since no allowance was to be made for inflation. Lasdun's reputation for financial control would have been ruined, and he might even have been held legally liable for unavoidable overspending. Everyone involved knew that the trick spelled out by Callaghan was being played, and Cottesloe's attempt to get Lasdun to take full blame for the effects of a prolonged and shared tactical budget fudge seems harshly cynical.

Lasdun could on occasion be intransigent in his dealings over the National Theatre, but with Cottesloe applying pressure, and Olivier's Building Committee savaging him personally as well as the design they had worked on together, it is hardly surprising that he squared his jaw and prepared to fight. He even discussed with his colleagues in Denys Lasdun & Partners the possibility of abandoning the job altogether.[55]

With the government expressing its refusal of funding to the opera as 'a postponement' it looked for a while as if the National Theatre might be built alone with an empty site next to it vulnerable to any later development – a prospect Lasdun was very unhappy about. The GLC, supportive as ever, rescued the situation by offering to exchange the site of the 1965 scheme for the land the building now occupies.[56] This enabled Lasdun to tie it visually to Waterloo Bridge by use of concrete similar in colour to the bridge's Portland stone,

A CONCRETE VIOLIN

Olivier doing a better job than Lasdun at acting cordially at a press conference

and by echoing its railings. Waterloo Bridge was constructed in wartime using temporary utilitarian railings that have never been replaced by the originally intended ornamental ones, with the happy result that the National Theatre was able to echo the tough industrial look of the long-lasting stopgap rails. The two structures were now also connected physically by a walkway a floor below the height of the bridge. Without the pairing of National Theatre and Opera House flowing together in cascading terraces, some of the architectural richness of the 1965 scheme was gone. In response, Lasdun and his team instead worked up the National Theatre design into a more complex and sophisticated composition on its own. They brought some vertical elements of the building forward, making them more prominent than they had been in the 1965 scheme, allowing lift shafts and service ducts to emerge as faceted masses up the exterior, sometimes cut by parapets, sometimes free-standing, and sometimes in front of the parapet.

Lasdun also needed to come to a final design for the open stage theatre. After the explosive rows of the previous months, Lasdun brought the Building Committee back to a more constructive attitude by proposing in May 1966 Scheme C, which was essentially a deliberate step back to something more traditional. It had its intended effect of reminding the Building Committee that there was much they had liked about Scheme B, at which point Lasdun admitted that Scheme C had been 'a gesture to show you we were not taking up an entrenched position, but we can never be philosophically behind the new model'.[57] Instead Peter Brook suggested that the Building Committee appoint a reconstituted mini-Building Committee to work more closely and faster with Lasdun:

> Out of Scheme B could come a most exciting theatre that might not accommodate the plays you want to do. Out of the new model [Scheme C] would come the conventional. The third possibility is that the National Theatre people now lock themselves up with models and the Architects and search for another solution.[58]

Olivier opposed the idea of a smaller committee, with his usual nervous anxiety in the face of taking personal responsibility for decision-making, but Brook pushed hard and carried the committee as a whole.[59] Lasdun now worked closely with only three directors (including Olivier and Hall), the stage designer Jocelyn Herbert and the National's General Manager, to finalise the design. With such an intimate committee rapid progress was made on general principles and then on specifics.[60]

The theatre design which this smaller committee achieved, the Olivier Theatre, was something new: it succeeded in uniting the embracing unity of the open stage with scenic capabilities even greater than those of a proscenium theatre.[61] To get large-scale

A CONCRETE VIOLIN

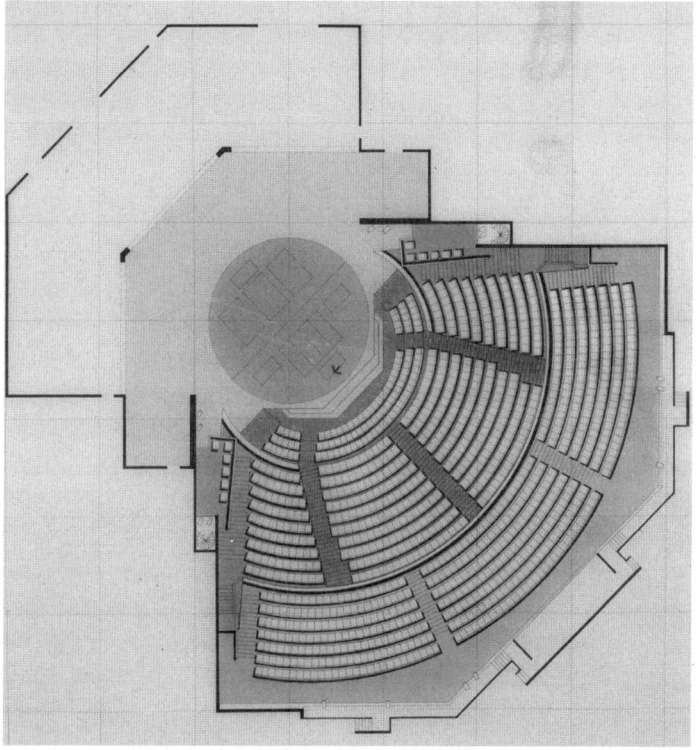

The open stage largely as built

scenery on to the stage it was to be placed on a prodigious rising and falling rotating stage, reaching far below the theatre level down an immense concrete shaft. The two halves of this revolve would be able to rise and fall independently and swap plain stage floor for huge structures of scenery – potentially one of the most dramatic spectacles available to any director in history, as my childhood memories of *Wind in the Willows* confirm.

Meanwhile for smaller scenery and props the Olivier Theatre was to be provided with a vast fly tower with up-to-the-minute computerised flying which could place any object precisely on any part of the sixty-foot stage. Yet if these remarkably bold steps were finally to resolve the prolonged discussion over the auditorium and stage shape, they were only the start of another challenging process: making the National Theatre buildable. As the clients and architects neared an agreed design the number and size of teams working on the project started to rise: structural engineers to work out how the shapes designed by the architects could most economically be achieved, more architects to draw up detailed drawings for the contractors to work from, mechanical engineers to work out the wiring, ventilation and so on, quantity surveyors to estimate costings, draw up contract documents, and hold the ring between client, architect and builders as arguments over budgets inevitably intensified.

Each of these specialist teams worked as fast as it could, rushing their latest work round to the next team that needed to work on it, so that the project could keep advancing as quickly as possible towards the tendering stage, where several firms of contractors would look at the design and offer the price they would be prepared to build it for. The headlong rush of 1968–69 to get to tender was given particular urgency by the fact that the budget was fixed definitively at £7.5 million: at least one tender needed to come in within that budget or the scheme would be cancelled. Each month that went by, inflation made that sum more inadequate and brought the National Theatre project nearer to disaster.

vi

Before the contractors could estimate what the project would cost them, consultant engineers needed to work out how the architects' designs could actually be structured and built. The firm chosen, Flint & Neill, were (and are) specialist civil engineers for such things as demanding bridge projects, but the National Theatre was to prove at least as tricky as any more conspicuously daring structure. The specifics of the job threw up a range of structural problems which the engineers took pride and pleasure in solving.

The difficulties would start from the very outset of the project: the National Theatre was to be erected on bad building land. Normally a structure this large and complex in its engineering would land on piles – deep posts driven or drilled into the ground to pin it immovably to the earth. Yet here the terrain was spotted with industrial remains. The huge hole needed for the Olivier drum revolve, for example, landed on a vast lump of concrete which had once supported a high tower through which molten lead was dropped, to cool into solid gunshot pellets as it fell. To save the immense cost of clearing this and other industrial foundations, they cut the Gordian knot and decided not to use piling at all for the National Theatre. Instead it stands on a series of concrete rafts, effectively floating above the industrial remains, on the soft, wet earth of the riverside. At the meeting points of the six separate rafts, wide joints run the height of the building to allow space for the outer parts to lean inwards as the dressing-room block at the centre – heavy because of its many floors – slowly sinks.[62]

As if the mix of soft riverside subsoil and surviving industrial foundations were not problem enough, the proximity to the river and the scale of the holes required for the Olivier's drum revolve and subterranean parking meant that much of the building would be beneath the level of the nearby Thames and therefore subject to tremendous water pressure. Valves were built into the basement to allow it to flood should the groundwater rise dangerously, rather than risk the walls crushing under the pressure and making the building collapse. Only the most critical parts of the substructure were built to sufficient strength to keep out flooding.[63]

Even greater challenges would await the contractors as they embarked on building the upper parts of the National Theatre. Although it looks a picture of robust solidity, the auditoria and stages need huge uninterrupted internal spaces that were always going to be tough to engineer. The biggest stage, the Olivier, requires an immense void beneath it for the drum revolve, and another above it for the huge, heavy fly tower, yet because the front of the stage is surrounded on three sides by audience there could not be columns interrupting their view.[64] The engineers worked out a structure for the Olivier's fly tower requiring it to be supported during construction on two enormous temporary concrete columns which would be demolished after the structure was complete.[65] Once these were removed, the front of the tower would hang from the back of the tower, like the overhanging top of a periscope, but in hundreds of tons of concrete, steel and scenery-flying equipment. To hold such an ambitious overhang in place the engineers specified that the reinforcing steel should be post-tensioned: steel cables would be cast into the concrete as usual, but once the concrete had set, the cables would be pulled very tight so that they strained hard against it.[66] Normally, the steel only starts to stretch and take the weight once tiny cracks have developed in the concrete. For most structures that works fine. Post-tensioned concrete is more difficult and therefore more expensive to construct, but holds the concrete together to avoid these cracks and prevent any sagging or weakness developing where special strength is required.

The design of the steel reinforcement in the fly towers and other key parts of the National Theatre's concrete was going to be highly complex, and the engineers were proud to boast that the locations and quantity of reinforcement bars had been calculated with the aid of computers – an early example of the forthcoming revolution in engineering.[67] Where normally contractors would determine the final positions of reinforcement along lines agreed with the engineers, in this case the engineers themselves decided that they could increase the overall speed and accuracy of the process by specifying every bit of the post-tensioned reinforcement. It would simply be too complex for even the best contractors.[68]

vii

It was only in this final sprint, 1968–69, that the all-important exposed in situ concrete was determined upon by the architects. Given how central a feature of the finished building the board-marked concrete is, it seems shocking that it should only have been chosen as the design was finalised.

Lasdun had consistently reserved an adequate sum of money for the finishes throughout the budget-slashing exercise of 1965–67, advising the South Bank Board that 'his firm considered advice to the Council would be not to build at all rather than to accept a lower standard'.[69] He had not, however, discussed finishes with either the Board or the Building Committee. By his own account, Lasdun tended to hold back his views on finishes until the client committee were convinced of the virtue of the design of the outline model: 'Each member of the committee will be dressing that skeletal model up as he thinks it is going to look, some in stone with mouldings, others in steel and glass.'[70] Certainly he did not rush to clarify the use of concrete when he met the GLC in January 1968. He records in a memo a question which arose and his response to it:

> What would the external material of the building be?
> Non committal answer by DL.[71]

A memo of a phone call from Cottesloe to one of Lasdun's partners shows the extent of the confusion caused by Lasdun's earlier non-committal answer:

> [Cottesloe] understood you [Lasdun] to have said at the GLC that the building was to be faced in Portland stone. He would like to know the saving if this were reduced to bare concrete, though he fully realised that bare concrete was out of the question.[72]

Lasdun rang Cottesloe back later to say that

> at no time whatsoever have I ever said that the building would be in Portland stone finish, and they have no reason to assume that whatever. No further savings can be made.[73]

The last word came the following month at a meeting at the GLC where Lasdun was

> questioned from various quarters as to what further economies they could make as architects. This included talk about terraces, walkways etc. DL SAID NIL, AND THEY COULD TAKE AS CERTAIN THAT THE FINISH OF THE BUILDING WOULD NOW BE CONCRETE.[74]

One suspects that his voice in the meeting will have made it perfectly clear that he was speaking in capital letters.

Yet this defence of the budget for concrete, and of Lasdun's own right to determine the finish, did not mean that he had a fixed idea on what the concrete finishes would be. He had one of his young architects drive him round London looking at a range of concrete buildings to examine their finishes: Were they well made? Were they weathering well?[75] As late as 1968 Lasdun had considered precast concrete for at least parts of the National Theatre – it was his normal preferred exterior material, with its factory-made reliability reassuring the perfectionist architect that his building would not be embarrassingly rust-streaked and crumbly looking within years.[76] Yet at the National Theatre the contractors advised that precast would be no cheaper than in situ – the number of different shapes for such a complicated and unrepetitive building would mean that economies of scale would be minimal.[77]

By choosing in situ, however, Lasdun was not adopting Le Corbusier's pleasure in rough workmanship and the beauty of the

A CONCRETE VIOLIN

bodge. Rather, in the face of the harder-to-control process, Lasdun's standards increased in exigency rather than diminished, and concrete design, in which Lasdun's practice was so experienced, became a huge part of the next stage of the design: detailing.

Today's architects have computer programmes and sophisticated catalogues offering short cuts to many parts of building design. As recently as the late 1960s, most details of most buildings were designed with pencil and paper by the architects, and made especially for the individual project. Lasdun's team had a great deal of work to do, under time pressure as prices rose continuously against their fixed budget: designing how materials would connect, what finishes would be used where, and how the building would be fitted out. This detailing stage included the tedious labour of producing measured drawings of endless unglamorous but necessary minutiae for offices, lavatories and workshops, but also included the much more aesthetically significant questions of concrete finish, glazing, metalwork, and lighting in front of house and auditoria. Large-scale models were used to test the designs of key elements including glazing, diagrid ceilings, metal balustrades, the Olivier ceiling, and the concrete panels which flank the Lyttelton auditorium.[78] A note between two of Lasdun's colleagues shows the attractively fanatical attention given to one small detail, how the railings would be fixed to the concrete parapets:

> Dave King spent a couple of days on these [railings] this week and I hope that Philip [Wood, Lasdun's in-house model maker] will now add a section to his large scale model. Having done some smaller scale drawings, I came to the conclusion that, contrary to what we had previously thought, the pads were better when lining up with the vertical slot, but the model will tell.[79]

viii

As soon as the design was advanced enough, it was put out to tender in spring 1969, but despite the crushing labour of cutting in the previous years, none came in low enough. It took further discussion and negotiation to obtain from Sir Robert McAlpine and Sons a deal that was acceptable both to them as contractors and to the funders, and by the winter of 1969 the work was under way. In a splendidly 1960s counterpart to the laying of a foundation stone, on 3 November 1969 a ceremonial concrete-pouring was held.[80]

The construction process was to prove anything but straightforward. It was always going to be a big and difficult project to build such a large, complicated, heavily engineered building, with unusual and specialised stage equipment, and a range of uses and components from light-industrial scenery workshops through to the foyers with their grand public architecture and exceptional concrete quality. The intrinsic difficulties of the project were, however, to be massively aggravated by the circumstances of the 1970s. With the oil crisis, wild inflation, labour shortages and industrial disputes, there had been no time since the 1940s when it was so difficult to put up a building.

The haste to get it under way meant that the construction process was split into two parts, and McAlpine's started to dig and to build the underground areas even before the design for the superstructure was complete. As they began work in 1969, the hope was that the theatre would host its first productions in 1972. Despite the challenges of the groundworks, the project made fairly good progress, and it was still hoped in 1971 that 'topping out' (the completion of the concrete work) would be possible by summer 1972, with a public opening in 1973.[81] Later in 1971, however, work started to fall seriously behind: the first strikes and shortages that were to plague construction in the 1970s were beginning to bite.

The 1960s property boom came to its greatest climax in the early 1970s with hundreds of substantial building projects in progress at once in London. At times there was simply not enough skilled building labour to go round, holding up work on the National Theatre. Lasdun's office reported that 'there was a national shortage of electricians in 1973' – a particular problem for this project given that 'there are over 200 miles of wire in the fly towers alone'.[82] Max Rayne, the new chairman of the South Bank Board from 1971, looked closely at the building process with his property developer's eye, and felt that the situation could be improved by the contractors. He wrote to Sir Edwin McAlpine in 1974 with elegant forcefulness, to say that in his view too many of the available electricians were being used for two major commercial McAlpine projects, including the Brent Cross shopping centre by another property developer, Hammerson:

> Knowing how deeply aware you are of the great importance attaching to accelerating completion of the new National Theatre, I felt sure you would wish to have your attention drawn to this situation and I know we may count on you to take such action as you can to remedy the matter.[83]

The labour shortage gave greater power to skilled workers and their trade unions, and the increasingly volatile political atmosphere of the 1970s led to strike after strike. The National Theatre was an attractively high-profile target for recurrent industrial action, and costs and delays piled on top of each other.

In 1973 Max Rayne began to send a representative along to all site meetings, but the next crisis a month later was far beyond his power to resolve: OPEC quadrupled the price of oil, and Britain's coal miners went on strike.[84] The massive energy demands of a construction project like the National Theatre became ruinously costly, and inflation shot up to remain consistently over 20 per cent. The agreed budget became ever more ludicrously inadequate to the fast-changing conditions, yet each agonising appeal to the Treasury for more money threw another 'spanner in the works', as an exasperated Lasdun recorded.[85]

The architects put huge pressure on the contractors to keep up the quality. In a phone call to McAlpine's:

> DL said that he had visited the site yesterday and had found the conditions on site intolerable and totally out of control, with steel all over the place lying on top of concrete.
>
> DL continued that supervision was slacking off and the standard of concrete was deteriorating and is unacceptable. That this [. . .] has got to change forthwith.
>
> DL continued that there is no supervision and no concrete engineer. This probably was due to the strike but was the responsibility of McAlpine.
>
> [The McAlpine representative] accepted the strafing, has already replaced the concrete engineer and will rectify the attitude.[86]

It is hard to believe, looking at the finished building, that the construction process was vexed by such endless difficulties; it is a Rolls-Royce of a concrete structure, magnificent in the ambition of its engineering and the elegance of its construction craft. The quality of the National Theatre's concrete began in the architects' office, with a carefully written specification to set out its ingredients and how it should be textured, focusing in particular on the clarity of the imprint of the wood shuttering and on the intended longevity of the building. Reinforcement near the surface was to be buried more deeply than was normally the case, and unusually it was to be galvanised to ensure that rust streaks would not escape – normally the roughness of the surface rust was used to bond the concrete firmly to the steel.[87] The amount of reinforcement used was increased to allow for possible weaker bonding, and to allow for an unusual concrete mix chosen because it was closer in colour to the

Portland stone cladding of Waterloo Bridge. The specific concrete mix and galvanised reinforcement were then subjected to testing to ensure that together they would be more than strong enough.[88]

As for the wood texture, Douglas fir was chosen for its straight, strong grain, and its resistance to distortion. The wooden planks used in the formwork were to be sawn to different thicknesses to heighten the visibility of individual boards and strengthen the texture when seen from a distance.[89] Each board was only to be used twice, as cement would otherwise begin to lodge in the grain and reduce the clarity of its texture.

Demanding as it was, the written specification was only part of the process of ensuring a perfect concrete finish: the real test of the quality of the concrete was a sample panel cast by the contractors and kept as a benchmark against which to verify the standard of later work – a sort of built contract document.[90]

Concrete work occupied a curious position on the post-war building site. Unlike carpentry or bricklaying – long-standing trades with established norms, guilds and unions – the newcomer trade, concrete, often attracted unskilled and semi-skilled labour, and had, on the face of it, a low status on the British building site.[91] Yet despite its theoretical humility, in reality the concrete work was where the big risks were taken, and the most heroic action occurred. Concrete pourers worked closely with the carpenters who built the formwork for their pours.

In the basement areas, where the finish would not be seen by so many, the concrete shows signs of experimentation to find the best techniques. On one part of a staircase up from the car park, the shuttering was so rough that shreds of its wood tore off in strips and can still be seen sandwiched into the concrete surface. By the time they got up into the foyer levels, though, they seem to have found their form.

Each pour was a major event on the site: steelworkers would place the reinforcement bars according to the instructions of the

engineers. Then for days highly skilled carpenters, many of them Sikh immigrants who used the tools of their regional tradition rather than those familiar on English sites, would work on the formwork, joining together the wooden planks with their varied thicknesses and strong texture.[92] The boards could then be soaked with water, to make them swell so that they fitted more tightly together to keep the concrete from seeping out.[93]

The boards which would produce the markings had to be secured to the backing framework without too much in the way of visible fixings which would also print into the concrete, yet the whole formwork structure needed to be strong enough to hold the tons of liquid concrete which would be poured into them. The formwork also had to be precisely positioned to ensure that everywhere the steel reinforcement would be buried deep enough. The surface of the wooden moulds needed to be treated with a releasing oil which would allow the wood to come smoothly off the 'green' (fresh) concrete without tearing it, yet the oil needed to be thin enough not to mute the texture of the wood, and carefully chosen to come off the completed concrete without causing any discolouration.[94]

Once all this painstaking preparatory craft had been completed the concrete needed to be mixed to precisely the same colour as the rest, and poured with skill and care so that the same mix of gravel, sand, cement and water made it to the bottom of the pour as was found at the top, otherwise appearance or structural strength could be problematically variable. This was made much harder because within the tall, narrow voids in the formwork, into which the concrete was to be poured, the dense steel reinforcement could act like a sieve, catching the gravel, or alternatively pieces of heavy gravel could fall to the bottom first. Even once the concrete was in the formwork there were hazards. Air bubbles which naturally cling to the rough wood texture needed to be knocked loose by vibrating the wet concrete mechanically after it was poured but before it set, but not too vigorously: overvibrating concrete would shake the gravel to the bottom.

The contractors and site architects would wait anxiously for each large concrete pour to emerge from the shuttering, not knowing for sure as the wood was stripped off whether so many man-hours of work and waiting would have resulted in perfect concrete that could be kept, or whether any of the many semi-controllable threats to in situ concrete would have struck: air bubbles in the surface (known because of its cellular appearance as 'honeycombing'), prominent changes of colour, gaps between planks producing unwanted extrusions of concrete, or distortions in the wooden formwork from the weight of the wet concrete, resulting in bulging walls. Some entire pours needed to be demolished, wasting tons of concrete and steel, but also the wood of the formwork, and hundreds of hours of highly skilled labour. Minor surface imperfections were sometimes resolved on the quiet by an expert craft plasterer simulating in concrete the texture of wood-shuttering in the affected spots.[95]

The exterior concrete, which would be exposed to the weather and dirt of London, received particular attention. A waterproof cement was chosen to reduce deterioration over time.[96] The parapets of the terraces were post-tensioned like the fly towers to keep them from cracking, and special care was taken in pouring and curing their concrete, as the unusually large monolithic sections of concrete could easily crack if there were any mistakes. The chemical reaction of setting concrete generates a lot of heat, which can cause networks of small surface cracks – 'crazing'. To prevent these, the concrete throughout the building was 'cured' by being covered in hessian kept cool by regular hosing, reducing and evening the temperature of the setting concrete.

Concrete then shrinks slightly in the period after it is taken out of the formwork. To allow for this, the parapets and fly towers were poured in sixteen-foot-wide horizontal bands with gaps between sections. These first sections were given four weeks to set and shrink before the linking sections were poured, minimising shrinkage cracking.[97]

This level of expert craft paid dividends: the National Theatre's concrete work is exceptional in its lack of bubbles, the evenness of its colour and tone, the crispness of its corners, the rarity of cracking and crazing, and the clarity with which it expresses the wood grain of the shuttering and the divisions between planks. The rejection of boards after two uses has indeed kept the texture emphatic and fresh throughout. Some of those working on the site recollected that the carpenters would make furniture from the discarded boards.[98]

ix

After its prolonged design and construction, the National Theatre building opened in 1976 after seven years of building work, and cost £16 million – considerably more than the £7.5 million agreed in 1969, but vastly less than its famous contemporary the Sydney Opera House, which came in at £59 million, opening in 1973 after fourteen years under construction. Lasdun acknowledged that the National Theatre was over time and over budget, but pointed out that it was hardly surprising: it was a 'development project' comparable in his view to a nuclear power station, or to the great experimental ship of the 1960s, the *QE2*.[99]

The longest delays, in fact, were some way from the architect's office. They arose from specialist subcontractors for the equipping of the theatres. Some of these had tendered too low for the prestigious National Theatre work, and then were only able to meet their contractual obligations by subsidising the inflation-stricken cost of the project through taking on other contracts, which in turn slowed them down. Much of their work on the National Theatre needed to be done in a particular sequence, so the overrun of one struggling subcontractor would mess up the planning of the next one down the line. The scale of the stage-equipment project was unprecedented, and new problems were encountered by firms which had never attempted anything like it.[100] The situation for the builders became even more challenging once Peter Hall, from 1973 director of the National Theatre in succession to Olivier, moved the company into the incomplete building. He did it for good reasons – the much larger company of actors that the new building would accommodate had already been hired and were costing a great deal extra, and they were becoming demoralised – but once the theatres were active in the day and evening the contractors could only finish the job at night, rushing on to the stage to start work almost as the audience left, and having to take the time to leave things safe and useable for actors each day.[101] It was a spectacularly messy and difficult end to a very challenging project, but by 1976 the Lyttelton Theatre was ready to open, and the other theatres joined it in receiving audiences soon afterwards. At last the thirteen years' hard work on the National Theatre's design and construction was nearing an end and it was open to the public.

After such an epic gestation, the National Theatre was inaugurated at precisely the wrong moment for its architectural style. The architectural world of the 1970s was dividing into vociferously opposed camps. The advocates of High Tech thought that buildings ought to be ultra-flexible, lightweight, tent-like structures which could be easily modified to meet the changing needs of their users. The rising Postmodernists disagreed, and thought that architecture should re-engage the public through returning to historical motifs, and adding bright colours that people would recognise and feel more comfortable with, all undercut with humour – sometimes somewhat sneering – for the architecturally sophisticated. The National Theatre, heavily inflexible in its beautiful concrete, and supremely abstract and serious in its shape, was the perfect Aunt Sally for both camps.

After an ambivalent initial reception, Lasdun's careful masterpiece and his main focus for thirteen years descended by the 1980s to one of the most prominent hate-objects in Britain. In 1989 it was voted 'the runaway winner as worst building in the country' in a poll of *Observer* readers.[102] Lasdun endured years when people would spontaneously abuse it to him, not knowing he was its architect. His son James reports an occasion when a taxi driver took Lasdun a different route than usual in order, so the driver said, not to have to see the National Theatre.[103]

Actors, too, piled in to attack it:

> When [Richard] Eyre suggested to [Albert] Finney that architects now realised that they should provide in their design of theatres an instrument on which the actor could play Finney looked round, paused and growled to Eyre "yes, and who would make a violin out of fucking concrete?"'[104]

How could one not be heartbroken by such hostility? Lasdun had not only worked very, very hard over many years with his team to get the National Theatre designed, funded and built, he had also made considerable sacrifices of money and career structure in its interests, taking on no new work at all from the end of 1963 when he got the job right through to 1968. This career gap lost him potential fees, of course, but it also cost him the continuity of new-project design effort which is what keeps architects flexible and up to date in stylistic terms.

Again and again, critics of Lasdun's work and other Brutalist buildings came back to their hostility to its concrete – it was ugly, grey and cheap; it weathered badly; it was OK for sunny, dry countries but bad in Britain . . . *Observer* readers took up the long tradition of insulting buildings through unflattering comparison: it 'looks like a prison', 'looks like a warehouse for tinned food', 'is it a theatre or a high security prison?', 'a German gun emplacement near Boulogne looks better', 'pretentious, platonically inhuman, sterile, dark and ominous mass'.[105]

Leading the charge of 1980s 'common sense' responses to Brutalism came the Prince of Wales, who wondered whether the National

Theatre was 'a clever way of building a nuclear power station in the middle of London without anyone objecting'.[106] There is something curiously satisfying about the fact that Lasdun should earlier have foreshadowed this attack by pointing out that the National Theatre had some of the complexity and innovativeness of a nuclear power station.

The National Theatre took up more of Lasdun's effort than any of his other projects, and absorbed the greatest share of his attention throughout the years of the height of his international acclaim. For it he turned down numerous prestigious jobs including a US airport terminal and a British embassy, and in return he suffered excoriating attacks on his architecture.

In these terrible years, Lasdun carried with him a piece of paper containing

> a quote from Edmund Burke, which sort of protects me from the onslaughts, and he said 'Those who carry on great public schemes must be proof against the worst delays, the most mortifying disappointments, the most shocking insults, and what is worst of all the presumptuous judgements of the ignorant upon their design.'[107]

Yet the worst moment of all was in the 1990s, when Lasdun was beginning once again to be recognised as a great architect: the management of the National Theatre proposed heavy-handed changes to the building. Through some sad sequence of miscommunications, and amidst deteriorating relations between Lasdun and the theatre, the proposals ended up being very damaging for his conception of the building. The new architects wanted to demolish one of the terraces, to build under another, and to mess with the interiors.[108] Lasdun summoned all his resources to fight the changes, and after an acrimonious public dispute the worst of them were cancelled, though an unsympathetic bookshop addition and very ill-judged signage were to afflict the building until 2014–15 when both were removed.[109]

The campaign against the 1990s alterations brought out many vociferous supporters of Lasdun's architecture, but even at its lowest moments in the 1970s and '80s the National Theatre had its real admirers. Unsurprisingly Jørn Utzon and other Modernist architects expressed their warm admiration for Lasdun's achievement.[110] The National Theatre has always held a particular appeal for another class of serious architectural commentator: the great architectural historians John Summerson and Mark Girouard, and perhaps most surprisingly the founder of the anti-Modernist 'Nooks and Corners' column in *Private Eye*, John Betjeman, who praised it to the skies:

> I was in a taxi with Osbert Lancaster last week on my way to the City from County Hall. It was a fine crisp morning, blue sky and a little mist about. As our cab crawled out of that hell hole they have dug in front of Waterloo Bridge, I gasped with delight at the cube of your theatre in the pale blue sky and a glimpse of St Paul's to the south of it. It is a lovely work and so good *outside*, which is what matters most. Osbert pointed out how shoddy it makes that dreary Hayward Gallery look. Your theatre looks good from so many angles, that I think it will survive even horrific chests of open drawers or whatever slabs they put up south of it. It has that inevitable and finished look great work does.[111]

Yet it was the comments from members of the non-specialist public that Lasdun seems to have received with the greatest gratitude and pleasure. One visitor wrote to him that 'there was a most refreshing sense of space in the foyers, and we did like the texture of the concrete and the satiny finish of the stainless steel'.[112] Lasdun's reply thanked the writer for 'the kind of letter which makes it all worthwhile'.[113]

X

Lasdun's National Theatre is perhaps the highest achievement of a decade in which practical understanding of exposed concrete work on building sites reached a level comparable with understanding of stone in the great ages of architectural masonry. No wonder that Lasdun resented profoundly the implications of thuggishness and crudity in the term 'Brutalist'.[114]

Where the auditorium designs were a team project between the architects and the clients, the rest of the architecture was, love it or hate it, the achievement of Lasdun and his architects. The obsessive attention given by the Building Committee to the Olivier stage and auditorium had freed the architects to design the rest of the building with remarkably little intervention. Almost none of the ample discussion from which the National Theatre building emerged touched on the foyer designs and exteriors. Here Lasdun and his team appear to have had nearly total artistic freedom, with no one even commenting on the designs as they developed. Both the unbuilt National Theatre and Opera House scheme of 1965 and the 1967 National Theatre design that was built were first shown to clients, funders and the public as faits accomplis. There were technical and financial discussions about catering facilities, but almost nothing at all about the architectural expression.

This was partly a peculiarity of the process – the various factions of the South Bank Theatre Board and Building Committee were locked in such absorbing conflict with each other that, like Moriarty and Holmes on the lip of the Reichenbach Falls, they were blinded to bigger issues. However, it was also surprisingly representative of the great buildings of the period.

Lasdun's view of the creative process had a characteristically Modernist clarity: the first stage was to talk to the clients until he really felt he understood their needs, in practical detail and in less definable terms to do with the flavour and spirit of the institution for which he was building. Once this stage was complete, and an outline model had been agreed by the clients as meeting their needs, Lasdun asserted his right to shut the client out of the architectural design of the building. One can see Lasdun defending the right to control the materials and appearance of the National Theatre right through. For example, when Olivier raised the question of finishes in the auditorium:

> How can we get the atmosphere of an old theatre in a new one? Plaster and wood is better for voice. Acoustically, the theatre at Antwerp, which has plaster and wood, is best for me.

This comes too close to affecting the aesthetic, so Lasdun jumps on it:

> 'Engaged intensity' is the central thing. We cannot duplicate the furbishings of an old theatre except by pastiche. We have looked at the Lincoln Center and Loeb [Drama Center, Harvard]. They are adaptable but they lack the operative intensity.[115]

Perhaps the feeling that non-architects had of being excluded from the discussion of aesthetics intensified the eventual backlash against Brutalism. If architects would not allow clients and the public to discuss the architecture in shared terms, then as the fashion turned against Brutalism people would find their own vocabulary to discuss it: concrete monstrosity, concrete jungle, ugly, oppressive . . .

Was there any justice in the wave of hostility to the National Theatre? Was it a fair accusation that, by not discussing his aesthetic decisions with the clients, Lasdun was freeing himself to indulge at public expense in esoteric architectural art for his own pleasure and that of a small group of like-minded aesthetes? Emphatically no. Having defended his own aesthetic autonomy, Lasdun used it not to produce something highly personal, but to draw a carefully judged depiction of his clients, as at Christ's College New Court. His use of concrete at the National Theatre – the glory of the building for its admirers, and its greatest flaw for its detractors – fits the same pattern. The concrete is discreetly a very high-quality material, yet you have to really look at it to notice that.

In the inconspicuousness of its luxury, the National Theatre's concrete echoes with striking fidelity the curious political consensus which had given it hope of life three decades before it opened. Just as the backers of the theatre ranged from the formality, elitism and traditionalism of Lyttelton to the egalitarian socialism of Hayward, so the building holds in simultaneous existence both high and low registers. Lyttelton's sense of a palace to maintain the highest traditions of the elite arts is reflected especially in the axis of symmetry which governs the Olivier Theatre and its foyers. This is reminiscent of the great Baroque theatres – Classical, formal and dignified. Stairs up through the foyers are symmetrically paired around the axis like the stairs at the Opéra Garnier in Paris, as are the terraces and monumentally simple lift towers, with the fly tower's faceted face showing on the outside the location and orientation of the stage. The staircase at the very front of the building juts out as a prow, forming an appropriately monumental entry point to the processional route that follows the axis right up to the auditorium. This planning derives from the high Beaux-Arts classicism in which Lasdun was trained as a student at the Architectural Association in the early 1930s, though he had long left behind the Classical columns and stone claddings he learned there.

This grandeur and formality is not the only mood of the National Theatre, though, just as Lyttelton was not its only backer. If, rather than going up to the Olivier, you turn right into the Lyttelton Theatre's ground-floor foyer, you come into a much less formal space, aimed at passers-by, and the young or poor who would turn up early to get cheap last-minute tickets from the original box office in the corner.[116] There was an area casually marked out by a change in floor surface (not a divisive step or stage) for musicians or performers to entertain audiences for free. Here you are enjoying the cool, free-for-all event space favoured by the avant-garde theatre world of the 1960s.

There are no processional routes or symmetrical axes. Very large floor areas with comparatively low ceilings reverse the pomp of older public buildings where height is used to impose formality. When the space opens up vertically it does so by irregular cut-aways in the decks, so that the resultant high area, whilst stunningly impressive, has the informal sublimity of a cave system rather than the grandiosity of a ballroom.

A café above overlooks it all, but mostly there is abundant unprogrammed space for theatregoers to mill around, passers-by to drop in and listen to music or have a sit-down, temporary exhibitions to be mounted, informal performances to be put on, or any other function people might choose for what amounted to free, warm, indoor space. As a teenager without much cash I was one of countless beneficiaries, over the decades, of a place where I could read for hours, wait for or talk to friends, or just watch the world go by without having to buy and force down pints of tea or coffee, or resist the increasingly indignant table-wiping and 'Can I get you anything else?' of harassed café staff.

It is currently seen as a difficulty by managements of many Brutalist buildings that it is impossible to divide up the public space into lettable chunks for corporate jollies and the like, but this is in fact their whole glory. Isaac Hayward and his successors contributed extensively to the provision on the South Bank of a series of facilities in which high culture could be demystified for a wider audience firstly by the provision of ample indoor and outdoor public space for eating and drinking, pottering, people-watching, sunbathing, rain-dodging, chatting and reading. At the Southbank Centre the architecture has, so far, won out against what often seems like hostility from its management, with the thriving skate park beneath and the rather lovely community garden on the roof.

The Royal Festival Hall has taken a more corporate route with its superabundance of chain restaurants and cafés. Together, though, all these facilities have provided a critical mass which has made the South Bank one of the liveliest and most popular strolling places in the world. Hayward's LCC wanted a South Bank that would represent the best of city life in one of the world's great capitals, and now, as the remaining Welfare State provision comes under yet more pressure, that is what it has achieved. For all its neo-liberal hot-dog stands, the massive success of the South Bank is a lasting memorial to the vision and courage of the London County Council.

The National Theatre is Lasdun's masterpiece. It manages simultaneously to represent national prestige and institutional grandeur, to be a cool, approachable venue for informal events and casual use, and above all to be a breathtakingly fine piece of abstract architecture and concrete craft.

Thank goodness he was successful in fighting off the worst changes, and now more sympathetic architects have reinstated a new version of the original beautiful signage, and have stripped out the worst of the 1990s changes. The National Theatre management is at last aware of what a superb building it has, and is celebrating its architecture. Lasdun did not live to see the rising fortunes of the building, and it has still not reached the high public admiration that it certainly will, just as it took many decades for the Houses of Parliament to go from near-universal hatred to their current untouchably venerated status.

I find myself returning to the National Theatre with almost neurotic repetitiveness. One of my favourite places in the building is the uppermost level of the Olivier foyers, the highest public floor in the theatre. From there you can still appreciate one of Lasdun's carefully considered architectural effects. The heavy concrete 'diagrid' – coffered roof slab – seems almost to crush one under its low height and obvious heaviness. Looking out from within, the shining white stone of Somerset House, across the river, is sandwiched tightly between the parapet of Lasdun's terrace and his concrete overhang above; the perspective effect makes Somerset House look much closer. Suddenly, rather than being one detail of a wide vista, the National Theatre frames the eighteenth-century facade as a magnificent spectacle for theatregoers. It is a technique Lasdun probably learned in architecture school, and applied with genius in the National Theatre. At present the views out are almost all lost to the absurd forest along the riverfront. If one day the trees are thinned out, the National Theatre foyers will return to their full magnificent power, and the building's careful composition will be clearly visible again from over the Thames.

The early feeling I had that the National Theatre gave me the same sort of pleasure as Hawksmoor's churches turned out not to be

coincidence: Lasdun had admired Hawksmoor from his student days on.[117] I suspect Lasdun's work, especially the National Theatre, will always have something of Hawksmoor's tendency to attract fierce admiration from many, and to frighten others. Peter Ackroyd's creepy thriller *Hawksmoor* would hardly have worked with a less gutsy architect – Wren or Nash – and similarly Lasdun will always intimidate some. Yet for me there is little to touch it. I have taken my baby daughter there more often than to any other building in London, and any time that pleasure or business brings me near it my eyes keep returning to the building. Mark Girouard said that it is 'a smoulderer rather than a fizzer', and it smoulders in me like the charcoal in a kiln.[118] It is my gold standard of concrete work, and its magnificent blend of complexity and simplicity is the base-point against which I measure all other large buildings. Yet still throughout the years it somehow retains its mystery for me. I get a buzz of fresh pleasure on every visit, and find new things to notice and admire.

Lasdun suffered terribly to make the National Theatre a reality, yet his decades of strain and worry left something truly worthwhile. For as long as it stands the National Theatre will carry the unmistakable imprint of his solemn thoroughness, and the spirit-lifting force of his visual creativity.

Epilogue

Destruction and Preservation

(barnabascalder.org/rce/)

i

Loving Brutalist architecture brings its sufferings as well as its joys. The demolition of beautiful buildings upsets me deeply. When the Paisley Civic Centre was being partially demolished in 2010, I climbed under the fence to steal the biggest chunk of its concrete that I could find and carry off. The architecture of this local government office block was a tribute to the great American Brutalist Paul Rudolph, emulating his hand-smashed concrete ribs. I was horrified at the sight of so much craft and labour going to waste, and was comforted to find a reasonably intact piece lying amidst the rubble. I love my fragment of the lost building. When I was getting ready to leave Glasgow I told the movers it was a fragile ornament, hoping they might mistake it for a sculpture or a fossil, and treat it with appropriate care. The man who packed it wrapped it well, but his label on the box was clear enough: 'lump o' concrete'. When I explained what it was he crossed out his label and wrote instead: 'precious relic of car park'.

My precious relic of council offices is not my only Brutalist *furtum sacrum*: I have some flakes of smooth render which fell off the Strathclyde Architecture Building and were kept for me by a former student, and a larger fragment of rough render which had broken from a hauntingly ruined 1960s Catholic seminary at Cardross, near Glasgow. I also have more standard objects of devotion. I wrote much of this book sitting in a Harry Bertoia Diamond Chair which used to belong to the architect of the Tricorn Centre, Rodney Gordon. Other parts were written in a tatty Eames chair which Ernö Goldfinger's assistant John Winter had used for decades as a piano stool in his beautiful rusty-steel house in Highgate.

Until I can get back to living in a concrete building, these household gods are my daily contact with the architecture I love. The hoots of derision which once greeted my veneration of such things are rarer now; the worst days of hostility to Brutalism are past. After more than a decade of pariah status, from the 1990s the architectural world started gradually to rediscover the best 1950s and '60s architecture. Many of these early admirers were drawn to it by the social project so much of it served. Others found themselves excited by the solidity and legibility of its materials, which appeared strikingly exotic and intellectually pure by contrast with the inelegant laminate of insulating fuzz, plastic bags and exiguous cladding panels which make up today's well-insulated but often flimsy new buildings. In most

Brutalist structures, what looks like reinforced concrete *is* reinforced concrete, and is the same stuff right through. You can see what it is made of and how it was made from the outside.

Added to this, at least for me and my fellow fans, was its evocative state of neglect, and the opportunity to rebel against an older generation's general loathing of it. It is such an addictive excitement to discover beauty and depth in things which others instinctively dismiss. The fact that these lost gems are hidden only by the blindness of their viewers gives an even greater sense of privilege than having been a rare visitor to an inaccessible Mayan temple.

The growing popularity of Brutalism has added more to my collection of memorabilia: mugs, plates and tea towels emblazoned with major Brutalist buildings; a T-shirt declaring life's three essentials: 'Eat – Sleep – Concrete'; a cut-and-fold paper model of Balfron Tower; badges declaring me to be a Brutalist, and so on. People regularly tweet images of pleasingly photogenic late-Modernist buildings worldwide to me, and audiences keep rising at the talks I and others give on the subject. Whilst there are still those who hate

concrete Modernism, they are an increasingly embattled minority. I will almost be sad when the last puffing, angry right-winger stops trying to demonise Brutalism as a Stalinist fifth column in our good British cityscapes.

ii

Looking at the stories of the buildings in this book, a number of recurrent themes emerge. Perhaps the most important is that concrete was rarely used as the cheap and easy option. Beneath a superficial camouflage of utilitarian functionalism, Brutalist concrete was a celebration of unprecedented creative freedom.

Immense new technical capabilities in structure and services coincided with the greatest building boom Britain had ever seen. A climate of enthusiastic optimism saw even tradition-minded clients employing excitingly progressive architects, drawn by the technical innovations and freer spaces that new buildings could introduce.[1] The ubiquitous influence of Sir Leslie Martin reinforced strong Modernist architecture as the new norm for any civilised and responsible institution.

The emphasis on visual excitement in the revival of interest in 1960s architecture is not a perversion of the real intentions of the style. Brutalism started out as a swing towards a politically neutral, self-propelling aestheticism cultivated by young architects afire with the thrill of Le Corbusier's post-war concrete primitivism.

The superficial aesthetic unfamiliarity of Brutalism, looking forwards to a hoped-for, technologically enriched future rather than backwards to the styles of an idealised past, gives many the feeling that this is an architecture of intimidating radicalism. In fact, though, the clients who commissioned the Barbican or Christ's College, Cambridge, and many of those behind the National Theatre, were using the new architectural language in the service of continuity not change. A stone-clad Classical building would have made the underlying conservatism of many 1960s British projects glaring and controversial, where Modernism could disguise it.

Concrete, in particular, was the ideal material for camouflaging social or economic conservatism and entrenched privilege by the inconspicuousness of its luxury. Its utilitarian associations and the tendency for the public not to be able or willing to distinguish between high-quality and low-quality concrete work meant that a project like the National Theatre, which would inevitably come under fire for costing the public money, could avoid accusations of wasting that money on opulent materials, yet at the same time the designers could have the quiet satisfaction for themselves and the architecture world that they had produced a very high quality and durable building. The rumour went round architecture schools in the 1970s that in fact, rather than produce such immaculate concrete finishes, it would have been cheaper to clad the National Theatre in marble.[2]

The National Theatre was amongst the last of these great monuments to a confident, optimistic architecture which could do anything. Whilst engineering has continued to advance in the decades since Brutalism fell from fashion, many things have closed in on today's architects, making them necessarily less gloriously free than the Brutalist generation. Rightly, the country is much more hesitant about mass-demolition of existing buildings; less appealingly, there are now more attempts to regulate the appearance of buildings, meaning that in many cases the safest option is to design with blandly conventional materials and elevations. Above all, we have moved on from the sense the 1960s had that energy had been getting cheaper decade on decade since 1800, and with nuclear energy getting started electricity would soon be 'too cheap to meter'.[3] We are acutely aware, as they were not, that the extent of our dependence on fossil fuels has the potential to cause global catastrophe; contemporary architecture is appropriately preoccupied with improving insulation and reducing energy consumption. This sense of mission can be inspiring to good architects, but the fact remains that it considerably curtails their freedom: the amount of outside wall needs to be minimised, the windows need to be limited in size and shaded from direct summer sunlight, and the meeting between materials now needs to be handled with meticulous care to determine whether any part of the building is letting the heat out more easily than others. Concrete, for all its wonderful qualities, is appallingly polluting during production in its release of carbon dioxide, and ought now to be used sparingly. Whilst there are many pleasures of ingenious thinking, elegant detail and careful material choice in today's best buildings, British architects are now painting on a smaller canvas than that available to the Brutalists. It is inconceivable in the current circumstances that any architect working in Britain could achieve the buccaneering magnificence and material integrity of the Barbican, the National Theatre or Trellick Tower.

iii

Brutalism's revival has been both delightful and tricky. It is unequivocally positive that there are more supporters for good buildings in danger, and pleasing that there are many who now derive pleasure not pain from the concrete around them. In some dark corner of my mind, though, I feel like the hipsters who move into poor areas and then complain about the gentrification of which they are themselves a part. I was amused at my own irritation when taking students to Balfron Tower and finding a music video being filmed in its service-road, and I half miss the disbelieving laughs which used to greet my response when I was asked what period of architectural history I specialised in.

Most of this effect is purely personal and rather absurd. There is, however, one sense in which the increasing appreciation of Brutalist architecture does bring with it potential for degradation of the architectural impact of these buildings. With acceptance as valued heritage comes a tendency to tidy things up: to prink and preen them. Some architecture suits pristine restoration and cleaning, and a charming planting programme. Brutalism absolutely does not.[4] The rugged, quotidian-looking surfaces of Brutalism are misread by users as being infinitely abusable, or even as profiting from a bit of jollying-up with a lick of beige paint, posters or the like. The same mistake is rarely made with stone facings, whose specialness as high-quality crafted finishes is much more widely recognised.[5]

Brutalism may be a recent style, but its buildings are as unrepeatable now, only fifty years on, as medieval Gothic cathedrals. At a pinch, either period's craft skills could be recovered, but they will never be brought back on the scale required, and the artistic energy and cultural context which produced them is gone for ever. It would not be right to build Brutalist buildings now, but the best of the ones we have will never be bettered.

As I write there are still some shocking omissions from heritage protection. The most outrageous of them all is the Southbank Centre in London, repeatedly put forward for listing by English Heritage, and repeatedly refused by a succession of government ministers, afraid of bad headlines or perhaps guided by their own idiot prejudice.

The Southbank Centre is Brutalism for Brutalists: the separate articulation of art gallery and concert halls is absolute; there is a terrifyingly uncompromising windowless hardness to much of it; the services wind round the buildings, enigmatic and malevolent-looking, like serpents round the doomed Laocoon; raised walkways go everywhere and are the only way of getting round the complex, tentacling out to the Royal Festival Hall on one side and under Waterloo Bridge to the National Theatre on the other. Above all, the materials are magnificent. The in situ concrete prefigures the National Theatre's in its perfectionism, and the metalwork of windows and doors, which could be incongruously smooth elements, was cast into wet sand to produce a granular roughness which sits perfectly with the sandy concrete. The fact that the metal used for them was aluminium means that the heavy-looking doors push open with an agreeably surprising ease.[6]

For me, the glory of the Southbank Centre's materials is neither of these finely crafted finishes, nor yet the Macedonian marble and warm-looking wood of the concert halls' foyers and interiors.[7] The best material for me is the least attractive: the harshly rough, glumly coloured precast panels which give the complex its boundless toughness, bleak and terrifying. I liked them even more when I realised that they were installed as a rebellious V-sign to the GLC Chief Architect, after he ordered the young designers to clad the building with stone-speckled panels, hoping this would soften it. They conformed to the letter of his diktat whilst defying its spirit.

The Southbank Centre is one of the most gloriously, irresponsibly expressive pieces of architecture ever designed, a shouting, spitting punk, sandwiched in permanent rebellion between the courteous prettiness of the Royal Festival Hall and the orderly Cubism of the National Theatre. Its designers were the quintessential high Brutalist architects: obsessive, aesthetically driven, confident in the worth of what they were doing, and perfectionistic in their pursuit of impeccable building craft. Theirs is architecture for those who do not fear architecture. Like much of the art and music that it hosts, the Southbank Centre's architecture is too strong a flavour, too thrillingly avant-garde even half a century on, for some. It may always remain so. But I, and an increasingly large number of others, are exhilarated by our every visit to its gloriously sinister undercroft or its thunderously sublime central canyon, spanned by a single overlong bridge.

Brutalism can be a source of pleasure and excitement to anyone who chooses to give it a chance. Not many will shelter from the coastal Scottish wind in the beautiful Hermit's Castle, but huge numbers have daily views of Trellick Tower or Balfron Tower, or find themselves threading their way through the futuristic

DESTRUCTION AND PRESERVATION

Southbank Centre

cityscape of the Barbican for a concert or exhibition. Dozens of students every year live in Lasdun's New Court, and hundreds study in Stirling and Gowan's Leicester Engineering Building. Millions of people from all over the globe walk, cycle, drive or bus past the National Theatre over Waterloo Bridge or along the South Bank pedestrian path. Millions more have frequent interactions with thousands of other Brutalist buildings up and down the country. As yet a relatively small proportion of all these encounters brings with it the sensory pleasure and intellectual satisfaction which is available once one recognises how special an architectural moment this was: how remarkable was its competitive aestheticism, and the fertility of its inventiveness.

I hope that, as time passes, more and more people will come to join those of us who admire Brutalism and get daily pleasure from concrete buildings. Although some still see in the architecture of the 1960s a moment of madness or malign conspiracy, it makes far more sense to view it as a glorious celebration of new technologies, new cheap energy, new opportunities to enhance all human activities. The architecture of the 1960s has floated through the rougher seas of the 1970s and '80s like a much-buffeted ark, carrying with it the confidence, the optimism and the competitive brilliance of its moment of creation. When you visit a good Brutalist building it is not only the marks of its construction, but also the joyful energy of the 1960s architectural world, which is preserved there, still vivid, in its raw concrete.

Endnotes

Introduction

1 David Cameron, 'Estate Regeneration', article published in the *Sunday Times* 10 January, 2016, https://www.gov.uk/government/speeches/estate-regeneration-article-by-david-cameron (accessed 25 January 2016).
2 This theme of the connections between energy availability and architectural development will be explored in my forthcoming book *Architecture* (Pelican).
3 The range of building types that flowered in the decades after the Second World War is captured in Elain Harwood, *Space Hope and Brutalism: English Architecture 1945-75* (London: Yale, 2015).
4 The forward-looking optimism of the period is encapsulated by the discussion in a government report of the potential future challenges of managing personal jet-packs as a form of traffic: Colin Buchanan, *Traffic in Towns: A Study of the Long Term Problems of Traffic in Urban Areas – Reports of the Steering Group and Working Group appointed by the Minister of Transport* (London: HMSO, 1963), p. 24.
5 Andrew Saint, *Architect and Engineer: A Study in Sibling Rivalry* (London: Yale, 2007).

6 The best source on this is an oral history research project led by Christine Wall: 'Constructing Post-War Britain: Building Workers' Stories 1950-70'. Each of the studies is published on their website, http://www.westminster.ac.uk/probe/projects/constructing-post-war-britain.

7 Alan Powers, *Britain: Modern Architectures in History* (London: Reaktion, 2007), p. 13.

8 Alan Powers, *Modern: the Modern Movement in Britain* (London: Merrell, 2005).

9 Andrew Saint, *Towards a Social Architecture* (New Haven, Yale, 1987), pp. 17-31.

10 The most celebrated was that drawn up for the London County Council: J H Forshaw and Patrick Abercrombie, *County of London Plan* (London: 1943).

11 Harwood 2015, pp. v-xix.

12 Saint 1987.

13 Reyner Banham, 'The New Brutalism', *Architectural Review* (December 1955), p. 356.

14 Reyner Banham, *The New Brutalism: Ethic or Aesthetic* (London: Architectural Press, 1966), p. 10.

15 Banham 1955; the renewed interest in renaissance theory was brought to the London architectural world primarily by Rudolf Wittkower, a German-Jewish émigré art historian whose interpretations of renaissance architecture as being tied into a rich intellectual and scientific understanding of the world spoke to the ambitions of the young to produce architecture which had some philosophical and cosmological claims beyond utility.

16 Very few took on the tag 'Brutalist', which was hardly calculated to endear architects to clients, but plenty pored over the deliberately tough photos of the Smithsons' school, for which they had all the furniture removed, and the photos taken from near ground-level to increase the apparent size, hardness and monumentality of the building. The result was splendidly polarised responses, one correspondent to the *Architectural Review* calling it 'the Thing [. . .] completely lacking in grace, charm and beauty [. . .] a sort of blind man's architecture.' [N. A. Cowburn, letter to the *Architectural Review* (November 1954), p. 282] Another wrote praising its 'purity of style', and advocating that more architects follow its example. However even this supporter felt

that it was 'unfriendly [. . .] the stairs give a grim promise of canings and theoretical physics on the first floor.' [Peter Beresford, letter to the *Architectural Review* (November 1954), p. 282].

17 Reyner Banham, 'Revenge of the Picturesque: English Architectural Polemics, 1945-65', in John Summerson, ed, *Concerning Architecture* (London: Allen Lane, 1968), pp. 265-73.

18 Barnabas Calder, '"The Sweetest Music You Will Ever Hear": Structural and Programmatic Uses of Concrete by Denys Lasdun & Partners', *Journal of Architecture* (June 2015), pp. 376–418.

19 Barnabas Calder, 'Brutal enemies? Townscape and the "Hard" Moderns', in John Pendlebury and Erdem Erten, eds, *Alternative Visions of Post-war Reconstruction: Creating the Modern Townscape* (London: Routledge, 2014), pp. 199-215.

20 The idea that post-war housing in Western Europe was used to give an appearance of change is touched upon in Adrian Forty, *Concrete and Culture: A Material History* (London: Reaktion, 2012), p. 164.

21 Adrian Forty, *Words and Buildings: A Vocabulary of Modern Architecture* (London: Thames and Hudson, 2000), pp. 142-48.

22 Astrid Kander, Paolo Malanima and Paul Warde, *Power to the People: Energy in Europe over the Last Five Centuries* (Princeton: Princeton, 2013), pp. 267-73.

23 Charles Windsor, Prince of Wales, 'A vision of Britain', 1989.

24 E.g. Sam Jacob, 'Cute nostalgia sits strangely with Brutalism', *Dezeen Magazine*, 11 July 2013, http://www.dezeen.com/2013/07/11/sam-jacob-opinion-brutalism-on-cushions/ (accessed 18 January 2016).

25 'A speech by HRH The Prince of Wales at the 150th anniversary of the Royal Institute of British Architects (RIBA), Royal Gala Evening at Hampton Court Palace', 30 May 1984, http://www.princeofwales.gov.uk/media/speeches/speech-hrh-the-prince-of-wales-the-150th-anniversary-of-the-royal-institute-of (accessed 18 January 2016).

Chapter 1

1 Forty 2012, p. 43.
2 Jean-Pierre Adam, *Roman Building: Materials and Techniques* (London: Batsford, 1994), p. 184.
3 Vitruvius, Book II, chapter 6.

4 Adam, pp. 69–70.
5 *OED*; the early history of modern concrete is still told best in a 1959 book, reissued more recently with extra essays: Peter Collins, *Concrete: The Vision of a New Architecture* (Montreal: McGill-Queen's University Press, 2004).
6 Forty, pp. 232–33.
7 The emergence of the consultant engineer is set out in Saint 2007.
8 Interview with Dr Anthony Flint, spring 2010.
9 Letter from Lasdun to the Librarian, Royal College of Physicians, 14 November 1984, RIBA Lasdun Archive, LaD/27/6.
10 Denys Lasdun, 'An Architect's Approach to Architecture: Denys Lasdun', *RIBA Journal* (1965), pp. 184–95 (p. 184).
11 Banham's PhD was later published as *Theory and Design in the First Machine Age* (New York: Praeger, 1960).
12 Calder 2014.
13 Most of the evidence other than the building itself comes from the artist Bobby Niven, who has made a meditative, haunting short film about the building (http://www.bobbyniven.co.uk/work/hermits-castle, accessed 23/08/2014). Niven has kindly given me access to his interview with Margaret MacLeod, who runs the Achmelvich campsite. She is the daughter of the crofter who gave David Scott permission to build there, and she was seven in 1955, the year that Scott constructed his hut. From a mixture of childhood memory and family legend she supplied details of the architect's origins and his time on their coast.
14 Bobby Niven interview with Margaret MacLeod.
15 Transcript of a discussion between Andrew Saint and Peter Moro, no date, lent to the author by Andrew Saint, pp. 76-77.
16 Bobby Niven interview with Margaret MacLeod.

Chapter 2

1 GLC press release of 12 February 1968: 'LEADER OF GLC TO OPEN EAST END'S TALLEST BLOCK', RIBA GolEr/171/2.
2 Miles Glendinning and Stefan Muthesius, *Tower Block: Modern Public Housing in England, Scotland, Wales and Northern Ireland* (London: Yale, 1994), p. 1. The authors have made the full book

available free as a pdf at: http://towerblock.org/; Mark Swenarton, *Homes Fit for Heroes* (London: Heinemann, 1981).
3 Harwood 2015, p. 49.
4 Harwood 2015, p. 49.
5 Beveridge identified 'giant evils' threatening Britain: squalor, ignorance, want and disease were the obvious targets of Welfare State improvement. He included a fifth giant evil, however, 'idleness', which has a much less left-wing ring to it, and recalls nineteenth-century efforts to identify and help the 'deserving poor' without giving succour to the 'idle poor'.
6 Glendinning and Muthesius, p. 1.
7 Aled Davies, '"Right to Buy": The Development of a Conservative Housing Policy, 1945–1980', *Contemporary British History*, (2013) 27:4, pp. 421–44 (p. 425).
8 The specific motivations behind the provision of council housing varied very extensively from place to place and moment to moment, generally involving some blend of ideological commitment, electoral expediency and competition with neighbouring councils: who could build most, or who could build highest. The housing types built after 1945 were also widely divergent. On a less well-known side-note, the Conservatives also introduced measures to support increasing levels of owner-occupation, and the proportion of owner-occupied housing rose from 29 per cent to 42 per cent during the 1950s (Davies, p. 425).
9 Glendinning and Muthesius, p. 4.
10 Glendinning and Muthesius, p. 2. The great benefit to these five-storey blocks was that fire brigades had ladders long enough to rescue people from their upper storeys, whereas taller blocks required special negotiations over fire permissions with their cautious local fire brigades, usually including extensive additional provision of fireproof escape stairs, costing extra space and money.
11 Glendinning and Muthesius, Chapter 22.
12 C. Pearson and N. Delatte, 'Ronan Point Apartment Tower Collapse and Its Effect on Building Codes', *Journal of Performance of Constructed Facilities*, May 2005, 19(2), pp. 172–77. Connections between panels which the system required were not in fact implemented on site, and even if they had been, the building had no structural backup: if the walls failed there was nothing else to hold it up.

ENDNOTES

13 Glendinning and Muthesius, p. 4.
14 Glendinning and Muthesius, Chapter 24.
15 Harwood 2015, p. 66.
16 The thrifty efficiency with which these blocks exploited the available resources to provide for an urgent need is nowhere more visible than in housing like the Kennings Estate, Lambeth, where the fencing of the block is composed of some of the huge surplus of emergency stretchers left over after the Blitz, welded to vertical steel posts and painted. Some of the stretchers are heartbreakingly child-sized: personal communication from Andrew Saint, *c.* 2003.
17 Harwood 2015, p. 65.
18 It was the wartime LCC Architect J. H. Forshaw who had first implemented this division into teams; Harwood 2015, p. 65.
19 National Heritage List for England, Brandlehow School, List entry Number: 1126541.
20 Nigel Warburton, *Ernö Goldfinger: The Life of an Architect* (London: Routledge, 2003), p. 3.
21 Warburton, p. 49.
22 The two best sources on Perret are: Peter Collins, *Concrete: The Vision of a New Architecture; a study of Auguste Perret and His Precursors* (London: Faber and Faber, 1959) and Institut Français d'Architecture, *Les Frères Perret: L'Oeuvre Complète* (Paris: Editions NORMA, 2000).
23 Warburton, p. 6.
24 Warburton, pp. 51–52.
25 Goldfinger's house, 2 Willow Road, is owned and opened by the National Trust.
26 Warburton, pp. 100–102.
27 The massing and composition of the blocks, now renamed Metro Central Heights, is still good, though the wonderful psychedelic cinema has gone, the offices have been divided into flats, and the whole thing has been painted a feebly conciliatory cream and blue.
28 Goldfinger's development of this planning idea seems likely to have been based on the LCC's recent blocks on the Pepys Estate, Deptford, whose vertical proportions, separate access and service tower, and bridging corridors closely prefigure Goldfinger's. Ross Brown, *Scottish Brutalism*, http://www.scotbrut.co.uk/archive/anniesland-cross-housing/.

29 James Dunnett and Nigel Hiscock, '"To This Measure of Man": Proportional Design in the Work of Ernö Goldfinger', *Twentieth-Century Architecture and its Histories* (Society of Architectural Historians of Great Britain, 2000), pp. 87-124 (pp. 109–110).
30 This draft specification proposed the use of board-marked concrete rather than bush-hammered, so its many pages of careful detail on the achievement of good finishes must have been supplanted in the final (lost) specification; September 1964, 'Specification for the Structural Engineering Works Rowlett Street Housing, Poplar', RIBA GolEr/172/2.
31 Warburton, p. 134.
32 Warburton, p. 133.
33 A characteristically oddly typed Goldfinger memo, 25 March 1968, RIBA GolEr/171/7.
34 GLC press release of 12 February 1968: 'LEADER OF GLC TO OPEN EAST END'S TALLEST BLOCK', RIBA GolEr/171/2.
35 Ursula Goldfinger, 'General Report – Balfron Tower 19th March, 1968', RIBA GolEr/170/7.
36 Ursula Goldfinger, 'General Report – Balfron Tower 19th March, 1968', RIBA GolEr/170/7.
37 Goldfinger memo, 25 March 1968, RIBA GolEr/171/7.
38 Note of meeting of Brownfield Estate Tenants' Association by Management Officer, P. D. J. McDermott, 7 March 1968, RIBA GolEr/171/7.
39 Handwritten table showing residents' jobs, RIBA GolEr/170/6.
40 Glendinning and Muthesius, p. 323.
41 Warburton, p. 168.
42 Warburton, pp. 168 and 185.
43 Warburton, p. 185.
44 The friend who first took me there had stumbled on Trellick by chance in 1990 and loved it at once. In 1994 he found a resident willing to sell, and after some effort an estate agent willing to value it. After a visit, however, the agent told him, 'I can't value it. It is in a concrete high-rise council block. It is worth nothing.' He and the prospective seller agreed a provisional price of £60,000, but it fell through. By the later 1990s flats there were selling for up to £400,000, making headlines and giving the impression of arty yuppification.

45 Alexandra Bullen, 'Trellick Tower: What is the Role of Social Media in the Current Popular Reassessment of Brutalist Architecture?', unpublished Part 2 Dissertation, University of Liverpool School of Architecture, 2014.
46 7 March 1968 Note of meeting of Brownfield Estate Tenants' Association by Management Officer, P.D.J. McDermott, RIBA GolEr/171/7.
47 Some, like the Pepys Estate in Rotherhithe, have had individual blocks refurbished for private sale; others, like the Heygate Estate, have been demolished to make way for new private development.
48 For example Benjamin Mortimer, 'How the Balfron Tower Tenants Were "Decanted" and Lost Their Homes', *East End Review*, 24 March 2015 (available at http://www.eastendreview.co.uk/2015/03/24/balfron-tower-poplar-harca/). The tone of anger is clear in the comments below the article: 'Balfron Tower remains standing, given a new life as a daily reminder of the relentless screwing given to the public by their trusted "servants" whose greed and ineptitude is rewarded handsomely.'
49 This was the subject of a fascinating study by Victoria Slater, 'Artists as the Agents of Gentrification: The Debate Surrounding "Artwashing" in Balfron Tower', unpublished Part 2 Dissertation at Liverpool School of Architecture, 2015.
50 Wayne Hemingway, 'Hipster-led Regeneration', Design Council website, 3 October 2014, http://www.designcouncil.org.uk/news-opinion/hipster-led-regeneration-wayne-hemingway.
51 Peter Hetherington, 'On Social Housing, Tory Ideology Trumps All Evidence', *Guardian*, 23 September 2015, http://www.theguardian.com/society/2015/sep/23/social-housing-tory-ideology-trumps-evidence-housing-associations.

Chapter 3

1 GLC press release, 12 February 1968, 'Leader of GLC to Open East End's Tallest Block', RIBA GolEr/171/2; Terence Bendixson, 'Many Takers for Life in a Grey, Baroque Pile', *Guardian*, 4 December 1969 (found via Martin Belam's blog on MartinBelam.com).
2 Advertisement, *The Sunday Times*, 3 June 1973, p. 48.

ENDNOTES

3   For the political and planning history of the City after 1945, see Michael Hebbert, 'The City of London Walkway Experiment', *Journal of the American Planning Association* (Autumn 1993), pp. 433–450.
4   Hebbert, p. 435.
5   David Heathcote, *Barbican: Penthouse Over the City* (Chichester: Wiley Academy, 2004), pp. 54–55.
6   Hebbert, p. 442.
7   Hebbert, pp. 438–39.
8   Hebbert, p. 440.
9   Hebbert, p. 442.
10 Donald McMorran's practice, McMorran and Whitby, was after this initial contact to go on to work for the City on several occasions, producing notably in 1963–66 a charming and highly expressive police station with an elegant mini-tower block of accommodation. Its limestone cladding is simplified and stripped of most of the traditional classical ornament, with those decorative features which are retained being heightened and strengthened. It is handsomely composed and has a kind of stocky dignity which suits both the police and the Corporation. Edward Denison, *20th Century Architects: McMorran and Whitby* (London: RIBA Publishing, English Heritage and the Twentieth Century Society, 2009).
11 Alison and Peter Smithson, *The Charged Void* (New York: Monacelli, 2005), p. 87.
12 Tom Heyden, 'Was There a Time British People Couldn't Buy Olive Oil?', BBC website, 16 September 2014, http://www.bbc.co.uk/news/magazine-29220046 (accessed 11 October 2015).
13 The best thing written on the architectural partnership is Elain Harwood, *20th Century Architects: Chamberlin Powell & Bon* (London: RIBA Publishing, English Heritage and the Twentieth Century Society, 2011), p. 20.
14 Harwood, 2011, p. 20.
15 Mark Goldie, *Corbusier Comes to Cambridge: Post-war Architecture and the Competition to Build Churchill College* (Cambridge: Churchill College, 2007, second edition 2012), p. 16.
16 Hebbert, p. 440.
17 These historical references are explored in Heathcote.
18 Elain Harwood, 'Chamberlin Powell and Bon', talk in the series 'The Architects Who Made London, with Maxwell Hutchinson', 20 April

2009, available from the Royal Academy: http://feedproxy.google.com/~r/RA-Architecture/~5/sOUKTkmqxvo/chamberlin-462.mp3.

19 Christine Wall, Linda Clarke, Charlie McGuire and Olivia Muñoz-Rojas, *Building the Barbican 1962–1982: Taking the Industry Out of the Dark Ages* (http://www.westminster.ac.uk/__data/assets/pdf_file/0018/160236/BarbicanPamphlet_lo.pdf 2012). The research work led by Christine Wall is exceptional within the history of the period for finding out so much about the realities of construction sites, material which tends to be very under-represented in archives and even in interviews with architects themselves.

20 Wall et al., 2012, p. 7.

21 Wall et al., 2012, p. 8.

22 Wall et al., 2012, pp. 12 and 17.

23 Wall et al., 2012, p. 12.

24 Wall et al., 2012, p. 17.

25 Wall et al., 2012, p. 10.

26 Wall et al., 2012, p. 15.

27 Wall et al., 2012, p. 18.

28 Wall et al., 2012, p. 19.

29 Wall et al., 2012, p. 20.

30 Wall et al., 2012, pp. 33–44.

31 Harwood, 2015, p. 74.

32 Barbican, Historic England Statutory Listing entry, no. 1352667.

33 Barbican, Historic England Statutory Listing entry, no. 1352667.

34 Wall et al., 2012, p. 41.

35 Harwood, 2012, p. 20.

36 Wall et al., 2012, p. 18.

37 Wall et al., 2012, p. 41.

38 Museum of London Archaeology Site: www.molas.org.uk/pages/site-SummariesDetailsAll.asp (accessed 19 August 2014).

39 This Modernist enthusiasm for walkways and multiple ground levels enables some very neat high-density planning, and some wonderful views and effects, though it is a major failing that it can make public areas inaccessible to disabled people, pram-pushers and the heavy laden. Only from the 1970s did architecture finally start to wake up to the ways in which it had always shared the indifference shown to

disabled people by 'the not yet disabled'. (This term for the non-disabled comes from the comedian Francesca Martinez.)
40 Harwood, 2009.
41 Barbican, Historic England Statutory Listing entry, no. 1352667.
42 Barbican, Historic England Statutory Listing entry, no. 1352667.
43 Somewhere in the remainder of my student trip I lost the contact details of the kind resident who showed us round so memorably, and I have regretted ever since that I could not thank him for his kindness to us. If ever he reads this I hope that he recognises himself in the description.
44 Information from Tony Chambers, who kindly showed me round his beautifully preserved flat in the Barbican, in November 2014. I also saw much of the Barbican and parts of Golden Lane, and had my enthusiasm for both fed generously when shown round by John McLean.
45 Harwood, 2011, p. 24.

Chapter 4

1 Richard Morrison, 'Those Who Want to List Brutalist Buildings Should Try Living in One', *The Times*, 25 September 2015.
2 My affection for the building was fed by reading William Curtis's writing on Lasdun – an unapologetically aesthetic exploration of his work, and one that avoided the unapproachable rhetoric of pared-down, austerity-influenced functionalism which the architects of the 1960s themselves generally favoured.
3 Denys Lasdun, National Life Stories Collection, National Sound Archive.
4 An institution which was, as he left, about to become a furiously controversial crucible of British Modernist architecture.
5 Denys Lasdun, National Life Stories Collection, National Sound Archive.
6 John Allan, *Berthold Lubetkin: Architecture and the Tradition of Progress* (London: RIBA, 1992).
7 Barnabas Calder, 'The Education of an Architect: Denys Lasdun in the 1930s', *Twentieth Century Society Journal* 8 (2007), pp. 117–27.
8 Denys Lasdun, National Life Stories Collection, National Sound Archive.
9 Barnabas Calder, ' "Unlearning Lessons": Denys Lasdun in the 1950s, Part 1', *Architectural Research Quarterly*, December 2007, pp. 301–10.

ENDNOTES

10 Letter from Lasdun to J. F. Cory Dixon, University of Liverpool Estates Officer, 20 December 1960, RIBA Lasdun Archive, LaD/74/6.
11 Denys Lasdun, 'An Architect's Approach to Architecture', *RIBA Journal* (1965), pp. 184–95 (p. 185).
12 The Robbins Report on higher education would shortly set the seal on an already well-advanced programme of expansion across all UK universities, and pressure Christ's to take a substantial addition to its undergraduate body. Letter from Prest to Lasdun, 6 November 1963, RIBA Lasdun Archive, LaD/39/1.
13 Notes of a meeting of Christ's College Development Committee, 4 February 1966, RIBA Lasdun Archive, LaD/39/2.
14 *Christ's College Magazine*, Easter Term 1954, letter by J. G. Parker, pp. 8–9.
15 Casson and Conder plan, 16 October 1958, Christ's College Archives, File 27; Alistair Fair, 'An ideal campus: The Sidgwick Site, Cambridge', in *Twentieth Century Architecture 11: Oxford and Cambridge*, pp. 102-121.
16 Christ's College Governing Body minutes, 14 July 1959.
17 Christ's College Governing Body minutes, 14 July 1959.
18 Letter from Brian Downs to Lasdun, 21 July 1960, LaD/39/1.
19 Christ's College Governing Body minutes, 7 March 1961.
20 Lasdun's first scheme has been lost, but its general disposition seems to have been close to what was eventually built. Christ's College Governing Body minutes, 9 May 1961; letter from Brian Downs to Lasdun, 11 May 1961, RIBA Lasdun Archive, LaD/39/1.
21 Harry Pugh memorandum of a conversation with C. K. Phillips, Bursar of Christ's College, 8 October 1971, RIBA Lasdun Archive, LaD/39/4.
22 Sainte-Baume, France, 1948 and Roc et Rob, Roquebrune-Cap-Martin, France, 1949.
23 Irénée Scalbert, 'Siedlung Halen: Between Standards and Individuality', *Architectural Research Quarterly*, 2, 1996, pp. 14–25.
24 Patrick Zamarian is currently doing research on the history of the Architectural Association in the post-war years, for a PhD at the University of Liverpool.
25 Mark Swenarton, 'Developing a New Format for Urban Housing: Neave Brown and the design of Camden's Fleet Road estate', *Journal of Architecture* (December 2012), pp. 973–1007.

26 Leslie Martin and Lionel March, eds, *Urban Space and Structures* (London: Cambridge University Press, 1972).
27 The Italian Futurists were highlighted in Banham's 1960 *Theory and Design in the First Machine Age*. Whether British architects would have been aware of Sauvage in the 1960s is less clear.
28 Lasdun was an early adopter of the stepped section, first proposing one for an unsuccessful competition design for Churchill College, Cambridge, in 1958–59, and then for another rejected scheme for Cambridge, at St John's College. RIBA Lasdun Drawings, Churchill College: PA2100/4(1-14); St John's College: PA2116/5(1-5). The Christ's College proposal of 1961 was the first of Lasdun's stepped-section designs to eventually get built. If it had been built at soon as it was designed it would have been a very early application of the idea. As it was, eight years of planning delays made it come in rather after the cutting edge, and indeed after Lasdun's own stepped-section residences at the new University of East Anglia which he and his practice designed outside Norwich.
29 Harry Pugh, draft explanatory text for *Architectural Review*, 17 June 1971, RIBA Lasdun Archive, LaD/40/5; minutes of Development Committee meeting, 29 November 1967, RIBA Lasdun Archive, LaD/39/3. Although there have been problems in places from water leaking through imperfectly sealed joints between components, the concrete itself shows none of the problems of corroding reinforcement or deteriorating surface which some in situ work elsewhere has suffered in the years since construction.
30 At the time Lasdun's proposal was first being drawn up there were plans for a multistorey car park opposite, which would have kept the overwhelming toughness of Lasdun's elevation in countenance, and as the scheme was finalised a road-widening with corresponding increase in traffic noise had been determined upon. Neither materialised in the end. Minutes of Development Committee meeting, 24 January 1968, RIBA Lasdun Archive, LaD/39/3.
31 Denys Lasdun, 'An Architect's Approach to Architecture', *RIBA Journal* (1965), pp. 184–95 (p. 184).
32 Lord Todd, 'A New Chapter', *Christ's College Magazine*, May 1966, pp. 3–5 (p. 5).
33 Lord Todd, 'The College Grows', *Christ's College Magazine*, May 1968, pp. 67–69 (p. 67).

ENDNOTES

34 Christ's College note of Building Committee, 29 March 1968, RIBA Lasdun Archive, LaD/39/3.
35 King Street Building Committee: Furnishing Sub-Committee, 27 November 1969, RIBA Lasdun Archive, LaD/39/3.
36 King Street Building Committee: Furnishing Sub-Committee, 27 November 1969, RIBA Lasdun Archive, LaD/39/3.
37 King Street Building Committee: Furnishing Sub-Committee, 27 November 1969, RIBA Lasdun Archive, LaD/39/3.
38 Student accommodation in 1960s Oxford and Cambridge was typically planned on the assumption that students would eat their meals communally in hall, using their shared, basic kitchenettes for little more than making toast and heating baked beans.
39 King Street Building Committee: Furnishing Sub-Committee, 27 November 1969, RIBA Lasdun Archive, LaD/39/3.
40 Letter from Prest to Lasdun, 29 May 1963, RIBA Lasdun Archive, LaD/39/1.
41 Letter from Fulton Roberts, Bursar of Jesus, to Alan Prest, Bursar of Christ's, 12 February 1964, RIBA Lasdun Archive, LaD/39/2.
42 Prest to Roberts, 24 March 1964, RIBA Lasdun Archive, LaD/39/2.
43 Letter from Pugh to C. K. Phillips (who had succeeded Prest as Bursar of Christ's on 1 July 1964), 28 January 1965, RIBA Lasdun Archive, LaD/39/2.
44 Letter from Pugh to Prest, 29 August 1963, RIBA Lasdun Archive, LaD/39/1.
45 Letter from Pugh to Prest, 29 Aug 1963, RIBA Lasdun Archive, LaD/39/1.
46 Meeting of Development Committee, 24 January 1968, RIBA Lasdun Archive, LaD/39/3.
47 Letter from Phillips to Lasdun, 16 March 1967, RIBA Lasdun Archive, LaD/39/2.
48 Edward Cullinan interviewed by William Fawcett and Barnabas Calder, 2004.
49 Whipplesnaith (pseudonym for Noel Howard Symington), *The Night Climbers of Cambridge* (London: Chatto and Windus, 1937). The author was (not entirely incongruously, somehow) later to write a book proposing new ways forward for fascism in the post-war world.

ENDNOTES

50 Casson Conder & Partners plan, 16 October 1958, Christ's College Archives, File 27.
51 The brief of slotting a building into the back of New Court had been a design training exercise for students at Cambridge Architecture Department since at least the early 1980s. Letter from Rowan Moore (then an architecture student in Cambridge) to Lasdun, 6 October 1981, RIBA Lasdun Archive, LaD/41/3.
52 Personal communication from Lady Lasdun.
53 Harry Pugh memo, 20 July 1971, RIBA Lasdun Archive, LaD/39/4.
54 Lasdun memorandum, 1 April 1971, RIBA Lasdun Archive, LaD/40/4.
55 Lasdun memorandum of telephone conversation with Tim Rock and Harry Pugh, 7 July 1971, RIBA Lasdun Archive, LaD/40/5.
56 Lasdun memorandum of telephone conversation with Tim Rock, 13 July 1971, RIBA Lasdun Archive, LaD/40/5.
57 Editorial: 'Anarchy', *Architectural Review* (September 1971), pp. 131-132 (p. 131).
58 Letter from Rock to Lasdun, 26 Aug 1971, RIBA Lasdun Archive, LaD/41/1.
59 Alan Powers, 'The Heroic Period of Conservation', in *The Heroic Period of Conservation, Twentieth Century Architecture 7*, 2004, pp. 7–18.
60 Letter from Daria Venerandi, Rome, published in *The Times*, 14 April 1968: 'I was in Cambridge three years ago and enjoyed so much my stay there that every stone or rail or "back" reminds me of a lovely conversation, a delicious walk, a nice face. Thus, I was dismayed when I read [. . .] that King Street will be deprived of its famous spike-topped railings. It is a pity that this lovely town should be altered. We love Cambridge and its colleges because they show us a peculiar character of England: her everlasting faith in tradition.'
61 RIBA Lasdun Archive, LaD/41/1.
62 Lasdun memorandum, 19 October 1971, RIBA Lasdun Archive, LaD/41/3. It is striking to compare it with the much more developed thinking about streets by Neave Brown at the same period, discussed in Mark Swenarton, 'Developing a new format for urban housing: Neave Brown and the design of Camden's Fleet Road estate', *Journal of Architecture* (December 2012), 973-1007.
63 Susan Lasdun in particular, the architect's wife, has been consistently helpful and supportive to me in my research on his work.

64 Lasdun memo of a meeting, 9 March 1960, RIBA Lasdun Archive, LaD/17/1.
65 Lasdun memorandum of telephone conversation with Robin Middleton, 31 March 1971, RIBA Lasdun Archive, LaD/40/4.
66 Personal communication from Susan Lasdun.
67 Letter from David Coombe to Lasdun, 10 November 1971, RIBA Lasdun Archive, LaD/39/4.
68 The college did parts of the renovation much more sensitively, notably in the treatment of the precast concrete, where a proposed coating which would have radically altered the appearance of the exterior was abandoned in favour of a much more appropriate finish. At least two members of the academic staff and one of the support staff whom I spoke to took the architecture seriously, and wanted to do the right thing by the building.
69 Marco Iuliano, 'The other Cambridge', in *Cambridge in Concrete: Images from the RIBA British Architectural Library Photographs Collection*, ed. by Marco Iuliano and François Penz (Naples: Paparo Edizioni, 2012), pp. 8-11.

Chapter 5

1 The UGC is described in Stefan Muthesius, *The Postwar University: Utopianist Campus and College* (London: Yale, 2000), p. 95.
2 The requirement for the tank is mentioned in John McKean and Alan Berman, 'Understanding the Engineering Department, Leicester', in Alan Berman ed., *Jim Stirling and the Red Trilogy: three radical buildings* (London: Frances Lincoln, 2010), 29-41, p. 31.
3 Mark Girouard, *Big Jim: The Life and Work of James Stirling* (London: Chatto & Windus, 1998), p. 111.
4 Obituary, 'Leslie Martin', *Telegraph*, 1 August 2000.
5 Oliver Wainwright, 'Obituary: James Gowan', *Guardian*, 21 June 2015.
6 Mark Crinson, *Stirling and Gowan: Architecture from Austerity to Affluence* (New Haven: Yale, 2012), pp. 58–59.
7 Crinson, p. 59.
8 Crinson, p. 59.
9 Girouard, pp. 7–11.

ENDNOTES

10 Girouard, pp. 21 and 23.
11 The dynamics of this generation of students is discussed in Patrick Zamarian's doctoral research on the Architectural Association in the post-war years, forthcoming.
12 Crinson, p. 61.
13 Crinson, p. 65.
14 Crinson, p. 64.
15 Crinson, p. 137.
16 Banham, 1966, pp. 87-88.
17 Girouard, pp. 64-66.
18 Girouard, p. 107.
19 Girouard, pp. 98–99.
20 The extent of Gowan's contribution to the design of their projects comes through most clearly in Mark Crinson's book, where it is clear that if both men were judged only on the work they did together they would have been seen as equals. It is only because Stirling's later career remained internationally famous and Gowan's receded into comparative obscurity that Gowan has been so underrated.
21 Michael Wilford, National Life Stories Collection, National Sound Archive.
22 Crinson, pp. 46–51.
23 Though it is sometimes said that Gowan did more on the workshops and Stirling on the tower, Crinson's research suggests that 'both partners worked flexibly across the whole scheme.' Crinson, p. 233.
24 Alan Berman, 'Building the Future: challenges and failures of post-war technology', in Berman, ed., pp. 68-73 (p. 71).
25 Crinson, p. 257.
26 Peter St John, in Berman, ed., pp. 106–7 (p. 107).
27 Crinson, p. 247.
28 McKean and Berman, p. 30.
29 Crinson, p. 243.
30 McKean and Berman, p. 36.
31 Banham, 1966, p. 134.
32 *DNB*, Leslie Martin.
33 RIBA Drawings & Archives Collections, MARTIN 0001/1.
34 *DNB*, Leslie Martin.

35 Adam Sharr and Stephen Thornton, *Demolishing Whitehall: Leslie Martin, Harold Wilson and the Architecture of White Heat* (London: Ashgate, 2013), p. 153.
36 Sharr and Thornton, p. 154.
37 'The LCC Architect's Department', *Journal of the Royal Institute of British Architects* (March 1965), pp. 126–31 (p. 126).
38 'The LCC Architect's Department', p. 127.
39 Crinson, pp. 200–205.
40 Peter Carolin, obituary, 'Sir Leslie Martin, 1908–2000', *Architects' Journal* (3 August 2000).
41 Paul Bolton, 'Education: Historical Statistics', House of Commons Library, SN/SG/4252, last updated 27 November 2012, p. 20, Table 8, available at http://researchbriefings.files.parliament.uk/documents/SN04252/SN04252.pdf, accessed 11 June 2015.
42 Barnabas Calder, 'Representing Science: the Architecture of the New Museums Site, Cambridge, 1952–71', *Oxford and Cambridge: Twentieth Century Architecture 11* (Twentieth Century Society, 2013), pp. 166–179.
43 Goldie, p. 15.
44 Goldie, p. 16.
45 Crinson, p. 224.
46 Crinson, pp. 248–49.
47 Girouard, p. 149.
48 Leslie Martin, 'Development Plan for the University of Leicester,' 1956, information provided by Professor Nicholas Ray.
49 Girouard, p. 152.
50 Girouard, p. 104.
51 Crinson, pp. 249-250.
52 Jørn Utzon, 'Making Architecture a Joy and Art for Others', *Architectural Research Quarterly*, (June 2000) p. 304.
53 Peter Jones, *Ove Arup: Masterbuilder of the Twentieth Century* (London: Yale, 2006), pp. 206-236.
54 Utzon, p. 304.
55 Utzon, p. 304.
56 Barnabas Calder, *Lasdun Online*, forthcoming. Graham Lane (of Denys Lasdun & Partners) memo 13 June 1966, of 8 June RFAC meeting, RIBA Lasdun Archive, LaD/43/4; Graham Lane memo of RFAC

meeting 26 July 1966, RIBA Lasdun Archive, LaD/43/3; Lasdun memo of telephone conversation with Basil Spence, morning of 27 July 1966, RIBA Lasdun Archive, LaD/43/4. The two meetings show Martin speaking as the University of London's master planner, and the conversation with Spence records Spence's confidence that Martin will support the scheme as a member of the RFAC.

57 For example, the University of Leeds, where having originally been shortlisted as a possible planner he advised against softer, older architects Casson and Brett, and pushed forward Stirling, Lasdun, CPB and Howell Killick Partridge & Amis (Vice Chancellor's notes of meeting on 25 June 1956). For refusal of fees, see letters 6 and 11 December 1958, in file '1958 "Resignation of Dr Lodge Committee"', University of Leeds archives. I am very grateful to Professor Nicholas Ray for this information.

58 Sharr and Thornton, p. 77.

59 The fullest publication of this theory came in Leslie Martin and Lionel March, *Urban Space and Structures* (Cambridge: CUP, 1972).

60 This was the orthodox view of what the car required, to the point where even Thomas Sharp, one of the fathers of the movement to conserve ordinary town centres, felt that the way to 'save' Oxford from the car was not to discourage car use but to build a relief road right through Christ Church Meadows; Thomas Sharp, *Oxford Replanned* (London: Architectural Press, 1948).

61 Macmillan's large-state modernisation moves were often later associated with Wilson, under whose administration they came to fruition. Yet it was Macmillan who set Dr Beeching to work on his overhaul of the railway network, still controversial today, and initiated the updating of Euston including the demolition of its ugly but widely loved propylaeum, the 'Euston arch' (Sharr and Thornton, p. 10). Macmillan's set of influential investigations also included the Robbins Report which set the seal on the rapid expansion of the university sector, and Professor Colin Buchanan's celebrated report 'Traffic in Towns'. With the exception of Martin, who was at Cambridge when the Whitehall report was commissioned from him, all of the new generation of technical experts leading the production of this wave of reports were non-Oxbridge based. In the face of the growing complexity of government-led planning, the traditional elite of Oxford and Cambridge

arts graduates was giving way to a newer body of professionals. These men, mostly in their early fifties when appointed, were technical specialists trained at, and mostly holding posts at, redbrick universities: Robbins at UCL and LSE, Buchanan and Beeching at Imperial College; Martin trained at the University of Manchester, though he was Professor at Cambridge.

62 Sharr and Thornton, p. 51.
63 David Croghan, quoted in Sharr and Thornton, p. 138, n. 22.
64 Sharr and Thornton, pp. 104–31.
65 Sharr and Thornton, p. 89.
66 The *Plan Voisin*, first published in 1925.
67 Calder, 2014.
68 Girouard, p. 111.
69 Eisenmann, 'Real and English: The Destruction of the Box I', *Oppositions*, 4 (October 1974), pp. 5-34.
70 Richard MacCormac, in Berman, ed., pp. 95–96 (p. 95).
71 Norman Foster, in Berman, ed., pp. 88–90 (p. 88).

Chapter 6

1 Raymond Fitzwalter and David Taylor, *Web of Corruption: The Story of John Poulson and T. Dan Smith* (Granada Publishing, 1981).
2 Oliver Marriott, *The Property Boom* (Second edition, London: Abingdon, 1989), p. 4.
3 Marriott, pp. 1 and 6.
4 *DNB*, Jack Cotton.
5 Marriot, p. 108; Michael Brawne, 'An Appraisal of the Architectural Achievements of Britain's New Universities', *Architectural Review* (April 1970), pp. 250–86.
6 Richard Savill and Will Bennet, 'Harry Hyams Loses Rare Antiques in Raid', *Telegraph*, online, 3 February 2006.
7 Marriott, p. 172, though in fact the law explicitly excluded losses made by the developer on account of planning restrictions on density or bulk: Desmond Heap, 'New Developments in British Land Planning Law – 1954 and after', *Law and Contemporary Problems* (July 1955), pp. 493–516 (p. 506).
8 Marriott, p. 7.

9 Marriott, p. 109.
10 Marriott, p. 11.
11 Marriott, p. 118.
12 Marriott, p. 117.
13 Marriott, pp. 170–71.
14 Marriott, p. 131.
15 Richard Seifert, National Life Stories Collections, National Sound Archive.
16 *DNB*, Richard Seifert.
17 Lynex annotation, 'Preliminary List of Architects', 10 June 1963, National Theatre Archive, Box 40 SBTB.
18 *DNB*, Richard Seifert.
19 *DNB*, Richard Seifert.
20 @Corb1887, tweet, 6 September 2013. This Twitter account is very witty and well worth following: tweets in the persona of Le Corbusier if he were alive today in Glasgow, written in thick Glaswegian with a good knowledge of his thinking.
21 Glendinning and Muthesius, pp. 1–2.
22 Mitchell Library, Glasgow, drawing D-TC 13/561.
23 Mitchell Library, postcard C8713.
24 Handwritten memorandum, 'Anderston Cross Comprehensive Development Area', Mitchell Library, AGN2269; the Clydeway Industrial Centre by Jack Holmes & Partners is discussed in the Scottish Brutalism Project: http://www.scotbrut.co.uk/archive/clydeway-industrial-centre/.
25 The housing estate is in that curious, exaggeratedly grim Scottish social-housing style where economical, simple elevations have been covered on completion in a rough grey render which I have always found singularly gloom-inducing under leaden skies in the dark winters so far north. It helps me to understand how concrete-haters must feel when confronted with Brutalism. Last time I passed, September 2015, the western range of the slab-blocks to Argyle Street was empty and partially demolished.
26 In a happy postscript the bridge has recently been completed as a component of an improving cycle network, landing not on the podium of the Anderston Centre as intended, but on the street. To my pleasant surprise it seems to be well used, unlike so many footbridges

over large roads, beneath which pedestrians obdurately wait for light after light as the traffic lanes take their long turns to fume by.

27 Letter from R. Verrico, City Estates Surveyor, to Town Clerk, 15 June 1967, Mitchell Library DTC8/1/3/9.

28 The assumptions behind social housing in the 1950s and '60s took it for granted to an extraordinary extent first that most people would form heterosexual marriages and have small numbers of children, and second that the residents and the housing list would act 'rationally' in moving families to appropriate sizes and locations of housing as their circumstances changed. The imagined resident around which schemes were designed would not wish to keep spare bedrooms, have adult children or grandchildren live with them at least part-time, convert a bedroom into some other use, or otherwise deviate from the planned pattern.

29 Corporation Minutes, Minutes of the Subcommittee on the Development Plan, 2632: 14 April 1964.

30 Handwritten memorandum, 'Anderston Cross Comprehensive Development Area', Mitchell Library, AGN2269.

31 'Anderston Cross Comprehensive Development Area. Commercial Centre. Report by Town Clerk', Town Clerk's General: Mitchell Library DTC8/1/3/8.

32 Letter from Gerald Eve, Chartered Surveyor, to James Falconer, Town Clerk, 9 June 1967, Mitchell Library DTC8/1/3/9.

33 Letter from 'Depute City Chamberlain' to Town Clerk, 8 June 1967, Mitchell Library, DTC8/1/3/9.

34 Letter from 'Depute City Chamberlain' to Town Clerk, 8 June 1967, Mitchell Library, DTC8/1/3/9.

35 Letter from 'Depute City Chamberlain' to Town Clerk, 8 June 1967, Mitchell Library, DTC8/1/3/9.

36 Letter from Gerald Eve, Chartered Surveyor, to James Falconer, Town Clerk, 9 June 1967, Mitchell Library DTC8/1/3/9.

37 *DNB*, Richard Seifert.

38 Richard Seifert, National Life Stories Collections, National Sound Archive.

39 Obituary, 'Richard Seifert', *The Telegraph*, 29 October 2001.

40 Marriott, pp. 100-119.

41 Marriott, p. 42.

ENDNOTES

42 John Betjeman, 'Nooks and Corners of the New Barbarism: 2', *Private Eye*, 18 June 1971. Although it is titled as the second edition of his column it was in fact the third.
43 *DNB*, Richard Seifert.
44 Obituary, 'Richard Seifert', *Telegraph*, 29 October 2001.
45 Michael Horsnell, 'Centre Point Occupied in Housing Protest', *The Times*, 19 January 1974.
46 Marriott, p. 27.
47 Marriott, p. 32.
48 Marriott, p. 110.
49 *DNB*, Richard Seifert.
50 *DNB*, James Stirling.
51 *DNB*, Richard Seifert.
52 The Tricorn Centre was demolished in 2004, Trinity Square in 2010.
53 'Gateshead's ' "Get Carter" Car Park Demolition Date Set', BBC News Website, 15 July 2010, http://news.bbc.co.uk/local/tyne/hi/front_page/newsid_8825000/8825818.stm.
54 Within months of the demolition of Trinity Square, the fine Brutalist bus station in Preston came under threat. Like Trinity Square, it is dominated by a car park, this one long and thin, and made very distinctive by surprisingly delicate-looking precast concrete parapets whose component parts curve up like petals. The sheer length and clarity of the building, the futuristically swooping car ramps up to the parking, and the wonderfully preserved 1960s interiors made it obvious to those who like post-war architecture that this was one to save. Initially there was not much enthusiasm from the surrounding population, and some noisy voices complained that the £300,000 which the building cost annually to run was a waste of tax money. However, attitudes have changed considerably, and the building is on the way to becoming a loved symbol of its city after a brilliant campaign led by local enthusiasts, supported by the Twentieth Century Society, and involving a local arts collaborative working with Manchester School of Architecture. The campaign garnered extensive local and national coverage, and when it was announced that the bus station had been listed dozens of people held a celebratory march, complete with a model of the building held up in separate parts by nearly thirty of the structure's admirers. 'Preston Bus Station Campaigners Celebrate Victory', *Lancashire Evening Post*, 3 November 2013.

55 The Tricorn Centre was not immune to legitimate criticism – the shops had failed to thrive, the architecture was so over-powerful as to be frightening, and its location was rather cut off for a shopping centre – but there is room in a rich country for some buildings which do not function with optimal contemporary efficiency, and the Tricorn Centre was one of the world's most energetic and full-blooded Brutalist buildings.
56 Quoted in Marriott, p. 28.
57 Quoted in obituary, 'Rodney Gordon', *The Times*, 15 August 2008.
58 In many British regions local practices produced very good commercial buildings which have tended not to receive as much attention as those by London-based, nationally active firms. Ryder & Yates in the north-east; Bradshaw, Rowse & Harker in the north-west; Building Design Partnership across the north of England; John Madin in and around Birmingham; Peter Womersley in the eastern Scottish Borders; Keppie Henderson in Glasgow; or Garner, Preston & Strebel in Dumbarton all designed and built office or shopping complexes, stadia or light-industrial premises where it is clear at once that enthusiastic attention and skilled care have been given to good detailing, and where it is evident that the architecture has been a source of pleasure, pride and artistic expression for the design team. Rutter Carrol, *Twentieth Century Architects: Ryder and Yates* (Twentieth Century Society/English Heritage/RIBA, 2009); Alan Clawley, *Twentieth Century Architects: John Madin* (Twentieth Century Society/English Heritage/RIBA, 2011); Ross Brown, *Scottish Brutalism project*, online at Scotbrut.co.uk.
59 Scotbrut.co.uk has some particularly good discussion of this phenomenon.
60 Marriott, p. 108.
61 The event, 'City Spaces and Strings', was held in September 2014. An evocative film of it is available here: https://www.youtube.com/watch?v=fg8jyACTBCA.

Chapter 7

1 Denys Lasdun, 'Tradition, Classicism and Myth: An Architect's Interpretation', talk at the Institute of Education Arts Centre, 31 October 1991, video cassette, LaD/489/1.

ENDNOTES

2 Much of the Newbery Tower material in this chapter was originally included in my conference paper at the Society of Architectural Historians' Annual Meeting 2011, in New Orleans, which in turn profited from research conducted by my student Ross Brown, especially his Freedom of Information request on the listing discussion concerning the building. For the University of Strathclyde Architecture Building I am indebted for much information to students who researched it, especially Ross Brown, Ruairidh Campbell Moir and Dale Munro Smith.
3 DNB, John Anderson.
4 The campus is not a distinguished piece of planning overall, and at its northern edge it is insultingly bad, with the buildings across the campus keeping parallel with the street to its south, and therefore meeting the angled street at the north of the site in a series of saw-teeth, on the abandoned triangles between which the litter can blow freely in eddies of Scottish winter wind as the bus-stop queues huddle against the bleak, trafficky street.
5 Frank Fielden & Associates with J. C. Cunningham, and Frank Walker.
6 The mural is by the prominent Scottish muralist Charles Anderson.
7 John Campbell Cunningham, speaking at a 'Celebration of the Architecture Building' event, 26 March 2013, at the Strathclyde Architecture Building, and organised by Architecture @ 131 and the New Glasgow Society.
8 Nikolaus Pevsner, *Pioneers of Modern Design: From William Morris to Walter Gropius* (Third edition, London: Penguin, 1975) p. 166.
9 http://www.scotbrut.co.uk/category/architect/keppie-henderson-partners/ (accessed 8 October 2015).
10 *Builder*, 18 August 1961, p. 322. Ross Brown's research suggests that the Foulis building was designed on its own, and the master plan came afterwards.
11 Wilder Green, 'Louis I. Kahn, Architect: Alfred Newton Richards Medical Research Building. University of Pennsylvania, Philadelphia, 1958–1960', *The Bulletin of the Museum of Modern Art* (1961: 1), pp. 3–23.
12 Ross Brown, 'Newbery Tower, Glasgow School of Art', Twentieth Century Society Building of the Month, July 2011, http://www.

c20society.org.uk/botm/newbery-tower-glasgow-school-of-art/ (accessed 10 October 2015).

13 Timothy Rohan, *The Architecture of Paul Rudolph* (New Haven: Yale, 2014).

14 Flora Samuel, *Le Corbusier in Detail* (Oxford: Architectural Press, 2007), p. 83.

15 Lasdun's New Museums Site scheme of 1961–63; Barnabas Calder, 'Representing Science: The New Museums Site, Cambridge', *Twentieth Century Society Journal* (2013). The Glasgow University Library is another example of a similar design approach of servicing towers, and phase 1 of it was being built as the Newbery Tower was being designed: http://www.scotbrut.co.uk/archive/library-phase-one/.

16 Shown on a photographic 35-millimetre slide which Ross Brown preserved when the GSA was disposing of parts of its slide collection.

17 The online version of the architecture magazine *Urban Realm* claimed that the university was still considering demolishing the building after its listing: http://www.urbanrealm.com/news/3949/Strathclyde_University_refuse_to_rule_out_demolition_of_brutalist_Architecture_Building.html (accessed 10 October 2015).

18 *University of Strathclyde Campus Plan 2011*, available at https://www.strath.ac.uk/media/ps/estatesmanagement/strategy/Campus_Development_Plan_2011.pdf (accessed 10 October 2015), p. 4.

19 *GSA Strategic Plan 2008–2012*, available at www.gsa.ac.uk/about-gsa/publications/strategic-plan.

20 *GSA Strategic Plan 04-08 (07/08 Update)*, available at www.gsa.ac.uk/about-gsa/publications/strategic-plan, p. 12.

21 *GSA Strategic Plan 04-08 (07/08 Update)*, p. 13.

22 Robert Proctor, 'Tradition and Evolution: Glasgow School of Architecture under Eugène Bourdon', in Ray McKenzie, ed., *The Flower and the Green Leaf: Glasgow School of Art in the Time of Charles Rennie Mackintosh* (Edinburgh: Luath, 2009), pp. 80–94 (pp. 88–89).

23 One referred to 'a pretty horrendous collection of faculty buildings [. . .] directly opposite the Mackintosh school'. Another picked this up: 'Absolutely! the existing neighbours look terrible and the new building will be a vast improvement.' Those commenting are not per se hostile to modern architecture. The writer goes on: 'It is much better, in my view, to put something genuinely modern and different

next to Mackintosh. The alternative would be a half-hearted bit of kitsch that would diminish, rather than enhance, the impact of the original.' (Online comments section beneath Rowan Moore, 'Outcry over Glasgow School of Art extension', *Guardian*, 25 February 2011, www.theguardian.com/artanddesign/2011/feb/25/mackintosh-glasgow-school-art-extension.)

24 Charles McKean, David Walker, Frank Arneil Walker, *Central Glasgow: An Illustrated Architectural Guide* (Edinburgh: RIAS, 1989), p. 149. They were writing in 1989, perhaps the absolute nadir of Brutalist popularity in Britain, but fifteen years later this attitude to exposed concrete had not disappeared entirely: architectural consultants reporting in 2005 on the possible future development of the art school, talked of the Newbery Tower's equally concrete neighbour as having 'considerable visual presence that could be said to border on the oppressive. Designed in what was known as the "brutalist" style, today most observers would say its weathered raw concrete appearance is a little too brutal.' (The Bond Bryan Partnership, *The Glasgow School of Art Estates Options Appraisal DRAFT February 2005*, page 11, paragraph 3.11.)

25 Dale Munro Smith, '"One is naturally sorry that many of the architects do not like their new building": Lessons from the Architecture Building and the Bourdon Building', unpublished fourth-year dissertation, University of Strathclyde (2011), p. 13. The quotation in the title relates to the Bourdon Building, the architecture school building for the Mackintosh School of Architecture.

26 Richard Carr, 'Bourdon Blues', *Building Design*, 31 October 1980.

27 Committee on Climate Change, *Meeting Carbon Budgets: 2013 Progress Report to Parliament* (available at https://www.theccc.org.uk/wp-content/uploads/2013/06/CCC-Prog-Rep_Chap3_singles_web_1.pdf), p. 109.

28 Mike Jackson, 'Embodied Energy and Historic Preservation: A Needed Reassessment', *APT Bulletin*, Vol. 36, No. 4 (2005), pp. 47–52 (Table 4, p. 51).

29 New buildings with lots of concrete have a particularly serious environmental impact because it not only requires a lot of energy to make cement, but the process in itself also releases large amounts of CO_2 through a chemical reaction during cement production. The cement

industry is responsible for around 5 per cent of human CO_2 release: Madeleine Rubenstein, 'Emissions from the Cement Industry', *State of the Planet: Earth Institute, Columbia University* (9 May 2012, available at http://blogs.ei.columbia.edu/2012/05/09/emissions-from-the-cement-industry/).

30 Saint 1987, p. 86.

31 Figure given for a three-bedroom, semi-detached house with gas central heating, by the Energy Saving Trust (http://www.energysavingtrust.org.uk/domestic/thermostats-and-controls).

32 For example, in the comments thread beneath *Building Design*'s publication of the news of the competition win: http://www.bdonline.co.uk/steven-holl-wins-glasgow-school-of-art-mackintosh-competition/3148238.article.

33 Open letter from William JR Curtis, 20 March 2011, available at http://www.architectsjournal.co.uk/news/opinion/facing-up-to-mackintosh/8607805.article.

34 'Historic Scotland: Glasgow School of Art Consultation: Proposal', undated document released with names obscured under Ross Brown's Freedom of Information request, January 2011. From another document in the release it seems to have been considered for listing in 2006.

35 Historic Scotland listing description, '131 Rottenrow, University of Strathclyde, Architecture Building (Ref:51962)'. Listed July 2012.

36 The preservation society is Friends of the Architecture Building. Articles discussing the fate of the building included: Laura Mark, 'Anger as Strathclyde School of Architecture Leaves Brutalist Home', *Architects' Journal*, 14 January 2013; Ruairidh Campbell Moir, 'Strathclyde University School of Architecture', 20th Century Society Building of the Month – September 2013, available at http://www.c20society.org.uk/botm/strathclyde-university-school-of-architecture/; 'Vessels', *RIAS Quarterly*, Spring 2013 (pp. 52–57), available at http://www.rias.org.uk/files/2013/166/5E8DDC0E-D3C0-8E3C-965D-772908312C84.pdf, in which students at all of Scotland's architecture schools reflect on their buildings, stimulated by the threat to Strathclyde's.

37 At the time of writing it seems fairly certain that Alison and Peter Smithson's Robin Hood Gardens housing estate in London is going to go, yet with each 'last visit' it seems less believable – people are still

living there, the concrete looks as robust as ever, the gardens as mature and permanent, and the whole thing so inescapably real and solid that it is impossible to imagine it disappearing from the cityscape.

38 'Particularly careful selection is required for buildings from the period after 1945', *Principles of Selection for Listing Buildings* (Department for Culture Media and Sport, March 2010), p. 5; Historic England: 'Listed Buildings', https://historicengland.org.uk/listing/what-is-designation/listed-buildings.

39 The 1966 Seifert scheme, 'River City', would have demolished the dock to replace it with a number of office towers which would have housed 50,000 workers. George Brown's ban on new offices in London made such schemes particularly financially attractive at this period. Strong-minded individuals can change the outcomes for buildings. If you know a good Brutalist building that is coming under threat, contact the Twentieth Century Society and then get your head down and fight.

Chapter 8

1 The best general history of the National Theatre is Daniel Rosenthal, *The National Theatre Story* (London: Oberon, 2013).
2 Gavin Stamp, 'The South Bank Site', *Twentieth Century Architecture 5, the Festival of Britain* (2001), pp. 11–24 (pp. 13–14).
3 Hansard, House of Commons Debate, 21 January 1949, vol. 460. The element of consensus which drew these apparently opposed groups together was a characteristically mid-century faith in the intrinsic value of 'high' culture. Even in the deep national poverty of the 1940s the opponents of the National Theatre Bill fought it not by questioning the value of subsidised theatre but by arguing that the best way to spend the subsidy was to share it around the country in smaller subsidies to more theatres.
4 *DNB*, Isaac Hayward.
5 Hansard, House of Commons Debate, 21 January 1949, vol. 460, cc. 446.
6 Hansard, House of Commons Debate, 21 January 1949, vol. 460, cc. 447.

7 'My father and mother were both concerned with the original project nearly 40 years ago, and I am very glad to think that my mother lived long enough to know of the introduction of this Bill. So I support the Bill wholeheartedly on its merits. I support it also out of filial piety and from the association, not a short one, which I have had with the project.' Hansard, House of Commons Debate, 21 January 1949, vol. 460, cc. 443. 'It has not been Lord Esher [another hereditary peer who helped to push through the bill]'s privilege or good fortune to live in an age when, as a Maecenas, he could have supported the drama out of his own resources, but within the limits of the possible in our age no one has worked more devotedly than he.' Hansard, House of Commons Debate, 21 January 1949 vol 460, cc449. When the National Theatre was opening, twenty-seven years later and after the death of Lyttelton, the second-largest auditorium was named after him. At his own earlier request it was named the Lyttelton Theatre, not, as the National Theatre Board preferred, the Chandos (after his title Viscount Chandos), because he wished it to commemorate his mother too; National Theatre Archive: National Theatre Board minutes (henceforth 'NTB minutes'), 13 March 1972 and 18 April 1972.

8 Joan Littlewood quoted by Stephen Mullin, in Samantha Hardingham and Kester Rattenbury, *Supercrit #1: Cedric Price: Potteries Thinkbelt* (Abingdon: Routledge, 2007), p. 103.

9 Rosenthal, p. 56.

10 LCC minutes, 18–19 July 1961, p. 502.

11 Richard Findlater, 'The Winding Road to King's Reach', in Simon Callow, ed., *The National: The Theatre and Its Work 1963–1997* (London: Nick Hern/National Theatre, 1997), pp. 79–83 (pp. 82–3).

12 Denys Lasdun & Partners (DLP) memorandum, 11 March 1968, Royal Institute of British Architects, Denys Lasdun Archive (RIBA), LaD/171/3.

13 Barnabas Calder, 'Committees and Concrete: the genesis and architecture of Denys Lasdun's National Theatre', unpublished PhD thesis, University of Cambridge, 2006, pp. 123–5. The Opera House committee had drawn up their brief by October 1962: National Theatre Archive, South Bank Theatre Board minutes (SBTB), 17 October 1962, 22, p. 2.

14 National Theatre Archive, Building Committee minutes (BC), 9 January 1963, p. 6.

ENDNOTES

15 The architectural advisory committee consisted of Sir Robert Matthew, LCC Architect 1946–53; Hubert Bennett, the current LCC Architect; and Sir William Holford, a planner of considerable influence. It also included the artist John Piper and the theatre specialist Norman Marshall.
16 National Theatre Archive: List of architects as at 1 July 1963, NTA, Box 40 SBTB.
17 National Theatre Archive: Lynex annotation, 'Preliminary list of Architects', 10 June 1963, Box 40 SBTB.
18 E.g. National Theatre Archive: List of architects as at 24 May 1963, Box 40 SBTB.
19 National Theatre Archive: Letter from Bill Howell to Lynex, 17 May 1963, in SBTB 13/13 Part 1.
20 National Theatre Archive: Small sheet headed 'Very confidential', SBTB 13/13 Part 1.
21 National Theatre Archive: [Lynex] to David McKenna and Lord Chandos, SBTB 13/13 Part 1, 29 October 1963.
22 Lasdun's archive shows this process in action. His first sketches for the National Theatre project are not the napkin-doodles of architectural legend, by which 'genius' architects leap straight to a magnificent solution to a complex brief. Rather they are rough outlines, in his child-like, scribbled 6B pencil, of the views to and across the National Theatre and Opera House site next to County Hall; RIBA Lasdun Drawings, PB909/1(1–5); the information on Lasdun's favoured pencil comes from Derek Potter, interviewed by author.
23 DLP memoranda, 17 and 30 November 1964, RIBA Lasdun Archive, LaD/171/1.
24 National Theatre Archive: BC minutes, 4 March 1964, p. 3.
25 The leading directors of subsidised theatre were indeed formidable when challenged, feeling perhaps a need to demonstrate their artistic independence by biting the hands that fed them. Olivier found himself figuring as the Establishment in such a fight with Peter Brook in 1968. Brook wanted to stage a grotesque dance to close his production of Seneca's *Oedipus*, arguing that this was the authentic conclusion of ancient tragedies. In 1968 National Theatre productions still ended with the National Anthem, and Brook proposed to accompany his grotesque dance with a jazzed-up 'God Save the Queen', in place of

the normal solemn rendition. Olivier, by his own account an ardent royalist, objected to the affront to the monarchy, and Brook replaced the dance with the slow and stagey unveiling of a vast, spotlit statue of a penis in the centre of the stage – ostensibly a release of feelings after the tension of the play, but undoubtedly also a very clear gesture to Olivier in response to his intervention; Laurence Olivier, *Confessions of an Actor* (London: Weidenfeld & Nicolson, 1982), pp. 286–87.

26 National Theatre Archive: Lynex to Cottesloe (SBTB 13/13 Part 1), 28 July 1963.

27 National Theatre Archive: BC minutes, 4 March 1964, p. 3.

28 National Theatre Archive: BC minutes, 3 January 1963, p. 1.

29 National Theatre Archive: BC minutes, 3 January 1963, p. 2.

30 DLP Memorandum, 9 December 1963, RIBA Lasdun Archive, LaD/170/6.

31 Calder PhD, pp. 10–16.

32 Laurence Olivier quoted in Richard Pilbrow, 'Notes on Barnabas Calder Thesis on the Design of the National Theatre', 12 November 2014, p. 14.

33 National Theatre Archive: BC minutes, 4 March 1964, p. 1.

34 National Theatre Archive: BC minutes, 5 February 1964, p. 4.

35 DLP memorandum, 7 April 1964, RIBA Lasdun Archive, LaD/170/6.

36 Letter from Jocelyn Herbert to Lasdun, received 28 April 1964, RIBA Lasdun Archive, LaD/190/1.

37 Lasdun made clear to the Building Committee that 'I would not like to take the responsibility for Scheme B without, say, six producers playing around with the model, and we should also, at some time, need a mock-up in a field somewhere.' National Theatre Archive: BC minutes, 7 October 1964, p. 5.

38 RIBA Robert Elwall Photographs Collection, 41798/14-41798/29.

39 Denys Lasdun, National Life Stories Collection, National Sound Archive.

40 Lever interview, p. 56.

41 A photograph survives of the heap of discarded models in the late 1960s. The contrast between the miniaturised delicacy of the balsa auditoria and terraces and the messy, spilling heap is poignantly evocative of the massive amount of effort used, reworking and sacrificing attractive design ideas in favour of even better ones. Lasdun

submitted the photo to the Royal Academy in place of a more conventional drawing, as the evidence of his worthiness to become a member; Royal Academy Archives, photograph accepted 1991, 04/2372.
42 Peter Sullivan, 'The National Theatre Plan – and How it Evolved,' *Sunday Times*, 21 February 1965; SBTB minutes, 21 April 1965, 116, p. 1.
43 DLP memorandum, 22 February 1965, RIBA Lasdun Archive, LaD/171/1.
44 Philip Wood, interviewed by author at the National Theatre, 18 May 2004.
45 National Theatre Archive: BC minutes, 1 April 1966, p. 6.
46 DLP memorandum, 27 April 1966. The meeting recorded was the previous day. RIBA Lasdun Archive, LaD/171/2.
47 It was enlarged from 700 seats to 850 by the South Bank Theatre Board, to increase its revenue at some cost to its feeling of intimacy: National Theatre Archive: SBTB minutes, 20 July 1966, 146, p. 2.
48 Quoted anonymously in Iain Mackintosh, *Architecture, Actor and Audience* (London: Routledge, 1993), p. 25. The Lyttelton provides perfect sight-lines from every seat, and decent acoustics, and by avoiding aisles gets all the audience as near as possible to the centre-line on which the best seats lie. This was understood in the 1960s to be the essence of proscenium design, but many have found the theatre disappointing.
49 DLP memorandum, 21 September 1964, RIBA Lasdun Archive, LaD/170/6.
50 RIBA Lasdun Models, MOD/LASD/24.
51 John Elsom and Nicholas Tomalin, *The History of the National Theatre* (London: Jonathan Cape, 1978), p. 178; National Theatre Archive: SBTB minutes, 20 October 1965, p. 2.
52 National Theatre Archive: SBTB minutes, 9 March 1966, 140, p. 1. Right through to the abolition of the LCC in 1965 its determined support was repeatedly to rescue the National Theatre building from threatened cancellation by the government. Its successor, the Greater London Council, was, as it transpired, to do likewise. By renegotiating their own contributions of site, building subsidy and ongoing subsidy the council repeatedly embarrassed or cajoled Westminster into not pulling out.

53 In the event the smallest theatre, the Cottesloe (now renamed the Dorfman), was to be postponed to save money, and eventually designed to ideas of the advisory firm Theatre Projects Consultants: Richard Pilbrow, 'Innocence and the National Theatre', *The Theatres Trust Newsletter* (March 2002), pp. 4–8 (pp. 6–7), and Iain Mackintosh, interviewed by author, at Theatre Projects Consultants, Camden, 3 December 2003.

54 National Theatre Archive: SBTB minutes, 10 August 1966, p. 2.

55 DLP memorandum, 6 May 1966, p. 1, LaD/171/2.

56 The White Report, Appendix D, p. 1. There may, too, have been practical advantages for the GLC from the swap: it left the large site next to County Hall more flexible for future development.

57 National Theatre Archive: BC minutes, 11 May 1966, p. 6.

58 National Theatre Archive: BC minutes, 11 May 1966, pp. 7–8.

59 National Theatre Archive: BC minutes, 20 May 1966, p. 1.

60 Calder PhD, pp. 106–108.

61 The magnificently ambitious stage machinery was specified by Richard Pilbrow of Theatre Projects Consultants.

62 You can see these settlement gaps in the foyers, for example around the indoor staircase nearest to Waterloo Bridge in the Lyttelton Foyer.

63 A. R. Flint and J. A. Neill, 'Engineering Aspects of the National Theatre', *Structural Engineer*, 55 (1977), pp. 19–40 (pp. 32–33).

64 Flint and Neill, p. 19.

65 Flint and Neill, p. 26.

66 Post-tensioning is a form of pre-stressing. Both terms can be used in 1960s and 1970s projects.

67 Flint and Neill, p. 32.

68 Flint and Neill, p. 27.

69 National Theatre Archive, SBTB minutes, 4 May 1965, 125, p. 3.

70 Denys Lasdun, 'An Architect's Approach to Architecture', *RIBA Journal*, 72 (1965), pp. 184–95 (p. 194).

71 DLP memorandum, 23 January 1968, p. 1, RIBA Lasdun Archive, LaD/171/3.

72 DLP memorandum, 19 February 1968, RIBA Lasdun Archive, LaD/171/3.

73 DLP memorandum, 19 February 1968, RIBA Lasdun Archive, LaD/171/3.

74 DLP memorandum, 7 March 1968, p. 2, RIBA Lasdun Archive, LaD/171/3.
75 Derek Potter, interviewed by author, at his home in Docklands, 20 September 2005.
76 DLP memorandum, 12 June 1968, p. 1, RIBA Lasdun Archive, LaD/171/3.
77 DLP memoranda, 26 June and 7 July 1969 (the dates here are of the memoranda, not the meetings they record), RIBA Lasdun Archive, LaD/171/3. Mr Rolt of McAlpine's was the specialist who dismissed the possibility of precast on a steel frame. I know nothing else about him, but I frequently think of him with gratitude: the National Theatre as built is for me the supreme monument of in situ concrete, and I simply cannot imagine it being so good clad in precast.
78 Models of diagrid (MOD/LASD/38) and Olivier ceiling (MOD/LASD/17) survive in RIBA; glazing and Lyttelton concrete information from Philip Wood interviewed by author.
79 DLP memorandum, 6 August 1969, LaD/171/5.
80 NTB minutes, 10 November 1969, 99/69 p. 4.
81 Elsom and Tomalin, p. 225.
82 DLP memorandum, 25 August 1976, RIBA Lasdun Archive, LaD/172/1.
83 Letter from Rayne to Sir Edwin McAlpine, 21 May 1974, RIBA Lasdun Archive, LaD/157/6-LaD/158/2.
84 DLP memorandum, 25 September 1973, RIBA Lasdun Archive, LaD/172/1.
85 DLP memorandum, 25 August 1976, RIBA Lasdun Archive, LaD/172/1.
86 DLP Memorandum of telephone conversation between Lasdun and Peter Scott of McAlpine's, 4 October 1972, RIBA Lasdun Archive, LaD/173/1.
87 DLP memorandum, 6 February 1973, LaD/171/6.
88 Flint and Neill, pp. 27–28.
89 DLP memorandum, 6 February 1973, LaD/171/6.
90 DLP memorandum, 8 October 1970, pp. 2–3, RIBA Lasdun Archive, LaD/171/6.
91 Forty, p. 226.
92 Patrick Dillon, *Concrete Reality: Denys Lasdun and the National Theatre* (London: National Theatre, 2015), p. 53.

93 It is not known whether this was done at the National Theatre, but it is featured in Ernö Goldfinger's draft specification for Balfron Tower, before he resolved to use bush-hammered concrete: 'Specification for the Structural Engineering Works Rowlett Street Housing, Poplar', September 1964, 5.85 (p. 36), RIBA GolEr/172/2.
94 'Specification for the Structural Engineering Works Rowlett Street Housing, Poplar', September 1964, 5.85 (p. 36), RIBA GolEr/172/2.
95 Christine M. Wall, '"Raw, Potent Concrete": The Architectural Use of Concrete in the Twentieth Century and its Effect on the Labour Process in the Construction Industry', Polytechnic of North London School of Architecture unpublished dissertation, 1991.
96 DLP memorandum, 6 February 1973, LaD/171/6.
97 Flint and Neill, pp. 26, 33 and 35. I have never managed to find marks in the concrete showing where the sixteen-foot sections, cast first, end and the infill sections begin – somehow the brilliant carpenters have disguised them entirely.
98 Wall dissertation.
99 DLP memorandum, 25 August 1976, RIBA Lasdun Archive, LaD/172/1.
100 'All contractors are losing money because they tendered too low', DLP memorandum, 25 August 1976, RIBA Lasdun Archive, LaD/172/1. The difficulties experienced by one of the main theatre-equipment subcontractors are set out in notes for a 'Meeting with Mole Richardson on 10 January 1977', a copy of which survives in the National Theatre Archive's SBTB Correspondence. The document is annotated in pen, 'Meeting did not take place.'
101 DLP memorandum, 25 August 1976, RIBA Lasdun Archive, LaD/172/1.
102 Charles Nevin, 'The Best and Worst Buildings in Britain', *Observer*, 11 June 1989, pp. 18–23 (p. 18).
103 James Lasdun, 'My Father', *Modern Painters*, 16 (2003), pp. 54–61 (p. 59).
104 Mackintosh, 1997, pp. 16–17.
105 Nevin, p. 22.
106 Charles Windsor, Prince of Wales, *A Vision of Britain*, BBC television programme, 28 October 1988.

107 Denys Lasdun, 'Tradition, Classicism and Myth: An Architect's Interpretation', talk at the Institute of Education Arts Centre, 31 October 1991, video cassette, RIBA Lasdun Archive, LaD/489/1.
108 Rosenthal, pp. 573–78.
109 The architects for the latest refurbishment (2014–15) were Haworth Tompkins. They conducted an exemplary investigation into the history of the National Theatre, and studied the qualities of its architecture. Their research and consultation would serve as a good model for any management of an important Modernist building to seek to emulate, and has resulted in interventions by Haworth Tompkins, led by Patrick Dillon, which have restored much of the original excitement and quality to the building, whilst contributing valuable updated facilities. I was among those consulted on the history of the building.
110 Letter from Jørn Utzon to Lasdun, 3 August 1995, RIBA Lasdun Archive, LaD/242/4.
111 Letter from John Betjeman to Lasdun, 1 November 1973, RIBA Lasdun Archive, LaD/191/2.
112 Letter from Vivien Bradford to Lasdun, 9 March 1976, RIBA Lasdun Archive, LaD/192/1.
113 Letter from Lasdun to Vivien Bradford, 17 March 1976, RIBA Lasdun Archive, LaD/192/1.
114 In this kind of concrete quality Lasdun was a very long way from the rough origins of 'Brutalism', or from the glorious crudity of Hermit's Castle. Here Lasdun was using the spectacular craft skill available among British concreters by the later 1960s in order to produce perfect, beautiful surfaces and durable, high-strength engineering. In things like the disguising of the joints between one pour and the next, this meant actively concealing details of the process by which the concrete had been produced, rather than exhibiting them with candour in the way that Brutalism claimed to favour. The craft of Lasdun's buildings is less like Le Corbusier's buildings than those of the great German-American Modernist Ludwig Mies van der Rohe. Mies's steel-framed buildings were welded and sanded with the highest perfectionism until, rather than being clear Modernist demonstrations of how they were made, they became pure expressions of

perfect order and flawless execution. Lasdun's concrete shows in general terms how it was made, but with an elegance of perfect surfaces and simple geometrical volumes that required – and got – impeccable concrete work: Calder 2015.
116 National Theatre Archive: BC minutes, 9 January 1964, p. 6.
117 Calder PhD, p. 167.
118 Curtis, p. 16.
119 Mark Girouard, 'Cosmic Connections', *Architectural Review*, 161 (1977), pp. 5–7.

Epilogue

1 Barnabas Calder, *Denys Lasdun's Royal College of Physicians: A monumental act of faith* (London: Royal College of Physicians, 2008).
2 Personal communication from William Fawcett, c. 2004.
3 Lewis L. Strauss, Speech to the National Association of Science Writers, New York City, quoted in 'Abundant power from atom seen', *New York Times*, 17 September 1954.
4 The chunky clarity of Brutalist detailing, and its avoidance of smooth textures, seem to be qualities which are hard to evoke in contemporary materials. The incongruity is often unflattering to both, the original building looking coarse and the new additions flimsy and dishonest. What the coming generation of Brutalism refurbishers need is to keep the overall environment hard and spare. Any planting should have a reasonably natural or wild look, and not be too small and fiddly. New materials should be clearly what they are, and should not be slick, or scratchily-thin. Colour should be used extremely cautiously – the monochrome environments of Brutalist architecture were intentional, and can suddenly look dull and tawdry when interrupted by bursts of brighter shades. Vivid new colours in a Brutalist setting can be as intrusive as a mobile ringtone during a two minute silence.
5 The single biggest thing that building owners and users can do to keep their Brutalist buildings looking good is to minimise clutter. There has been an extraordinary proliferation in recent decades of emergency exit signs mounted on prominent doors, generations of fire equipment and signage perhaps superseded but apparently

rarely removed, extra lights trailing tacked-on wires across brick and concrete, IT-related cabling taped and pinned to every wall, and a zoo of speakers, flat-screen monitors, CCTV installations, notice boards, and endless other shabby bric-a-brac.

6 Harwood, 2015, p. 490.
7 Harwood, 2015, p. 490.

Acknowledgements

My understanding of post-war architecture owes more to Elain Harwood than to anyone else. Her endless generosity and nearly omniscient knowledge of the period have been a constant resource to me both in published form – including her listing descriptions which are never signed but often recognisable – and by conversation and e-mail.

The Twentieth Century Society has also been an unfailing source of inspiration and support, and I have profited greatly from conversations and events with Catherine Croft, Alan Powers, Alistair Fair, Tim Brittain-Catlin, Otto Saumarez Smith and many others of those who form its backbone.

In my research at the Royal Institute of British Architects, with its unmatched collection of papers, drawings and photographs, and its superb library, I have been helped more than I can say by many including in particular Catriona Cornelius, Lisa Nash, Suzanne Waters, Justine Sambrook, Vicky Wilson, Charles Hind, Eleanor

ACKNOWLEDGEMENTS

Gawne, Jonathan Makepeace, Irena Murray, Kent Rawlinson, Kurt Helfrich, and the late Robert Elwall.

This book has been much improved by comments and corrections from people who have read chapters or provided information, including Ross Brown, Mark Crinson, Catherine Croft, Steven Croft, Elain Harwood, Susan Lasdun, Ruairidh Campbell Moir, Gordon Murray, Helia Neto, Steven Parnell, Robert Proctor, Nicholas Ray, Adam Sharr, Mark Swenarton, Dirk Van den Heuvel and Christine Wall.

My research has been encouraged and guided at crucial stages by William Fawcett, Adrian Forty, and Murray Fraser, and most particularly Andrew Saint, whose supervision made my PhD a pleasure. Susan Lasdun has been unendingly kind and supportive in my work on Denys Lasdun.

Colleagues at the University of Strathclyde and the University of Liverpool have discussed my work and advised me on it, and conversations with students at both institutions have helped me immeasurably in developing and clarifying my thinking – I owe a particularly heavy debt to the wonderful students of my 'Ideal Worlds?' special subject course at Strathclyde, some of whom appear by name in the notes of this book.

This project would not have come about without my agent, Jon Elek, and my editor, Tom Avery, who got it started. I have waited ever since for Tom's patience or his enthusiasm to flag, but they never have.

Lastly, and most importantly of all, my family, and particularly my wife Helen, have helped and cheered me on at every stage of this project, discussing my ideas with me, visiting building after building, and tolerating my solipsism during writing. My lovely daughter Charlotte invariably cheers me up when I close the laptop for the evening.

Index

Page numbers in *italics* indicate illustrations.

A

Achmelvich, Highlands, 24–5, *34–5*, 36–9, *40*, 41–5, *46*, 47–9, 109, 140, 340
Ackroyd, Peter, 329
adaptability, 260
aesthetics, 11–15, 25, 27, 29, 32, 53, 55, 96–7, 109, 110–11, 118, 145, 157, 164, 174, 175, 200, 245, 252, 261, 262, 293, 324, 336, 341
aggregate, 26, 29, 42, 69, 109, 135, 252
Albert Dock, Liverpool, 271
Alexander Fleming House, Elephant and Castle, 63
Alton Estate, Roehampton, 83
Anderston Centre, Glasgow, *204*, 214, *215*, 215, *216*, 217–18, *218*, 219–27, 234, *235*, 235, 236
Anderston Cross CDA, Glasgow, 219–25
Andrewes, Lancelot, 94
Angry Young Men, 281, 282
anti-Semitism, 213
antisocial behaviour, 76
Antwerp, Belgium, 324
Architectural Association, 125, 131, 325
Architectural Review, 32, 151, 153
architecture
 adaptability, 260
 aesthetics, 11–15, 25, 27, 29, 32, 53, 55, 96–7, 109, 110–11, 118, 145, 157, 164, 174, 175, 200, 245, 252, 261, 262, 293, 324, 336, 341
 Art Nouveau, 247, 258
 Arts and Crafts, 247

INDEX

Baroque, 33, 88, 115, 136, 168, 276
Beaux-Arts, 125, 170, 325
Classical, 10, 26, 27, 62, 67, 97, 101, 125, 138, 160, 185, 217, 325, 336–7
commercial, 56, 95, 126, 172, *204*, *205*, *206*, 206–15, *215*, *216*, 217–18, *218*, 219–22, *222*, 223–31, 232–3, 234–5, *235*, 236
conservationism, 152–3, 226, 258, 265–6, 269
Constructivist, 33, 249
education, 4, 33, 110, 125
environmental performance, 261–4, 337–8
Futurist, 134
Gothic, 28, 67, 88, 126, 138, 250, 254, 339
High Tech, 250, 319
origin of, 39
patronage, 15, 60, 126, 157, 179, 181–201, 281
planning, 30, 45, 55, 90, 93–7, 100, 108, 112–14, 118, 130–1, 138, 141–3, 149, 150, 152, 155, 184, 185, 186, 188, 192, 194–6, 197, 201, 208, 209, 211, 219–26, 244, 278–310, 323–5
Postmodernist, 71, 147, 217, 319
private practice, 12, 56, 60–1, 126, 172, 183, 207, 228
proportion, 12, 26, 27, 67
Scots Baronial, 247
set pieces, 33
speculation, 56, 95, 207–36
tourism, 4, 199
arms trade, 259
Art Nouveau, 247, 258
art, 82–3, 97, 126, 181, 209, 236, 279, 283
art theory, 12
Arts and Crafts, 247
Arts Council, 299

artwashing, 81
Atelier 5 partnership, 131, 134
Athens, Greece, 33, 39
Attlee, Clement, 280
austerity, 18
Australia, 191, 318
Austria, 280
axis, 33
Aztecs, 115, 135

B

balconies, 17, 75, 88, 90, 96, 105, 114, 115, 117, 123, 151
Balfron Tower, Poplar, 55, 60, 61, *64*, 65, 67–77, *69*, 79–80, *80*, 80–4, 92, 108, 123, 151, 335, 338, 340
Ballard, James Graham 'J. G.', 17–18, 78, 227
Bangor, Gwynedd, 223
Banham, Peter Reyner, 11–12, 14, 32–3, 172, 180, 197
banking, 87, 209, 225
Barbican Arts Centre, City of London, 102–3, 104, 107–9, 113–15, 296
Barbican Estate, City of London, 48, *86*, 87–8, *89*, 89–90, *91*, 92–7, 98–9, 100–5, *106*, 107–15, *116*, 117–19, 123, 151, 157, 175, 196, 296, 336, 339, 340–1
Baroque architecture, 33, 88, 115, 136, 168, 276
Bartlett, University College London, 213
bathrooms, 59, 65, 107, 139, 141
Bauhaus, 10, 171, 182
Bavaria, Germany, 23, 47
Beatles, The, 4, 194
Beaux-Arts, 125, 170, 325
bed-makers, 140

bedheads, 140, 141
bedrooms, 74, *139*, 140–1, 149–51, 187
Beethoven, Ludwig van, 280, 281
Belgrano, 149
Bern, Switzerland, 131, 134
Bernini, Gian Lorenzo, 198
Bertoia, Harry, 334
bespoke design, 8
Betjeman, John, 226, 229, 322
béton, 12, 27
betterment tax, 208
Beveridge, William, 57
Birmingham, West Midlands, 196
Blackfriars Bridge, London, 231
Blackwell, Ursula, *see* Goldfinger, Ursula
Blenheim Palace, Oxfordshire, 90
Bloomsbury, Camden, 192, 196
boilers, 65, 67, 79, 131, 135
Bolton, 227
Bon, Christof, 97, 100
Boundary Estate, Tower Hamlets, 56
Brâncuși, Constantin, 182
Brandlehow School, Putney, 61
Brecht, Bertolt, 291
Brent Cross shopping centre, London, 311
Breuer, Marcel, 182, 229
bricks, 6, 12, 14, 26, 31, 60, 63, 111, 112, 115, 123, 146, 147, 152, 164, 168, 188, 189, 198, 199, 217, 239, 241, 245, 246, 250, 254
bridge to nowhere, 220
British Empire, 56, 102
British Library, St Pancras, 196
Britten, Benjamin, 297
Bronowski, Jacob, 182
Brook, Peter, 284, 286, 292, 294, 297, 302
Brown, Capability, 186

Brown, George, 210–11
Brown, Ross, 265, 269
Brutalism
    backlash against, 5, 17–18, 123, 160, 259, 319–25
    energy, 6–9, 13, 17, 67, 261–4, 337, 341
    geometry, 48, 67, 113, 174, 175
    historical inspiration, 31–3
    modernity, 16, 30, 41
    motivations for building, 15
    name, 11–14, 126–7, 172
    roughness of, 3, 39, 48, 110, 340
    revival, 334–42
    massing and form, 3, 4, 7, 24, 28, 31, 33, 37, 39, 41–2, 48, 65, 67, 88, 92, 110, 113, 141, 166, 173, 179, 188, 217–18, 229, 252, 256, 276, 319
    and welfare state, 15, 18, 31, 55, 61, 78, 82, 83, 84, 92, 182, 207, 228, 234, 281, 327
Buchanan, Colin, 196
Bullring, Birmingham, 196
bunkers, 39
Burke, Edmund, 321
Burton-upon-Trent, Staffordshire, 223
buses, 220, 235
bush-hammering, 68, 92, 103

C

Caine, Michael, 205–6
Callaghan, James, 283, 299, 300
Cambridge, Cambridgeshire, 100, 169, 254
Cambridge University, *122*, 124–5, 127–9, *130*, 130–1, *132*–3, 134–6, *137*, 138–9, *139*, 140–57, *158*–9, 160, 183, 184, 185–6, 190, 194, 325

INDEX

Christ's College, *122*, 124–5, 127–9, *130*, 130–1, *132–3*, 134–6, *137*, 138–9, *139*, 140–57, *158–9*, 160, 325, 336, 341
Churchill College, 185
History Faculty, 190
Jesus College, 141–3, 152
Selwyn College, 186
Sidney Sussex College, 141, 152
Camden, London, 175
Cameron, David, 4–5
Canada, 125
cantilever, 166, 244
car parks, 79, 136, 205–6, *206*, 212, 214, *215*, *222*, 230
Cardross, Argyll, 334
Carlton House Terrace, Westminster, 101
carpentry, 8, 28, 42–4, 62, 67–8, 108–9, 175, 181, 252, 313, 315–16, 318
cars, 100, 194–5, 209
casinos, 220
Casson, Hugh, 213
Casson Conder & Partners, 128–9, 131, 146
Catford, Lewisham, 230
cathedrals, 9, 87–8, 90, 95, 100, 102, 225, 254, 275, 322, 339
Catholicism, 6, 334
cement, 26, 27, 38, 42, 135
central heating, 7, 31, 59, 65, 74, 92, 115
Centre Point, Camden, 225, 226
chairs, 147, 334
Chamberlin, Peter 'Joe', 97, 117
Chamberlin Powell & Bon (CPB), 96–119, 183, 185, 228
Charles, Prince of Wales, 18, 320–1
chemical lavatories, 102
Chermayeff, Serge, 182

Chichester Festival Theatre, 282, 288, 289
chimneys, 7, 179
Christ's College, Cambridge, *122*, 124–5, 127–9, *130*, 130–1, *132–3*, 134–6, *137*, 138–9, *139*, 140–57, *158–9*, 160, 336, 341
churches, 9, 87–8, 90, 95, 100, 102, 112, 136, 196, 225, 254, 275, 276, 322, 328, 339
Churchill, Winston, 185, 208
Churchill College, Cambridge, 185
Churchill Gardens, Pimlico, 171
cinema, 63, 107, 276, 283, 290
Circle, 182, 201
City of London, 48, *86*, 87–8, *89*, 89–90, *91*, 92–7, *98–9*, 100–5, *106*, 107–15, *116*, 117–19, 123, 151, 157, 175, 196, 211, 225
City Spaces & Strings, 236
Civic Trust, 152
cladding, 28, 79, 164, 230, 241, 254, 269, 313, 325, 337, 340
Classical architecture, 10, 26, 27, 62, 67, 97, 101, 125, 138, 160, 185, 217, 325, 336–7
clay, 26, 27
climate change, 17
climbing buildings, 144–5
Clore, Charles, 230
CO_2 emissions, 261, 263, 337–8
coal, 6, 17, 27, 65, 311
Coates, Wells, 125
coffee-shops, 260
College Court, Leicester University, 186–7, *187*, 188, *189*, 189–90
columns, 6, 7, 14, 26, 29, 62, 108, 112, 114, 115, 136, 138, 160, 168, 175, 178, 179, 180, 188, 190, 205, 229, 260

388

INDEX

commercial architecture, 56, 95, 126, 172, *204*, 205, *206*, 206–15, *215*, *216*, 217–18, *218*, 219–22, *222*, 223–31, *232–3*, 234–5, *235*, 236
Commonwealth, 102
Communism, 33, 63, 94, 104, 125–6, 219, 228, 336
Comprehensive Development Areas (CDAs), 33, 143, 218–25
Compulsory Purchase Orders, 208, 221, 222
concierges, 77, 78, 115
concrete
   aggregate, 26, 29, 42, 69, 109, 135, 252
   cheapness of, 15, 25, 29, 320, 336
   colours, 3, 29, 37, 112, 113, 135, 175, 217, 312–13, 316, 318
   consultant engineers, 28–9, 304
   corduroy, 252, *253*, 254, 333
   cracking and crazing, 316, 318
   etymology, 27
   exposed, 12, 30, 59, 65, 92, 102, 180–1, 246, 254, 261, 307, 323
   fireproofing, 27
   formwork, 8, 28, 42–4, 62, 67–8, 108–9, 175, 181, 252, 313, 315–16
   hammering, 68, 92, 102–3, 109
   honeycombing, 316
   in situ, 28, 42, 109, 135, 175, 254, 268, 307, 308–9, 316, 339
   mixing of, 26–7, 44
   and modernity, 41
   moulds, *see* formwork
   nature, conflict with, 25, 42
   pollution, 338
   pouring, 8, 18, 30, 70, 109, 313, 315–16, 338
   pre-cast, 28, 136, 308
   reinforcement of, 7, 15, 27–8, 63, 68, 261, 312, 313, 315, 335
   shapes, 24, 28
   shuttering, 30, 41, 69–70, 103, 109, 135, 313, 316, 318
   straw waddling, 246
   textures, 3, 24, 29, 30, 37, 42, 43, 67–8, 80, 92, 102–3, 109, 175, 181, 252, 268, 276, 312, 313, 315–16, 318, 322, 339
   unreinforced, 27, 29
   water staining, 3, 29, 55, 252, 320
Conservation Areas, 153
conservationism, 152–3, 226, 258, 265–6, 269
conservatism, 15, 57–8, 94, 95, 96, 118–19, 157, 279, 280, 325, 336, 337
Conservative Party, 57–8, 81, 185, 195, 208, 235, 283
Constructivism, 33, 249
consultant engineers, 28–9, 304
Le Corbusier, 10, 14, 39, 62, 65, 71, 100, 101, 125, 131, 171, 172, 173, 179, 182, 197, 201, 229, 252, 308, 336
corduroy concrete, 252, *253*, 254, 333
Corporation of the City of London, 90, 92–7, 100–1, 118, 157
corruption, 4, 205–7
cottage estates, 58
Cottesloe, Lord, *see* Fremantle, John
Cotton, Jack, 209
council housing, 5, 9, 10, 11, 15, 16, 52, 53, *54*, 55–6, 60, 61, *64*, 65, 66, 67–9, *69*, 69–80, *80*, 80–4, *86*, 87–8, *89*, 89–90, *91*, 92–7, *98–9*, 100–5, *106*, 107–15, *116*, 117–19, *204*, 208, 214, *215*, 215, *216*, 217–18, *218*, 219, 221, 227, 234
County Hall, Lambeth, 185, 275, 279, 322

INDEX

County of London Plan, 61, 278
Courtauld Institute, 87–8, 89, 123, 276
courts, 136, 138
courtyard theatres, 290
Coward, Noël, 281
cranes, 103, 135
crazing, 316, 318
crime, 4, 5, 53, 77–8, 205–7
Crinson, Mark, 179
Crittal, 178, 241
Crosse & Blackwell, 63
Crudens, 59
Cubism, 41, 340

D

D-Day, 126
Dad's Army, 182
Dalston, Hackney, 88
Dannatt, Trevor, 187
darkrooms, 148
Darwin Garden, Christ's College, 157, *158*
David, Elizabeth 100
daylight, *see* natural light
democratic outdoor space, 138, 249
demolitions, 4, 33, 57, 79, 153, 166, 192, 195–7, 207, 209, 211–12, 218–19, 221, 222, 223, 230, 231, 234, 244, 249, 256–69, *270*, 271, 333–4, 337
Denmark, 191
Derby, Derbyshire, 223
desks, 139, 140, 245, 259
detailing, 309
developers, 205–36
Devine, George, 284, 288
Dexter, John, 284
DiMaggio, Joe, 97
Docklands, London, 275
Dolphin Square, Westminster, 101
Doncaster, Yorkshire, 223

door bells, 73
doors, 8, 39, 41, 42, 72, 73, 107, 109, 114, 117, 215, *216*, 217, 340
Dorchester Hotel, Mayfair, 209
double glazing, 79, 261
Douglas fir, 313
Drapers Gardens, City of London, 210
drugs, 78
Dunlop Rubber Co. Ltd, 220
dyslexia, 170

E

Eames chairs, 334
East Germany (1949–90), 104
Eastern Europe, 102, 219
Easton, John Murray, 193
École des Beaux-Arts, Paris, 62, 125, 126
Economist Building, St James, 235
Edenham Street Estate, Kensington, 52, 53, *54*, 55, 60, 61, 65, *66*, 67–8, 76, 77–9, 83–4, 87, 108, 339
Edinburgh, Scotland, 39, 261
education, 4, 6, 16, 33, 57, 128, 183, 207, 234, 279; *see also* schools, universities
Edwardian era (1901–10), 4, 111, 123, 220, 260, 289
Egypt, 6, 33
electricians, 311
electricity, 6, 7, 65, 67, 168, 211, 246, 337
Elephant and Castle, London, 63
elitism, 280, 281, 325
Elizabeth II, Queen of the United Kingdom, 279
Elliott, Michael, 284, 297
Empire State Building, New York City, 103
energy, 6–9, 13, 17, 67, 261–4, 337, 342

engineering, 6–8, 11, 26–31, 41, 49, 55, 62–3, 94, 109, 138, 157, 163–4, 166, 168–70, 172–3, 175, 178–80, 181, 189, 259, 304–6
Engineering Building, Leicester University, *162*, 163–4, *165*, 166, *167*, 168–9, 172–5, *176–7*, 178–81, 186–8, 190, 197–200, 341
English Baroque architecture, 88, 276
English Heritage, 339
English New Universities, 244
Enlightenment, 278
Entertainer, The, 282
environmental performance, 261–4, 338
Eros House, Catford, 230
Escorial, Madrid, 181
Eton College, Berkshire, 280
Euston Road, London, 196
experimental theatres, 282, 289, 300
exposed concrete, 12, 30, 59, 65, 92, 102, 180–1, 246, 254, 261, 307, 323
extensions, 211
Eyre, Richard, 320

F

Faber & Faber, 182
factories, 27, 28, 181, 219, 220
Fallingwater, Pennsylvania, 38
Farnsworth House, Illinois, 48
Fascism, 33
Fellows' Garden, Christ's College, 129, 148
Festival of Britain (1951), 171, 213, 279
Fielden, Frank, 244
filial piety, 281
Finney, Albert, 320
Finsbury, London, 96–7
fire hydrants, 76, 77
fireproofing, 27, 105

First World War, *see* World War I
Fitzroy Robinson, 231
Fleming, Ian, 61
Flickr, 78
Flint & Neill, 304–5
floor decks, 112, 254, 261
Florence, Italy, 9
La Fontaine, Jean de, 266
formwork, 8, 28, 42–4, 62, 67–8, 108–9, 175, 181, 252, 313, 315–16
Foster, Norman, 199, 256
Foster Associates, 229
Foulis Building, Glasgow School of Art, 257
France, 9, 12, 14, 27, 30, 43, 62, 63, 65, 88, 97, 101, 125, 156, 170, 172, 197, 201, 252, 275, 280, 325
Freedom of Information, 265
Fremantle, John, 4th Baron Cottesloe, 287, 300, 307
Fry, Maxwell, 182, 193
Futurism, 134

G

Gabo, Naum, 182
Garchey waste-disposal systems, 117
gardens, 31, 53, 58, 95, 100, 105, 112, 115, 117, 156
gargoyles, 52, 55
gas, 17, 59
Gaskill, Bill, 284
Gateshead, Tyne and Wear, 205, *206*, 206–7, 212–13, 230, 231
Gaudí, Antoni, 4
gender roles, 140
gentrification, 81–3, 338
geometry, 48, 67, 113, 174, 175
Georgia, 125
Georgian era (1714–1837), 4, 33, 56, 113, 192, 214, 219, 261

INDEX

Germany, 23, 27, 33, 47, 104, 229, 280, 297, 320
Gervais, Ricky, 213
Get Carter, 205–6, 231
Gibberd, Frederick, 193
Girouard, Mark, 322, 329
Glasgow, Scotland, 23, 83, 214, *215*, 215, *216*, 217–18, *218*, 219–25, 226, 227, 234, *235*, 235, 236, *238*, 239, *240*, 241–2, *242*, 243–7, *248*, 249–50, *251*, 252, *253*, 254, *255*, 256–71, 278, 333
    Anderston Centre, *204*, 214, *215*, 215, *216*, 217–18, *218*, 219–27, 234, *235*, 235, 236
    Glasgow School of Art, 170–1, 243, 247, *248*, 249–50, *251*, 252, *253*, 254, *255*, 256–61, 264–5, 267–8
    Queen Elizabeth Flats, 83
    Strathclyde University, *238*, 239, *240*, 241–2, *242*, 243–7, 256–7, 259–61, 265–7, 269, 271, 278, 334
    Trongate, 219
glass, 7, 24, 25, 27, 37, 39, 43, 48, 65, 74, 75, 111, 112, 136, 150, 166, 168, 174, 178, 180, 181, 188, 198–9, 245, 254, 256, 261–2
glass bricks, 43, 168
Glenfinnan Viaduct, Highlands, 29
Golden Lane Estate, Finsbury, 96–7, 113
Goldfinger, 61
Goldfinger, Ernö, 55, 61–3, 65, 67–81, 92, 126, 183, 193, 285, 334
Goldfinger, Ursula, 63, 72–5
Google, 24
Gordian knot, 305
Gordon, Rodney, 229–34, 334
Gothic architecture, 28, 67, 88, 126, 138, 250, 254, 339

Gowan, James, 164, 168–74, 178–81, 183, 185, 187–91, 198, 200, 285, 341
Grafton Street, Westminster, 209
Great Western Railway, 55
Greater London Council (GLC), 72, 299, 300, 307, 308, 340
Greece, 33, 39, 62, 290
grit-blasting, 135
Gropius, Walter, 128, 171
group value, 153
Guardian, 258
Guildhall School of Music and Drama, 107
Gut Garkau farm, Germany, 33
gutters, 52, 55, 135, 147

H

Hall, Peter, 284, 294, 296, 302, 319
Halle-Neustadt, East Germany, 104
Ham, Richmond, 172
hammering, 68, 92, 102–3, 109
Hammerson, 311
Handley, Mervyn, 129
Häring, Hugo, 33
Harry Potter, 29
Harvard University, 324
Harwood, Elain, 100
Hawksmoor, Nicholas, 88, 90, 136, 276, 328, 329
Hawksmoor, 329
Hayward, Isaac 'Ike', 279, 281, 283, 325, 326, 327
Hayward Gallery, South Bank, 322
health, 6, 15, 31, 56, 207, 218, 279
health and safety, 103, 144, 245
heating, 7, 31, 59, 65, 74, 92, 115, 217, 263
Hemingway, Wayne, 81
Hepworth, Barbara, 63, 182
Herbert, Jocelyn, 292, 302

heritage protection, 79, 82, 199, 258, 260, 265, 266, 269, 339
Hermit's Castle, Achmelvich, 23–5, *34–5*, 36–9, *40*, 41–5, *46*, 47–9, 109, 140, 340
hierarchy, 139, 157
High Tech architecture, 250, 319
High-Rise (Ballard), 17–18, 78
high-rise towers, 52, 53, *54*, 55, 60, 61, *64*, 65, *66*, 67–84, *69*, 69–80, *80*, 80–4, *89*, *91*, 98–9, 105, *106*, 112, 115, *116*, 117–19, 197, *204*, 214, 215, *215*, 216–18, *218*, 219, 243, 247, *248*, 249–50, *251*, 252, *253*, 254, *255*, 256–61, 264–5, 267–8, *270*, 275
Highgate, London, 63, 126, 334
Highpoint I, Highgate, 63, 126
hipsters, 336
Historic England, 82
Historic Scotland, 265
Holl, Stephen, 264–5, 267
Hollywood, 282, 290
homelessness, 226
honeycombing, 316
Honeyman & Keppie, 247
hospitals, 15
hot-desking, 259
hotels, 210, 220
Houses of Parliament, Westminster, 101, 275, 277, 327
housing, 5, 9, 10, 11, 15, 16, *52*, 53, *54*, 55–6, 60, 61, *64*, 65, *66*, 67–9, *69*, 69–80, *80*, 80–4, *86*, 87–8, *89*, 89–90, *91*, 92–7, 98–9, 100–5, *106*, 107–15, *116*, 117–19, 207, 208, 214, *215*, 215, *216*, 217–18, *218*, 219, 221, 227, 228, 234
housing, private, 126, 172, 207, 209, 212
Howell Killick Partridge & Amis, 285

Hull College of Art, 181, 186
Hungary, 61
Hungerford Bridge, London, 293
Hunstanton Secondary Modern School, Norfolk, 12, *13*, 14, 180
Hyams, Harry, 209–11, 225, 226, 227

I

Île-de-France, 88
immeuble à gradins, 134
in situ concrete, 28, 42, 109, 135, 175, 254, 268, 307, 308–9, 316, 339
incandescent bulbs, 7
industrial aesthetic, 27, 28, 181, 219, 220
Industrial Revolution, 6, 27, 56, 244
inflation, 300, 304, 309, 310, 318
inheritance tax, 227
insulation, 71, 73, 78, 144, 150, 217, 254, 261–3, 334, 337–8
Inverness, Highlands, 23
Ireland, 102, 103
Iron Curtain, 219
Italy, 9, 26, 33, 97, 101, 134, 153

J

jazz, 172
Jenga, 188
Jesus College, Cambridge, 141–3, 152
Jewish people, 213
JM Architects, 264
John, Augustus, 63
Johnson Wax Headquarters, Racine, Wisconsin, 166
Jonson, Ben, 94

K

Kahn, Louis, 250
Kensington, London, 278, 279

INDEX

Keppie Henderson & Partners, 247, 249, 250
King Street, Cambridge, 128, 136, 141–4, 145, 146, 151, 152
King, Dave, 309
Kingston, London, 171
Kingston Polytechnic, 97
Kingston School of Architecture, 171
kitchen-sink drama, 281, 282
kitchens, 59, 65, 71, 130
Kuwait, 191–2

L

labour, 102–4, 118, 246, 310–11
Labour Party, 57, 93, 210, 235, 278, 279
Lagonda, 100
Lambeth, London, 60
Lancashire, England, 181, 212, 230
Lancaster, Osbert, 322
Langham House Close, Ham, 172
Lasdun, Denys, 30, 31, 33, 124–9, 134–6, 139–49, 151–7, 183, 185, 192, 197, 243, 254, 278, 283, 284–7, 289, 291–4, 296–300, *301*, 301–2, 307–9, 311–12, 318–25, 327–9, 341
Lasdun, James, 320
Lasdun, Susan, 155–6
lavatories, 59, 65, 102, 105, 106, 139, 141, 173, 187, 242, 246
Leger, Fernand, 63
Leicester University, *162*, 163–4, *165*, 166, *167*, 168–9, 172–5, *176–7*, 178–81, 186–7, *187*, 188, *189*, 189–91, 197–200, 278, 341
Lenin, Vladimir Ilyich, 94
Lewis, Lou, 104
lifts, 65, 67, 73, 76, 77, 108, 115, 250, 254, 301, 325
lighting, 7, 72, 108, 114, 142, 168, 174, 211, 242, 245, 246, 260, 266

limestone, 26, 27, 31, 149
Lincoln Center, New York, 324
Lincoln's Inn Fields, Camden, 175
Lissitzky, Lazar Markovich 'El', 182
Littlewood, Joan, 281
Liverpool, Merseyside, 23, 123, 170–1, 173, 271
  Albert Dock, 271
  School of Architecture, 170
  University, 127
Livery Companies, 93
living rooms, 71
Lochinver, Highlands, 24
Loeb Drama Center, Harvard, 324
Logie, Gordon, 143
Loire Valley, France, 275
London, England, 4, 12–13, 18, 19, 29, 33, 48, 52, 53, *54*, 55–61, 63, *64*, 65, 67–9, *69*, *86*, 87–8, *89*, 89–90, *91*, 92–7, *98–9*, 100–5, *106*, 107–15, *116*, 117–19, 123–4, 171, 172, 175, 195–7, 209–12, 213, 225–8, 230, 231, *274*, 275–7, *277*, 278–313, *314*, 315–16, *317*, 318–28, *327*, 329, 336–41
  Alexander Fleming House, Elephant and Castle, 63
  Alton Estate, Roehampton, 83
  Balfron Tower, Poplar, 55, 60, 61, *64*, 65, 67–77, *69*, 79–80, *80*, 80–4, 92, 108, 123, 151, 335, 338, 340
  Barbican Estate, City of London, 48, *86*, 87–8, *89*, 89–90, *91*, 92–7, *98–9*, 100–5, *106*, 107–15, *116*, 117–19, 123, 151, 157, 175, 196, 296, 336, 339, 340–1
  Bloomsbury, Camden, 192, 196
  Boundary Estate, Tower Hamlets, 56

INDEX

Brandlehow School, Putney, 61
Brent Cross shopping centre, 311
British Library, St Pancras, 196
Carlton House Terrace, Westminster, 101
Centre Point, Camden, 225, 226
Churchill Gardens, Pimlico, 171
County Hall, Lambeth, 185, 275, 279, 322
Dolphin Square, Westminster, 101
Dorchester Hotel, Mayfair, 209
Drapers Gardens, City of London, 210
Economist Building, St James, 235
Eros House, Catford, 230
Golden Lane Estate, Finsbury, 96–7, 113
Grafton Street, Westminster, 209
Hayward Gallery, South Bank, 322
Highpoint I, Highgate, 63, 126
Houses of Parliament, Westminster, 101, 275, 277, 327
Langham House Close, Ham, 172
Lincoln's Inn Fields, Camden, 175
London Eye, South Bank, 275
Natwest Tower, City of London, 225
National Gallery, Trafalgar Square, 18–19
National Theatre, South Bank, 18, 29, 30, 124, 213, 228, *274*, 276–7, *277*, 278–90, *291*, 292, 294, *295*, 296–8, *299*, 299–302, *303*, 303–13, *314*, 315–16, *317*, 318–28, *327*, 329, 336–8, 339, 340, 341
Oxford Street, Westminster, 196
Ronan Point, Newham, 59
Royal Festival Hall, South Bank, 228, 279, 283, 327, 339, 340
Shell Centre, South Bank, 293
Somerset House, Westminster, 327–8
Southbank Centre, 279, 326, 332, 339–40, *341*
St Paul's Cathedral, City of London, 95, 100, 102, 275, 322
Trellick Tower, Kensington, 52, 53, *54*, 55, 60, 61, 65, 66, 67–8, 76, 77–9, 83, 87, 108, 123, 151, 338, 340
University of London, 186, 192, 196
Victoria and Albert Museum, Kensington, 278
Waterloo Bridge, 119, 275, 300, 301, 313, 322, 339, 341
Whitehall, Westminster, 195–6, 275
York Terrace, Regent's Park, 172
London County Council (LCC), 12–13, 56, 60–1, 65, 92, 93, 94, 95–6, 182–3, 184, 186, 225, 278–9, 283, 293, 294, 299, 327
London Symphony Orchestra, 107
London Underground, 100, 107, 108, 111
London Wall, 96
Lubetkin, Berthold, 63, 93–4, 125–6, 193
Lutyens, Sir Edwin Landseer, 190, 278
Lynex, Richard, 286
Lyons Israel & Ellis, 172
Lyttelton, Oliver, 280–1, 282, 297, 309, 325
Lyttelton Theatre, National Theatre, 319

M

M8 motorway, Scotland, 215, 220, 249
Macedonian marble, 340
Mackintosh, Charles Rennie, 247, 249, 254, 257, 258, 260
MacLeod, Margaret, 36, 39

Macmillan, Harold, 195
Madame Tussauds, 157
Maisons Jaoul, Neuilly-sur-Seine, 101, 172
Mall, Westminster, 101
Manchester, England, 181, 223
    Piccadilly, 223
    University, 181
marble, 338, 340
Marlowe, Christopher, 94
Marseille, France, 14, 65, 252
Marsh, George, 226
Marshall, Norman, 287–9, 294
Martin, Leslie, 60, 129, 134, 169–70, 172, 181–201, 207, 336
Marxism, 63, 94
mathematics, 8, 12, 67, 184
Matthew, Robert, 60
Sir Robert McAlpine and Sons, 30, 102, 310, 312
McAlpine, Edwin, 311
McAlpine, Robert 'Concrete Bob', 30
McMorran, Donald, 96, 97, 193
mechanical ventilation, 7, 211, 246, 266
mechanisation, 7, 8, 10
Medieval period, 4, 6, 9, 87, 93, 103, 111, 112, 147
Mediterranean Europe, 100–1
memorabilia, 335, *335*
middle class, 10, 17, 57, 92, 97, 125, 126
Middle East, 191–2, 228
Mill Hill, Barnet, 227
mining, 279
Ministry of Health, 63
Miró, Joan, 63
models, *291*, *292*, *294*, *295*, *296*, *298*, *309*
Modern Architectural ReSearch (MARS), 193
Modernism, 8, 9–16, 29, 31, 32–3, 48, 62, 71, 74, 77, 79, 90, 92, 95, 96, 97, 100, 108, 109, 110, 119, 124, 126, 128, 129, 139, 140, 145, 154, 155, 157, 160, 166, 168, 171, 172, 182, 184, 193, 197, 199, 201, 219, 243, 247, 250, 254, 262, 278, 322, 323, 335–6, 336–7
Modigliani, Amedeo Clemente, 178
Mohican House, 210
Moholy-Nagy, László, 182
Mondrian, Piet, 182
Monroe, Marilyn, 97
Moore, Henry, 63, 182
More, Thomas, 94
Moro, Peter, 38
mortgages, 210
moulds, *see* formwork
movement studies, 286
mugging, 78
murals, 244

N

Nash, John, 101, 329
Natwest Tower, City of London, 225
National Gallery, Trafalgar Square, 18–19
National Theatre Bill (1949), 281, 282
National Theatre Company, 281, 282, 284
National Theatre, South Bank, 18, 29, 30, 124, 213, 228, 274, 276–7, *277*, 278–90, *291*, *292*, 294, *295*, 296–8, *299*, 299–302, *303*, 303–13, *314*, 315–16, *317*, 318–28, *327*, 329, 336–8, 339, 340, 341
National Trust, 79, 81
nationalism, 280
natural light, 7, 59, 174, 211, 245, 246, 266

Neolithic period, 45
Netherlands, 178
New Brutalism (Reyner Banham), 14
New Court, Christ's College, *122*, 124–5, 127–9, *130*, 130–1, *132–3*, 134–6, *137*, 138–9, *139*, 140–57, *158–9*, 160, 336, 341
New Humanism, 11
New York, United States, 103, 125, 324
Newbery Tower, Glasgow School of Art, 243, 247, *248*, 249–50, *251*, 252, *253*, 254, *255*, 256–61, 264–5, 267–8
Newby, Frank, 180
Newcastle, Tyne and Wear, 205, 206–7
Nicholson, Ben, 63, 182, 188
Norfolk, England, 13, *13*, 14, 180
Normandy, France, 170
Notley Abbey, Buckinghamshire, 282
Notre Dame du Haut, Ronchamp, 101
Nottingham University, 193
nuclear power, 16, 18, 318, 320–1, 337

O

objets trouvés, 12
Observer, 319, 320
Office, The, 213
offices, 207, 208, 210–11, 212, 213, 215, 219, 221, 222, 225–6, 228, 230, 236, 260, 271, 298
oil, 6, 16, 17, 259
oil crisis (1973), 16, 310, 311
Old Vic Company, 283, 284, 288
olive oil, 100
Olivier, Laurence, 282, 284, 287–9, 294, 297, 300, *301*, 302, 319, 323, 324
Olivier Theatre, National Theatre, 276, 302–6, 309, 325

Olympic Games, 78
OPEC (Organization of the Petroleum Exporting Countries), 311
open theatres, 290–1, *291*, *292*, 297, 298, 302
Open University, 145
Opéra Garnier, Paris, 324
opera houses, 191, 283–5, 293, 297–9, 318, 323
Orkney, Scotland, 45
Osborne, John, 282
outdoor space, 7, 31, 113, 114, 115, 126, 138, 249, 250, 326
Owen Luder Partnership, 229, 231
Oxford Conference (1958), 183
Oxford Street, Westminster, 196
Oxford University, 138, 144, 183, 189, 190

P

paganism, 265
Paisley, Renfrewshire, 170
  Civic Centre, 333, *334*
Pantheon, Rome, 26
Paris, France, 62, 63, 101, 125, 126, 134, 197, 201, 325
Park Hill, Sheffield, 83
Parkes, Edward, 163, 179, 180
Parthenon, Athens, 39
Partick, Glasgow, 170
Paterson, Toby, 236
patronage, 15, 60, 126, 157, 179, 181–201, 281
Peabody Trust, 56
peeping toms, 148–9
Perret, Auguste, 62–3, 67, 68, 126, 252
Peru, 114
Pevsner, Nikolaus, 32
Philipe, Gérard, 97

photocopying, 8
photography, 148
physics, 8
Piccadilly, Manchester, 223
pigeons, 113, 164
piling, 305
Pilkington, 178
pillboxes, 39
Pimlico, Westminster, 171
pinboards, 150, 245, 246
Piper, John, 63
Piranesi, Giovanni Battista, 14, 114, 230
planning, 30, 45, 55, 90, 93–7, 100, 108, 112–14, 118, 130–1, 138, 141–3, 149, 150, 152, 155, 184, 185, 186, 188, 192, 194–6, 197, 201, 208, 209, 211, 219–26, 244, 278–310, 323–5
plot-ratio planning, 95
Plowright, Joan, 282
pollution, 56, 220, 338
polystyrene, 175
pop-art, 97
Poplar, London, 55
Portland stone, 300, 307–8, 313
Portsmouth, Hampshire, 230, 231, 232–3, 334
Postmodernism, 71, 147, 217, 319
pound shops, 213
pouring of concrete, 8, 18, 30, 70, 109, 313, 315–16, 338
poverty, 13, 56, 81
Powell, Geoffry, 97, 100
Powell & Moya, 171
precast concrete, 28, 136, 308
Preston, Lancashire, 212, 230
primitivism, 11, 14, 30, 43, 110, 336
Private Eye, 226, 322
private housing, 126, 172, 207, 209, 212

private practice, 12, 56, 60–1, 126, 172, 183, 207, 228
property developers, 205–36
proportion, 12, 26, 27, 67
proscenium theatres, 289–90, 291, 297, 298, 302
prostitution, 78
Pugh, Harry, 143
Punch, 321
Putney, London, 61

Q

QE2, 318
quartz aggregate, 135
Queen Elizabeth Flats, Glasgow, 83

R

R. G. Minter Ltd, 68
racism, 102
radiators, 117, 150
radio, 148
railways, 6, 55, 100, 105, 107, 108, 111, 220, 223
Rape of Persephone (Bernini), 198
rationing, 10, 60, 208
Rattigan, Terence, 281
Rayne, Max, 311
Read, Herbert, 182
Regent's Canal, 55
Regent's Park, London, 172
reinforced concrete, 7, 15, 27–8, 63, 68, 261, 312, 313, 315, 335
Rembrandt van Rijn, 209
Renaissance, 9, 12, 26, 181
Richard Rogers Partnership, 229
Richards Laboratories, University of Pennsylvania, 250
Richardson, Albert, 128, 136

Right to Buy, 81
Riley, Bridget, 174
riots, 4–5
roads, 6, 10, 32, 94, 95–6, 105, 194–6, 197, 207, 212, 214, 215, 220, 222
Roberts, David, 129
Robertson, Howard Morley, 193, 293
Rolls-Royce, 209, 227
Roman Empire (27 B.C.–395 A.D.), 6, 26, 27, 33, 62, 67, 112, 147
Rome, Italy, 26
Ronan Point, Newham, 59
Ronchamp, France, 101
roof gardens, 31, 105, 115, 117, 326
roofs, 27, 31, 43, 101, 111, 123, 130, 135, 138, 147, 148, 149, 160, 172, 173, 174, 175, 181, 188, 198, 266
room proportions, 71, 74, 130, 150, 187
Route 11, London, 96
Rowe, Colin, 171
Rowlett Street Estate, Poplar, 55, 60, 61, 64, 65, 67–77, 69, 79–80, 80, 80–4, 92, 108, 123, 151, 335, 338, 340
Royal Air Force (RAF), 170
Royal College of Physicians, 155
Royal Court Company, 282, 284, 294
Royal Festival Hall, South Bank, 228, 279, 283, 327, 339, 340
Royal Fine Arts Commission, 143, 192
Royal Institute of British Architects (RIBA), 96, 129, 284–5
Royal Shakespeare Company (RSC), 107, 283, 284, 294, 296
Rubens, Peter Paul, 209
Rudolph, Paul, 229, 250, 252, 333
Rugby School, Warwickshire, 125
Russia, 33, 63, 94, 125–6, 249
rust, 123, 308, 312, 334

S

Sadler's Wells, Clerkenwell, 283, 299
safety, 103
Sainte Marie de La Tourette, Éveux, 30
Salisbury Cathedral, Wiltshire, 88, 90
San Gimignano, Tuscany, 254
satanic mills, 179
Sauvage, Henri, 134
schools, 11, 12, 13, 14, 15, 61, 100, 112, 180, 208, 228
Schwitters, Kurt, 63
scotbrut.co.uk, 269
Scotland, 23–5, 29–30, 34–5, 36–9, 40, 41–5, 46, 47–9, 55, 83, 109, 140, 170, 214, 215, 215, 216, 217–18, 218, 219–25, 226, 227, 234, 235, 235, 236, 238, 239, 240, 241–2, 242, 243–7, 248, 249–50, 251, 252, 253, 254, 255, 256–71, 278, 333–4, 340
  Anderston Centre, Glasgow, 204, 214, 215, 215, 216, 217–18, 218, 219–27, 234, 235, 235, 236
  Edinburgh, Scotland, 39, 261
  Glasgow School of Art, 170–1, 243, 247, 248, 249–50, 251, 252, 253, 254, 255, 256–61, 264–5, 267–8
  Hermit's Castle, Achmelvich, 23–5, 34–5, 36–9, 40, 41–5, 46, 47–9, 109, 140, 340
  Paisley, Renfrewshire, 170, 333, 334
  Queen Elizabeth Flats, Glasgow, 83
  Strathclyde University, Glasgow, 238, 239, 240, 241–2, 242, 243–7, 256–7, 259–61, 265–7, 269, 271, 278, 334
  Trongate, Glasgow, 219
Scots Baronial, 247
Scott, David, 36–7, 39, 41, 48
Scott, John Oldrid, 250

INDEX

Second World War, *see* World War II
Seifert, Richard, 207, 213, 225–9, 231, 234, 235, 271, 285
Seifert clauses, 225
Selwyn College, Cambridge, 186
Shakespeare, William, 94, 107, 280, 290
Shakespeare Tower, Barbican Estate, 90
Shand, Morton, 182
Shaw, George Bernard, 278
Sheffield, Yorkshire, 83
Shell Centre, South Bank, 293
Sheppard Robson & Partners, 185
Sherlock Holmes, 76, 323
shops, 207, 208, 212, 213, 214, 219, 221, 230
showers, 130, 139, 141, 187
shuttering, 30, 41, 69–70, 103, 109, 135, 313, 316, 318
Sidney Sussex College, Cambridge, 141, 152
Siedlung Halen, Bern, 131, 134
Sikhs, 102, 315
Silkin, Lewis, 208, 211
single glazing, 261
Skara Brae, Orkney, 45
skateboarding, 326
Skidmore Owings & Merrill, 229
skylights, 245
Skylon, 171
slab-blocks, 58, 105, 112–13
slums, 10, 56, 57, 58, 87, 212, 218, 219
Smith, Ivor, 142, 152
Smithson, Alison and Peter, 11, 12, 33, 96, 101, 180, 185, 197, 235, 285
Soane, John, 33, 175
social cleansing, 81
social conservatism, *see* conservatism

social hierarchy, 139, 157
social housing, 5, 9, 10, 11, 15, 16, *52*, 53, 54, 55–6, 60, 61, *64*, 65, *66*, 67–9, 69, 69–80, *80*, 81–4, *86*, 87–8, *89*, 89–90, *91*, 92–7, *98*–9, 100–5, *106*, 107–15, *116*, 117–19, *204*, 208, 214, *215*, 215, *216*, 217–18, *218*, 219, 221, 227, 234
socialism, 10, 18, 57, 93, 100, 104, 118, 207, 279, 325
sociology, 12
Somerset House, Westminster, 327–8
soundproofing, 73, 105, 144, 150
South Bank, London, 279, 283, 293, 326–7
Southbank Centre, 279, 326, 332, 339–40, *341*
South Bank Theatre Board, 286, 287, 298, 300, 307, 311, 323
Soviet Union (1922–91), 33, 63, 94, 104, 125–6
Space Race, 179
Spain, 181
speculation, 56, 95, 207–36
St Giles-without-Cripplegate, Barbican, 196
St Paul's Cathedral, City of London, 95, 100, 102, 275, 322
staircases, 105, 111, 115, *116*, 138, 175, 188, 250, 254, 260, *314*
stalactites, 149, 217
Stalin, Joseph, 336
Standard Life, 224
state-funded building activity, 208
steel, 7, 12, 14, 27–9, 31, 48, 68, 103, 115, 117, 145, 148, 175, 180, 261, 306, 312, 313, 322
Stephen Holl Architects, 264–5, 267
stepped sections, *130*, 130–1, *132*–3, 134

Stevenson Building, Christ's College, 146
Stirling, James, 164, 168–74, 178–81, 183, 185, 187–91, 198, 200, 227, 285, 341
Stirling, Scotland, 39
stone, 6, 10, 24, 26–9, 39, 41, 43, 45, 62, 68, 88, 90, 104, 113, 146–7, 160, 185, 214, 219–20, 249, 252, 257, 300, 307–8, 313, 323, 339
storage, 130, 139
Strathclyde University, Glasgow, *238*, 239, *240*, 241–2, *242*, 243–7, 256–7, 259–61, 265–7, 269, 271, 278, 334
straw waddling, 246
streets, 153–4
strikes, 104, 118, 310, 311
studios, 83, 105, 110, 241–2, *242*, 243, 245–7, 250, 254, 259–60, 266, 271
subcontractors, 174, 318–19
Sublime/Sublimity, 14, 16, 49, 58, 88, 147, 151, 153, 217, 241, 326
Summerson, John, 322
Sunday Times, 92, 296
Sweden, 33
swimming pools, 220
Switzerland, 14, 30, 97, 131, 134, 213
Sydney Opera House, New South Wales, 191, 318
symmetry, 12, 326

T

taxation, 208–9, 227
Taylor Woodrow, 224
technology, 8, 9
Tecton, 125, 126
Tempest, The, 291
Ten Books on Architecture, 26
Tenants' Associations, 74–5
textures, 3, 24, 29, 30, 37, 42, 43, 67–8, 80, 92, 102–3, 109, 175, 181, 252, 268, 276, 312, 313, 315–16, 318, 322, 339
Thatcher, Margaret, 57, 81, 229
theatres
  courtyard, 290
  experimental, 282, 289, 300
  open, 290–1, *291*, *292*, 297, 298, 302, *303*
  proscenium, 289–90, 291, 297, 298, 302, *303*
Third Schedule, 211
ticks, 38
tiles, 114, 164, 168, 174, 175, 178, 186, 198, 199, *205*, 247
Times, The, 123, 153
Tintin, 179, 198
topiaries, 156
topping out, 310
Tottenham Court Road, Camden, 226
La Tourette, *see* Sainte Marie de La Tourette
tourism, 4, 199
Towards an Architecture, 179
Tower Bridge, London, 275
Town and Country Planning Act (1947), 208, 211
Townscape movement, 14
trade-unions, 103–4, 118, 279, 310, 311
Transport and General Workers Union, 279
transportation, 6, 55, 57, 100, 105, 107, 108, 111, 211, 219–20, 221, 235
  buses, 220, 235
  car parks, 79, 136, 205–6, *206*, 212, 214, *215*, 222, 230
  cars, 100, 194–5, 209

INDEX

railways, 6, 55, 100, 105, 107, 108, 111, 220, 223

roads, 6, 10, 32, 94, 95–6, 105, 194–6, 197, 207, 212, 214, 215, 220, 222

Treasury, 163, 298, 312

Trellick Tower, Kensington, 52, 53, *54*, 55, 60, 61, 65, *66*, 67–8, 76, 77–9, 83, 87, 108, 123, 151, 338, 340

Tricorn Centre, Portsmouth, 230, 231, 232–3, 334

Trinity Square, Gateshead, 205, *206*, 206–7, 212–13, 230, 231

Trollope, Anthony, 141

Trongate, Glasgow, 219

Tube, *see* London Underground

Twentieth Century Society, 269

Twitter, 78, 217

Twyfords, 107

Tynan, Kenneth, 281, 282

Tyne and Wear, England, 205, *206*, 206–7, 212–13, 230, 231

U

United Kingdom

1714–1837 Georgian era, 4, 33, 56, 113, 192, 214, 219, 261

1837–1901 Victorian era, 4, 32, 33, 56, 111, 146, 152, 196, 212, 219, 220, 236, 260, 289

1890 construction of Boundary Estate begins, 56

1901–10 Edwardian era, 4, 111, 123, 220, 260, 289

1914–18 World War I, 56, 280

1933 foundation of MARS, 193

1937 Cambridge University rejects scheme by Gropius, 128; Martin publishes *Circle* journal, 182

1938 site secured for National Theatre, 278

1939–45 World War II, 10, 39, 56–7, 93, 94, 101, 126, 170, 182, 184, 208, 278, 280

1940–1 Blitz, 10, 57, 93, 94, 101, 182, 208, 278

1942 Beveridge Report, 57; Goldfinger holds art sale in Hampstead Heath, 63

1943 preparation of *County of London Plan*, 61, 278

1944 City of London prepares reconstruction plans, 94, 95

1947 Albert Richardson begins work on Christ's College, 128; Town and Country Planning Act, 208, 211

1948 Attlee government brings forward bill on National Theatre funding, 280

1949 Robert Matthew takes control of public housing in London, 60; dissolution of Tecton, 126; National Theatre Bill, 281, 282

1950 Smithsons win architectural competition for Hunstanton Secondary School, 12

1951 City of London holds Golden Lane competition, 96; Festival of Britain, 171, 213, 279; Kenneth Tynan holds mock funeral for National Theatre site, 281

1953 Comprehensive Development Plan for London approved, 33; Richardson finishes work on Christ's College, 128; Martin appointed LCC Architect, 182; cancellation of betterment tax, 208

1954 rationing ends, 10, 60, 208

1955 construction of Hermit's Castle, 42, 109; planning of Barbican Estate begins, 90, 100; construction of Langham House Close begins, 172

1956 Casson Conder & Partners approached for work on Christ's College, 128–9, 146; Martin resigns from LCC, joins Cambridge faculty, 183; Martin judges Sydney Opera House competition, 191

1957 foundation of Victorian Society and Civic Trust, 152; University College Leicester granted full university status, 163; Martin receives knighthood, 184; first production of *The Entertainer*, 282

1958 construction of Langham House Close completed, 172; Oxford Conference, 183; Stirling and Gowan receive first commission from LCC, 183; planning for Churchill College begins, 185; construction of Leicester Univeristy College Hall begins, 187

1959 Casson Conder & Partners dropped by Cambridge University, 129; Stirling and Gowan commissioned for work on University of Leicester, 163–4, 172–4; Martin proposes design for Selwyn College, 186; Glasgow Council determines boundaries of Anderston Cross CDA, 222

1960 construction of Leicester University College Hall completed, 187

1961 Lasdun commissioned for work on Christ's College, 129; construction of University of Leicester Engineering Building begins, 164, 180

1962 construction of Barbican Estate begins, 100; foundation of National Theatre Company, 281, 282

1963 Stirling and Gowan win commission for Cambridge History Faculty, 190; Third Schedule cancelled, 211; Glasgow Council makes deal with developers on Anderston Cross CDA, 221, 223; planning of Newbery Tower begins, 250

1964 RSC plans residency in Barbican, 107, 296; construction of University of Leicester Engineering Building completed, 164; Labour Party wins general election, 210; planning of Strathclyde Architecture Building begins, 243

1965 establishment of GLC, 72, 283, 299; construction of Balfron Tower begins, 55; plans for Open University begin, 145; Lasdun begins work on University of London, 192; planning of Anderston Cross CDA begins, 223

1966 publication of Banham's *New Brutalism*, 14; Lou Lewis launches strike at Barbican

403

construction site, 104; opening of St George's Shopping Centre in Preston, 212, 230; National Theatre Building Committee rejects Scheme B; Scheme C proposed, 297, 302

1967 Lasdun's plans for Christ's College approved, 144; completion of Trinity Square, 207; developers pull out of Anderston Cross CDA project, 223; Strathclyde Architecture Building completed, 243

1968 Ronan Point gas explosion, 59; construction of Trellick Tower begins, 55; opening of Balfron Tower, 55, 76; Barbican Arts Centre redesigned, 107; Lasdun's proposal for built in desks at Christ's College vetoed, 140; riots and protests, 145

1969 Lasdun begins construction work at Christ's College, 134, 144; construction of Newbery Tower begins, 250; construction of National Theatre begins, 310

1970 construction of Willis Faber and Dumas Headquarters begins, 256

1971 release of *Get Carter*, 205–6

1972 completion of Trellick Tower, 55, 77; fire hydrants discharged in Trellick Tower, 77

1973 oil crisis, 16, 310, 311; Thomas Daniel Smith arrested on corruption charges, 206–7

1974 Direct Action occupy Centre Point, 226

1975 publication of J. G. Ballard's *High-Rise*, 17–18, 78; Willis Faber and Dumas Headquarters completed, 256

1976 opening of National Theatre, 30, 318

1978 death of Peter Chamberlin, 117

1982 end of work on Barbican Estate, 90, 104

1987 concierge introduced to Trellick Tower, 78

1989 good architectural guide criticises Brutalism at Glasgow School of Art, 259; National Theatre voted worst building in *Observer* poll, 319

2001 death of Richard Seifert, 227

2004 demolition of Tricorn Centre, 230

2006 burglary of Harry Hyams' Wiltshire estate, 209

2009 opening of Darwin Garden at Christ's College, 157

2010 demolition of Trinity Square, 207, 212, 230; partial demolition of Paisley Civic Centre, 333

2011 England riots, 5

2012 London Oympics, 78; demolition of Newbery Tower, 267, *270*

2014 City Spaces & Strings performance at Anderston Centre, 236; Glasgow School of Art Mackintosh Building damaged by fire, 258

United States, 38, 48, 103, 125, 166, 214, 229, 250, 321, 324, 333

Unités d'habitation, 14, 65, 71, 252

universities, 15, 101, *122*, 124–5, 127–9, 130, 130–1, *132–3*, 134–6, *137*, 138–9, *139*, 140–57, *158–9*, 160,

162, 163–4, *165*, 166, *167*, 168–9, 172–5, *176–7*, 178–81, 186–7, *187*, 188, *189*, 189–93, 197–201, 207, 209, 214, 228, *238*, 239, *240*, 241–2, *242*, 243–7, *248*, 249–50, *251*, 252, *253*, 254, *255*, 256–61, 264–5
University College London, 213
University Grants Committee, 163
University of East Anglia, 134, 144, 148–9, 209
University of Harvard, 324
University of Leicester, *162*, 163–4, *165*, 166, *167*, 168–9, 172–5, *176–7*, 178–81, 186–7, *187*, 188, *189*, 189–91, 197–200
University of Liverpool, 127
University of London, 186, 192, 196
University of Manchester, 181
University of Pennsylvania, 250
University of Strathclyde, *238*, 239, *240*, 241–2, *242*, 243–7, 256–7, 259, 260–1, 265–7, 269, 271
Yale University, 250
University of York, 209
unreinforced concrete, 27, 29
upper class, 10, 61, 63, 92, 97, 126, 281
uPVC double glazing, 79, 262
utilitarianism, 10, 15, 27, 60, 301, 336
Utzon, Jørn, 191–2, 322
Uzès, France, 97

V

van der Rohe, Mies, 48
Vanbrugh, John, 88
vandalism, 76, 77, 87
Vauban, Sébastien de, 39
Venice, Italy, 101
ventilation, 7, 173, 211, 246, 266
Versailles, Île-de-France, 156

viaducts, 29, 101
Victoria and Albert Museum, Kensington, 278
Victoria Park, Leicester, 191
Victorian era (1837–1901), 4, 32, 33, 56, 111, 146, 152, 196, 212, 219, 220, 236, 260, 289
Victorian Society, 152, 153
vista, 33
Vitruvius, 26
Vivien Leigh, 282
volcanic stone, 26

W

Wales, 279
walkways, 4, 31, 36, 53, 55, 65, 79, 87, 96, 105, 107, 111–12, 123, 215, 217, 220–2, 241, 249, 301, 308, 339
Warburton, Nigel, 70
warehouses, 27
Wassily chairs, 147
waste-disposal systems, 117
water staining, 3, 29, 55, 252, 320
water tanks/pipes, 166, 175, 178, 181, 300
water, hot and cold, 59, 65
Waterloo Bridge, London, 119, 275, 300, 301, 313, 322, 339, 341
Waterloo Street, Glasgow, 217
waterproofing, 174, 181, 316
wealth gap, 208
weatherproofing, 178
Welfare State, 15, 18, 31, 55, 61, 78, 82, 83, 84, 92, 182, 207, 228, 234, 281, 327
Westbourne Park, London, 55
Westminster Abbey, London, 88
Where's Wally? 275
whisky, 246
Whitby, George, 193

405

INDEX

white finger, 103
Whitehall, Westminster, 195–6, 275
Wi-Fi, 260
Wilford, Michael, 173
Willis Faber and Dumas
    Headquarters, Ipswich, 256
Wilson, Effingham, 278
Wilson, Harold, 210
Wiltshire, England, 209
Wimpey, 59
Wind in the Willows, 276, 303
windows, 7, 25, 37, 39, 43, 65, 74, 75,
    112, 150, 166, 168, 174, 188, 198, 211,
    230, 241, 245, 261–2, 266, 338
Winter, John, 70, 334
wiring, 73, 108, 200, 247, 250, 260, 311
Wisconsin, United States, 166
wood-textured surfaces, 42, 274,
    276, 313
Wood, Philip, 294, 309
working class, 6–7, 65, 87, 96, 279, 281
World War I (1914–18), 56, 280
World War II (1939–45), 10, 39, 56–7,
    93, 94, 101, 126, 170, 182, 184, 208,
    278, 280
world-power status, 10
Wren, Christopher, 33, 213,
    275, 329
Wright, Frank Lloyd, 38, 166
Wyatt, James, 88

X

Xenakis, Iannis, 252

Y

Yale University Art and Architecture
    Building, 250
York Terrace, Regent's Park, 172
York, Yorkshire, 209

Z

Zurich, Switzerland, 97, 213